Talker Variability in Speech Processing

Talker Variability in Speech Processing

Edited by

KEITH JOHNSON
Department of Linguistics
The Ohio State University
Columbus, Ohio

JOHN W. MULLENNIX
Department of Psychology
University of Pittsburgh at Johnstown
Johnstown, Pennsylvania

ACADEMIC PRESS
San Diego London Boston New York Sydney Tokyo Toronto

This book is printed on acid-free paper. ∞

Academic Press, Inc.
525 B Street, Suite 1900, San Diego, California 92101-4495, USA
http://www.apnet.com

Academic Press Limited
24-28 Oval Road, London NW1 7DX, UK
http://www.hbuk.co.uk/ap/

Library of Congress Cataloging-in-Publication Data

Talker variability in speech processing / edited by Keith Johnson,
John W. Mullennix. -- Ed. 1.
p. cm.
Includes index.
ISBN 0-12-386560-3 (alk. paper)
1. Psycholinguistics. 2. Speech perception. 3. Automatic speech recognition. 4. Language and languages--Variation. I. Johnson, Keith, date. II. Mullennix, John W.
P37.T24 1996
401'.9--dc20 96-31802
CIP

PRINTED IN THE UNITED STATES OF AMERICA
96 97 98 99 00 01 BB 9 8 7 6 5 4 3 2 1

Contents

Contributors

Numbers in parentheses indicate the pages on which the authors' contributions begin.

Stephen D. Goldinger (33) Department of Psychology, Arizona State University, Tempe, Arizona 85287

Keith Johnson (1, 145) Department of Linguistics, The Ohio State University, Columbus, Ohio 43210

Jody Kreiman (85) Voice Laboratory, Division of Head and Neck Surgery, UCLA School of Medicine, Los Angeles, California 90095

James Magnuson (109) Department of Brain and Cognitive Sciences, University of Rochester, Rochester, New York 14627

Richard S. McGowan (211) Haskins Laboratories, New Haven, Connecticut 06511

John W. Mullennix (1, 67) Department of Psychology, University of Pittsburgh at Johnstown, Johnstown, Pennsylvania 15902.

Howard Nusbaum (109) Department of Psychology, University of Chicago, Chicago, Illinois 60637

David B. Pisoni (9) Speech Research Laboratory, Department of Psychology, Indiana University, Bloomington, Indiana 47405

Sonya M. Sheffert (133) Speech Research Laboratory, Department of Psychology, Indiana University, Bloomington, Indiana 47405

Nikko Ström (167) Department of Speech, Music, and Hearing, KTH (Royal Institute of Technology), Stockholm, Sweden

D. H. Whalen (133) Haskins Laboratories, New Haven, Connecticut 06511

Yunxin Zhao (191) Beckman Institute and the Department of Electrical and Computer Engineering, University of Illinois at Urbana-Champaign, Urbana, Illinois 61801

Preface

In September 1995 a number of researchers in human auditory word recognition, human speech perception, voice perception, and automatic computer speech recognition met in Indianapolis for a National Institutes of Health-funded one-day workshop on talker variability and speech processing. The time was right to bring together researchers from different disciplines to discuss recent developments in research on talker variability in speech processing. We saw an interdisciplinary convergence toward a new type of solution to the talker variability problem. This book emerged from that workshop.

Before launching into the contributions, we must thank the people and institutions that made the workshop and this book possible. First, the NIH provided financial support through NIDCD Grants DC-00111 and DC-00012 to David Pisoni and Grant R29 DC-01645 to Keith Johnson. Scott Bentley of Academic Press has also been very supportive of our efforts to put the book together, while remaining appropriately demanding.

Without the enthusiastic support of David Pisoni and Jody Kreiman, we would not have gone forward with what was at first a rather tentative idea for a workshop; David gave us some very helpful suggestions as we organized the meeting. Several participants contributed significantly to the success of the workshop, although they are not contributors to this volume. In particular, Robert Remez, James Jenkins, and Terrance Nearey contributed humor and wisdom to the discussion that day, and on behalf of all of the authors we thank them for their insights and suggestions.

Keith Johnson
John W. Mullennix

1

Complex Representations Used in Speech Processing

Overview of the Book

KEITH JOHNSON
JOHN W. MULLENNIX

The chapters in this volume represent a diverse range of research topics: from theories of perception and cognition, to issues in clinical speech pathology, and the practical concerns of speech technology. Despite this diversity, the common theme is that speech researchers are converging in a new approach to an old problem. When such interdisciplinary convergences occur in the field, it is important to pay attention, because the inherent variability and complexity of speech make it an almost intractable problem from any one point of view.

Traditional accounts of speech processing emphasize that canonical linguistic representations are derived from the speech signal. In these accounts, after the system makes a response to variation in the signal and derives the canonical representation, information about nonlinguistic variation is discarded. This view holds that the mental representations used in speech communication are simple and that the mapping from the speech signal to representations is complex. Detailing this complex mapping has proven to be a very difficult problem (the lack of invariance problem). The approach in this volume is to treat variability not as a nuisance variable but as valuable information that is retained and used. From this point of view, the mapping is simple and the representations are complex. This approach is a radical departure from the traditional view of speech processing.

Talker Variability in Speech Processing

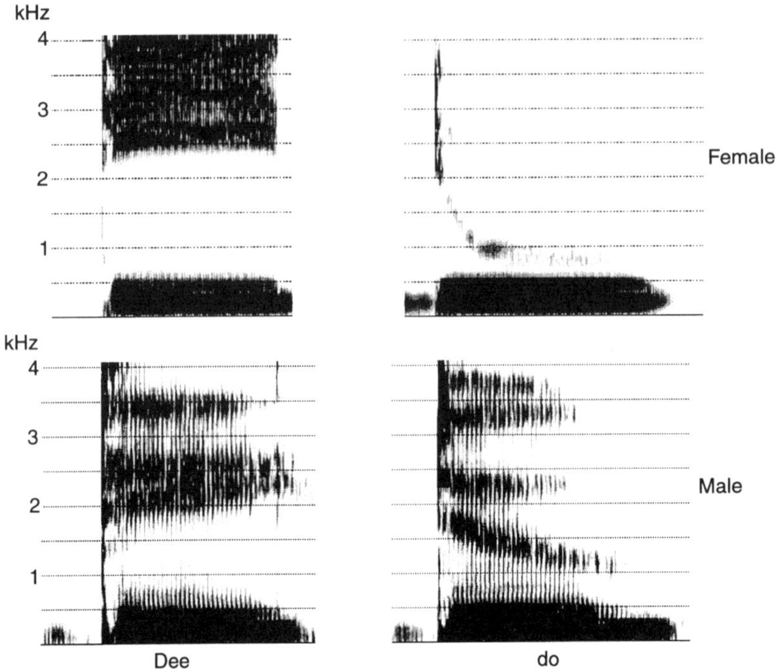

FIGURE 1 Spectrograms of *Dee* and *do* as spoken by a male and female speaker. These spectrograms illustrate both talker variability and contextual variability, two sources of lawful variation in the speech signal that contribute to the lack of invariance problem.

1.1 COMPLEX MAPPING: TALKER VARIABILITY AND CONTEXTUAL VARIABILITY

It is necessary in the traditional account to have a complex procedure to map the speech signal onto the mental representation of speech because it is assumed that each item in the mental lexicon is associated with (or contains) only one phonetic form. We call this the mental dictionary assumption because, in this view, words in the head are exactly analogous to dictionary entries. Like a dictionary entry, an item in the mental lexicon is assumed to have syntactic, semantic, phonological, phonetic, and orthographic information, and the process of recognizing words in the speech stream involves choosing the entry with a phonetic form that is closest to the phonetic form manifested in the signal.

When speech spectography became available in the late 1940s, the acoustic complexity of speech became apparent. Researchers were surprised by the large acoustic differences between speakers (see Figure 1) and sought to account for the listener's ability to recognize the phonetic forms of words produced by different speakers by positing perceptual "normalization" processes (Joos, 1948;

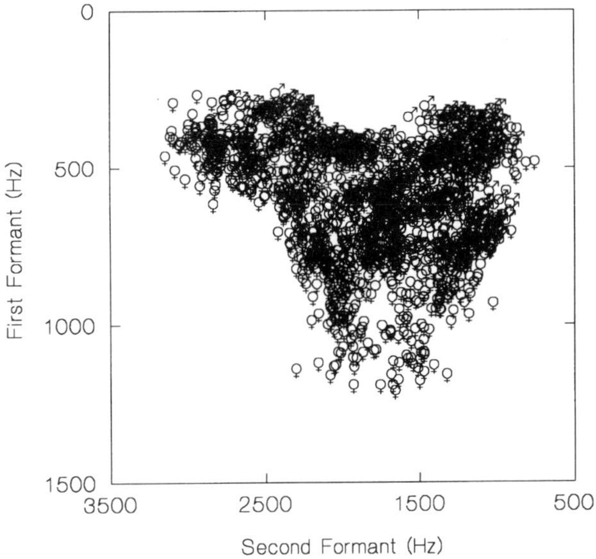

FIGURE 2 Scatter plot of the first and second formant values in vowels produced by 39 speakers of English.

Potter & Steinberg, 1950). The mental dictionary assumption makes speaker normalization necessary, because if each word is stored in the mental lexicon with only one canonical phonetic form, then the main problem in speech perception is to take speech signals that do not exactly match the canonical form and transform them so that predictable sources of variation (such as, vocal tract length and vocal fold vibration pattern) are eliminated. The assumption of any normalization scheme is that if one succeeds in finding the right transformation, then all productions of a particular linguistic form (dictionary entry) will look about the same.

The classic example of this approach is vowel normalization. In dealing with the acoustic values of vowels produced by different speakers (see Figure 2), the goal of a normalization routine is to reduce the amount of scatter within the vowel categories while maintaining separation between the vowels (assuming that no other acoustic properties are relevant for vowel identification). Several of the chapters in this volume discuss normalization strategies, so we will not go into details here. Our point is that a scatter-reduction technique of some sort is made necessary by the mental dictionary assumption.

In addition to talker variability, speech researchers in the early 1950s also noticed that speech exhibits a large amount of contextual variability. At that time, the contextual variability problem resulted from the assumption that each speech sound has a unique context-independent feature description, something like a dictionary entry. We call this the alphabetic writing assumption because we write the initial *d* in *Dee* using the same letter as the initial *d* in *do*. Because the formant transitions from the stop closure to the vowel steady state in these two words are quite different (Figure 1), and because we assume that they are merely positional variants of the same linguistic unit, it is necessary to describe a perceptual mapping that captures the lawful variation of linguistically identical entities in the speech signal. This contextual variability problem, typically referred to as the lack of invariance problem, has occupied the attention of speech researchers since it was pointed out by early researchers at Haskins Laboratories (e.g., Liberman, 1957). Although this problem spurred the development of a wide variety of theoretical viewpoints (Diehl & Kluender, 1989; Elman & McClelland, 1986; Fowler, 1986; Liberman & Mattingly, 1985; Stevens & Blumstein, 1978), research on contextual variation has (it seems to us) degenerated into repeating the same claims and counter-claims over and over, with no agreed-upon definitive experiment to distinguish the theories.

Although the chapters in this volume do not address this problem explicitly, we believe that the rich-representation, simple-mapping approach to talker variability that is emphasized in the work presented here suggests that a similar theoretical tack might also be fruitful in dealing with contextual variation (this change has already taken place in automatic speech recognition). By turning our attention to the flip side of the lack of invariance problem (that is, talker variability), we hope to find new ways to talk about variability in the speech signal, perhaps giving us a new frame of reference for discussing the contextual variation of speech sounds.

1.2 COMPLEX REPRESENTATIONS FOR SPEECH PROCESSING

Each chapter in this volume reflects, to a greater or lesser extent, an orientation toward viewing talker variability in speech processing in terms of a system with complex representations, in which variability is retained rather than normalized out. In this section we give brief previews of the chapters, highlighting some ways that the authors address this general theme.

1.2.1 Auditory Word Recognition

The first two chapters emphasize that memory for particular instances of auditorily presented words (episodic memory) has a significant impact on speech perception and word recognition. David Pisoni (Chap. 2) focuses on the contrast between (a) previous accounts of speech perception that treat variability as a source of noise in the signal that must be reduced or eliminated through perceptual normalization and (b) a new view based on ideas from nonanalytic cognition that says stimulus variability is "lawful" and "informative" for perceptual analysis. Pisoni reviews some recent experiments on talker variability and perceptual learning that indicate that listeners encode fine stimulus details about the talker and use them during word recognition and sentence perception. He suggests that this new approach to handling talker variability provides a new way of dealing with a number of long-standing issues in the field.

In a slightly different vein, Stephen Goldinger (Chap. 3) reviews the details of a number of recent perception and memory experiments, showing that episodic memory traces of words contain indexical information about the speaker. In addition, he describes the results of a number of modeling simulations using memory traces of "spoken words" with Hintzman's (1986) MINERVA 2 exemplar model of memory. He interprets his results as being consistent with the existence of an episodic mental lexicon. Goldinger concludes that there is no evidence in the literature related to the old abstractionist view to support the idea that normalization reduces information.

1.2.2 Voice Perception

Two chapters on voice processing and perception emphasize that much more needs to be understood about how speech signals are mapped to voice percepts.

John Mullennix (Chap. 4) reviews a number of recent findings in voice and speech perception that, when taken together, begin to form a more complete picture of the manner in which voice information and acoustic-phonetic information are extracted from the signal during speech perception. Mullennix suggests that although both voice information and phonetic information are encoded and retained during speech perception, they may be extracted in different ways or at least different rates from the signal. He also reviews evidence indicating that perceptual adjustments to talker voice are attention-intensive, capacity-limited processes. He concludes that more research needs to be conducted on determining the microstructure of the interactions between voice information and phonetic information during perception.

Jody Kreiman (Chap. 5) sent her chapter to us without a title and requested that we suggest one. These were some of our suggestions: "Back to basics in voice perception research: A critical reevaluation," "Research without theory is pointless: Evidence from voice perception," and "Theory avoidance: Twenty years of voice perception research." In this very important critical review of the literature Kreiman argues that "only the development of a theoretical basis for research into voice quality can stem the proliferation of repetitive, inconclusive studies." After reviewing decades of research she states, "it is unlikely such studies will ever explain why results differ from paper to paper." The theoretical foundation that she sketches—the prototype and deviations model—differs from previous approaches precisely by assuming that listeners' perceptual representations for voice are complex and listener-specific.

1.2.3 Speech Perception

Three chapters on speech perception discuss new views of speaker normalization in speech perception.

Howard Nusbaum and James Magnuson (Chap. 6) argue against the balkanization of speech perception research, in which talker normalization is segregated from later processes that compensate for contextual variation. They point out that most speech perception research has searched for a level of description that is not subject to the lack of invariance problem, assuming that speech perception is a passive, deterministic process. In contrast to this view, Nusbaum and Magnuson review an impressive array of evidence in support of a view of speech perception as an active process "more akin to hypothesis testing than pattern matching," in which talker normalization is an integral part. Central to their argument is a complex-representations view of linguistic–phonetic categories, in which the traditional view of phonemes is replaced by representations that encode, for example, "a theory of what a /b/ is." This novel viewpoint represents a way to look at talker variability in a new non-balkanized approach to speech perception.

Doug Whalen and Sonya Sheffert (Chap. 7) present evidence that speaker normalization occurs when synthetic vowel stimuli are preceded by a recorded inhalation noise. In one condition, they found a perceptual shift that was conditioned by the sex of the speaker doing the inhaling. As Whalen and Sheffert argue, this indicates that speech perception is guided by a model of the speaker. Although they do not explicitly argue against a complex mapping view, their results suggest that earlier accounts of vowel perception that rely on traditional cues like vowel formant range or vowel fundamental frequency in a normalization algorithm are vastly oversimplified. Whalen and Sheffert's finding pushes the complex mapping hypothesis to an extreme.

Keith Johnson (Chap. 8) describes an exemplar model of vowel perception and demonstrates that this model simulates human vowel identification performance without speaker normalization. He goes on to show that the model produces a speaker normalization effect for stimuli used in an earlier study and, by allowing attention to acoustic properties to vary, the model can simulate the presentation type effect found in that earlier experiment.

1.2.4 Automatic Speech Recognition

The book concludes with three chapters on speaker adaptation in automatic speech recognition (ASR). It is important to emphasize that studies of speaker adaptation are exploring ways to fine-tune ASR systems that already retain and use a great deal of speaker-specific information (the mixed Gaussian distributions that are ubiquitous now in ASR encode multimodal distributions of the sort needed to model certain types of talker variability). Speaker adaptation can be seen as yet another way to use complex speaker-specific representations in ASR because it involves adapting an existing speaker-independent recognition device given a partial analysis of some speaker-specific patterns. That is, speaker adaptation in ASR is an efficient way to construct, on the fly, a speaker-dependent recognition device.

In the first chapter in this section, Nikko Ström (Chap. 9) describes a technique for incorporating talker information directly into a vowel recognition neural network. In his technique, an explicit (but simple) representation of the talker is used to tune a vowel recognition network, in essence changing the internal representations of vowels in response to talker information. Unlike exemplar models in which talker variation is retained explicitly, this approach finds regularities in the relationship between talker and linguistic information and uses these regularities to tune the mapping between the signal and vowel categories.

Yunxin Zhao (Chap. 10), in the most technically demanding chapter in the book, describes an adaptation technique that includes both a data transformation stage, which is analogous to traditional normalization techniques because it involves modifying the input signal prior to comparison with stored representations, and a model adaptation stage. Zhao's iterative acoustic normalization technique is unique in that it involves phone-specific spectral bias removal. She demonstrates that her implementation of acoustic normalization is very good at compensating for spectral differences caused by varying recording circumstances. The second stage of the model, phone model adaptation, involves adapting the representations used to encode phonetic categories. By adapting the Gaussian mixture density parameters in a Hidden Markov Model (HMM) recognizer, Zhao is able to tune the model to the vocal tract and pronunciation habits of a particular speaker.

In Chapter 11, McGowan outlines a procedure for recovering an articulatory description of speech given the acoustic waveform (a gesture recovery procedure). Gesture recovery provides important knowledge for those employing articulatory representation in ASR. Although articulatory representation is on the speculative side of ASR research, articulatory variability due to talker differences has not yet received much attention. McGowan addresses this gap by extending his previous research on gesture recovery with a discussion of articulatory talker normalization. He proposes a technique that deals with talker variability in gesture recovery by characterizing intertalker variation in both vocal tract geometry and motor control patterns. Central to McGowan's strategy is the postulation of a normalizing map that represents the talker's vocal tract in terms of a standard vocal tract used in articulatory synthesis. He argues that by identifying talker-specific aspects of articulation and then using this information in ASR, the speech-recognition task is greatly simplified.

To some extent Kreiman's critique of voice perception research is relevant to speech perception and word recognition theory and ASR research as well. Theories exist in these areas to a greater extent than they do in voice research, but the same arguments seem to appear over and over. We hope that the alternative perspective presented in this collection will serve as a catalyst (or lightning rod, as the case may be) for future speech research.

REFERENCES

Diehl, R. L., & Kluender, K. R. (1989). On the objects of speech perception. *Ecological Psychology, 1,* 121–144.

Elman, J., & McClelland, J. (1986). Exploiting lawful variability in the speech wave. In J. S. Perkell & D. H. Klatt, (Eds.), *Invariance and variability in speech processing* (pp. 360–380). Hillsdale, NJ: Erlbaum.

Fowler, C. A. (1986). An event approach to the study of speech perception from a direct-realist perspective. *Journal of Phonetics, 14,* 3–28.

Hintzman, D. L. (1986). Schema abstraction in a multiple-trace memory model. *Psychological Review, 93,* 411–428.

Joos, M. (1948). Acoustic phonetics. *Language,* V *24* (Suppl. 2), 1–136.

Liberman, A. M. (1957). Some results of research on speech perception. *Journal of the Acoustical Society of America, 29,* 117–123.

Liberman, A., & Mattingly, I. G. (1985). The motor theory revised. *Cognition, 21,* 1–36.

Potter, R., & Steinberg, J. (1950). Toward the specification of speech. *Journal of the Acoustical Society of America, 22,* 807–820.

Stevens, K. N., & Blumstein, S. E. (1978). Invariant cues for place of articulation in stop consonants. *Journal of the Acoustical Society of America, 64,* 1358–1368.

2

Some Thoughts on ``Normalization'' in Speech Perception

DAVID B. PISONI

2.1 INTRODUCTION

The theoretical problems confronting researchers working in the field of speech perception are, in principle, no different from the problems studied in other areas of perception and cognition. Basically, they involve issues of invariance and variability of the speech signal, the neural representation of speech in the auditory system, and the perceptual constancy maintained by human listeners in the face of diverse physical stimulation. These are well-known problems in speech perception that have occupied psychologists, linguists, and engineers for close to a half-century, since the beginning of modern speech research in the late 1940s (see Klatt, 1989, for a review).

When compared to other perceptual systems, there can be little doubt that speech perception is extremely robust and adaptive over a wide range of environmental conditions that introduce large physical changes and transformations in the acoustic signal. For example, normal hearing listeners can adapt easily to changes in speakers, dialects, speaking rate, and speaking style, as well as a wide variety of acoustic transformations, including the presence of noise, reverberation, and the use of different transducers without any noticeable decrease in performance. Even the most sophisticated state-of-the-art speech-recognition systems cannot compare to the speed and efficiency of the human listener. It has always seemed that one of the principle tasks of speech science was to explain these remarkable perceptual and cognitive abilities and to model how the nervous system accomplishes this task so quickly and effortlessly in the face of continuous changes in the listener's environment.

For the last several years, I have been interested in the problems of stimulus variability in speech, in particular, the effects of stimulus variability from different talkers and different speaking rates on word-recognition performance. Recent findings have suggested to me that some of the long-standing theoretical assumptions that speech researchers have held about the existence of abstract units such as phonemes and words need to be reexamined and substantially revised. More specifically, the assumption of an idealized symbolic representation for spoken language has encouraged researchers to search for simple first-order physical invariants and to ignore the problem of stimulus variability in the listener's environment. Variability is simply treated as a troublesome source of "noise" in the acoustic signal. Following recent accounts of memory and concept learning by Jacoby and Brooks (1984), we will call this the traditional "abstractionist" or "analytic" approach to speech perception, an approach that places primary emphasis on the search for idealized categories that encode the linguistic content of speech into abstract symbolic units.

Findings from our laboratory on stimulus variability have suggested an alternative view of speech perception that is compatible with a large and growing body of literature in the field of cognitive psychology that deals with categorization. This view of speech perception focuses on the encoding of specific instances and assumes that very detailed stimulus information in the speech signal is processed by the listener and becomes part of the memory representation for spoken language. One of the assumptions of this "nonanalytic" approach is that stimulus variability is, in fact, a lawful and highly informative source of information for the perceptual process; it is not simply a source of noise that masks or degrades the idealized symbolic representation of speech in human long-term memory. According to this view, listeners encode particulars rather than generalities. Our research has shown that source information about the talker's voice and detailed information about speaking rate is, in fact, encoded into memory and forms part of the neural representation of speech. Rather than discarding the "indexical" attributes of speech in favor of a highly abstract symbolic code like a string of segments or phonemes, the human perceptual and memory systems appear to encode and retain very fine details of the perceptual event. Our results have a number of implications for future research on spoken-language processing as we continue to gain new insights into the "nonanalytic" aspects of speech and to reconsider the long-standing problems of invariance and variability in speech perception.

In this chapter, I consider the problem of perceptual normalization, specifically, talker normalization, in light of some recent findings and new theoretical developments in the field of perceptual learning and categorization. In past theoretical accounts of speech perception, a strict dissociation has been made between the linguistic properties of speech that carry the speaker's intended message and the indexical features of the signal that provide information about the talker's voice (Studdert-Kennedy, 1974). The dissociation between the form and content of the speech signal has a long history in the fields of linguistics and phonetics, which has been carried over to theoretical accounts of speech perception despite the obvious fact that both sources of information are carried simultaneously and in parallel by the same acoustic signal. An excellent example of the functional parallelism of the indexical and linguistic properties of speech can be seen in Figure 1, which shows the encoding of speech in the auditory periphery (Hirahara & Kato, 1992). The absolute frequencies of the formants provide cues to speaker identification (A), whereas the relative differences among the formants specify information for vowel identification (B). Both sets of attributes are carried simultaneously by the same acoustic signal.

Our recent findings suggest that the indexical attributes of a talker's voice are perceived and encoded in memory by the perceptual system along with the linguistic message, and that information about the talker's voice is not lost or discarded as a consequence of perceptual analysis. A variety of behavioral studies involving perceptual identification, speeded classification, and recognition memory tasks have demonstrated that very detailed information about the talker's voice and the specific stimulus tokens is encoded and retained in memory and subsequently affects spoken-word-recognition performance. Other studies have shown that listeners acquire information about unfamiliar voices that improves the intelligibility of novel words and sentences from these same talkers.

These results imply that the indexical and linguistic attributes of speech are not neatly partitioned into two independent channels of information by the nervous system. Indeed, the mutual dependencies observed in perceptual analysis between these two sources of information suggest very close interactions between the form and content of the linguistic message and the listener's linguistic knowledge. Thus, what a listener learns about a talker's voice—the acoustic correlates of gender, dialect, speaking rate, and so forth—are encoded and subsequently used to facilitate a phonetic interpretation of the linguistic content of the message.

These recent findings raise fundamental questions about the nature of the traditional symbolic representations that have been routinely assumed in previous accounts of speech perception. Current views about the neural representation of speech and the basic perceptual units will need to be revised and substantially enriched to accommodate the additional fine details of stimulus encoding that listeners carry out in speech perception and spoken-language processing tasks in the laboratory and real world. I believe these new perceptual findings are important because they suggest an alternative approach to traditional accounts of speech perception and spoken word recognition, which have relied heavily on abstract, idealized symbolic representations of the linguistic message with little or no concern about the contribution of the talker's voice and the indexical features of speech to the perceptual process and the neural representation of speech in memory. The findings from these recent studies also raise several interesting questions

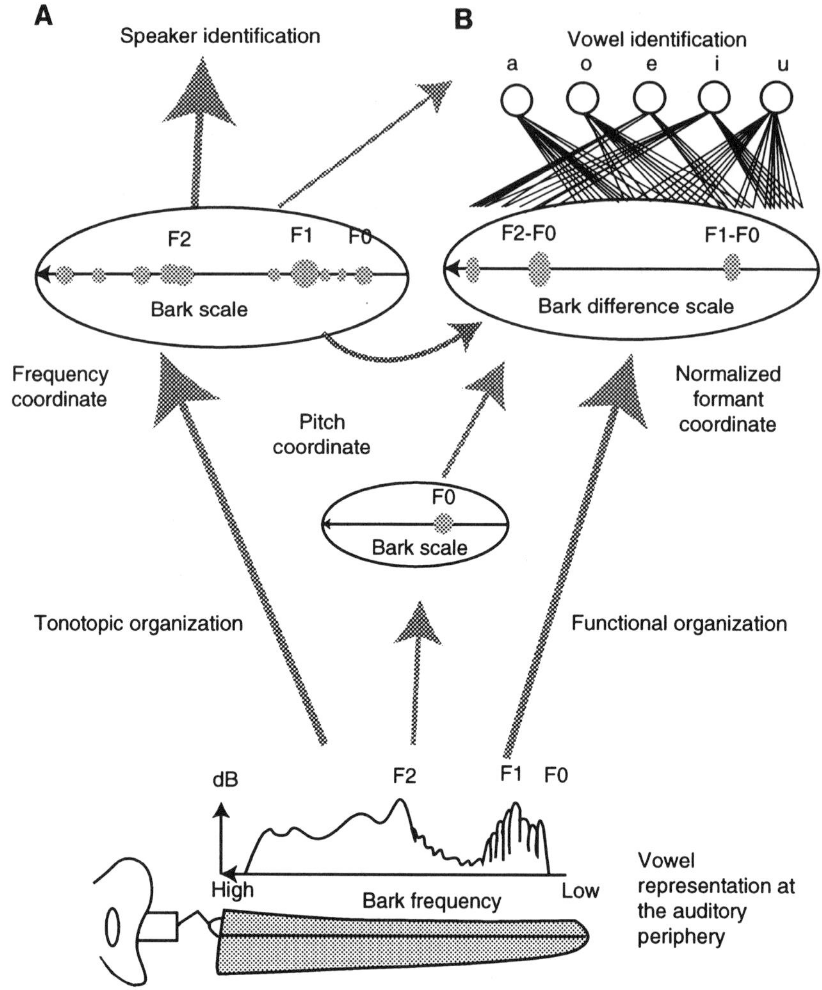

FIGURE 1 Vowel projections at the auditory periphery show that information for speaker identification (A) and perception of vowel quality (B) is carried simultaneously and in parallel by the same signal. The tonotopic organization of frequencies using a bark scale provides cues to speaker identification, whereas the relations among the formant (F) patterns in terms of difference from F0 in barks provide cues to vowel identification. (From Hirahara & Kato, 1992.)

about the theoretical assumptions that have been made over the years concerning the process of normalization in speech perception.

This chapter is divided into three sections. First, I begin by reviewing several definitions of the term *normalization* and consider the implications that follow from adopting the traditional meanings of this term. Then I briefly summarize several recent findings on the contribution of the talker's voice to speech perception and spoken word recognition. Finally, I describe an alternative approach to perceptual normalization that can accommodate these new findings within a theoretical framework that emphasizes the role of nonanalytic cognition and the contribution of specific instances to perception, learning, and cognition, especially memory and perceptual learning in speech perception and spoken-word recognition.

My goal in putting these ideas together at this time is to argue that it is possible to approach some of the old traditional problems in speech perception and spoken-word recognition, such as invariance, variability, and the need for perceptual normalization, in novel ways that can lead to new knowledge and insights into the fundamental process of speech perception. I believe this was not possible because of the traditional prevailing metatheory that was adopted by everyone working in the field and because of the experimental methodologies routinely employed in the past to study speech perception. However, this is a new era in the study of brain, behavior, and computation. Recent developments in cognitive and neural science, ecological psychology, and neural modeling, along with the widespread availability of high-speed computing technology, have provided new tools and powerful methods to study speech perception under much more demanding and robust conditions; thus many different sources of variability can be manipulated and studied.

Two key features of the traditional approach to speech perception are quite striking when viewed from the nonanalytic perspective, which emphasizes the role of specific instances to perception and cognition, that I am suggesting here. First is the dissociation, mentioned earlier, between the linguistic and indexical properties of the speech signal. Second is the assumption that stimulus variability is a source of noise and is not informative to the listener. Both of these assumptions have had profound effects on the study of speech perception and have strongly affected the kind of research problems that speech scientists have investigated over the years. These two assumptions have also affected the specific experimental methodologies used to study speech perception. Because stimulus variability was thought to mask or obliterate the underlying idealized symbolic message, factors known to create variability in the speech signal were deliberately reduced or eliminated. These factors were viewed as nuisance variables that needed to be controlled in experiments. For example, the traditional approach to acoustic-phonetic research typically used a small number of talkers, usually only one or two, reading carefully constructed experimental materials in citation format under extremely good recording conditions in the laboratory (Byrd, 1992). Also, each experiment typically addressed only a single specific research issue using a very small sample of highly controlled test materials, such as isolated nonsense syllables, words, or short sentences. In contrast, the current approach to acoustic-phonetic research relies very heavily on the use of large speech databases, such as the TIMIT corpus, which was collected with many different talkers producing speech under a wide variety of different conditions. Moreover, the test materials were specifically constructed to sample a larger and more diverse phonetic space, permitting computation of a variety of lexical statistics and the development of different types of models that can be used to characterize the structure and organization of lexical patterns in a given language (see Huttenlocher & Zue, 1984; Pisoni, Nusbaum, Luce, & Slowiaczek, 1985; Shipman & Zue, 1982; Zue, 1985).

The consequence of this traditional research strategy in acoustic-phonetics was that little if any effort was made to study the contribution of different sources of variability directly or to try to understand how variability affected speech perception or spoken-word-recognition performance in human listeners. Based on our recent findings, I believe that we have made some progress in understanding the role of stimulus variability in speech and how it affects performance in a variety of tasks with different populations of listeners. Also, a substantial body of new knowledge has been obtained about the interdependencies between the indexical and linguistic attributes of the speech signal. Listeners are sensitive to fine phonetic details in the signal, and they encode and represent acoustic changes in their listening environment that are potentially useful.

2.2 WHAT IS MEANT BY NORMALIZATION?

My observations and conclusions about stimulus variability and the encoding of fine phonetic details in speech are not entirely novel and should not be too surprising to people working in the mainstream of speech research. About 15 years ago, Dennis Klatt (1979) made a similar proposal about the need to preserve potentially useful acoustic-phonetic information in the context of his LAFS (Lexical Access From Spectra) model of speech recognition. His proposal was based on the idea that an optimally efficient speech-recognition system should be one that can recover gracefully from incorrect labeling or identification without catastrophic effects on performance. Klatt argued that models of speech perception that assume some form of intermediate level of discrete symbolic representation like phonemes or segments discard potentially useful acoustic-phonetic information that might be necessary if backtracking were required. Without retaining fine stimulus details, it would be impossible, according to Klatt, to recover from an errorful interpretation based on ambiguous or incorrect information in the signal.

Without remembering very much about Klatt's earlier proposal concerning the importance of retaining fine phonetic details, I initially found our results on talker variability troublesome for traditional accounts of speech perception that assumed that the speech signal is quickly encoded into a sequence of discrete abstract symbolic units like phonemes or phonetic segments. Of course, at that time, there were not many other viable alternatives to the traditional view of speech or competing accounts of speech perception. Everyone just assumed that phonemes or segments or some kind of symbolic units were perceived during the process of speech perception and constituted the basic perceptual units employed in accessing words from the mental lexicon. These theoretical views about the nature of speech have been around for a long time and have been prominent in discussions of speech perception and speech recognition. One of the best examples of the traditional idealized view of speech is expressed in Charles Hockett's well-known description of speech as a sequence of Easter eggs:

> Imagine a row of Easter eggs carried along a moving belt; the eggs are of various sizes, and variously colored, but not boiled. At a certain point, the belt carries the row of eggs between the two rollers of a wringer, which quite effectively smash them and rub them more or less into each other. The flow of eggs before the wringer represents the series of impulses from the phoneme source; the mess that emerges from the wringer represents the output of the speech transmitter. At a subsequent point, we have an inspector whose task it is to examine the passing mess and decide, on the basis of the broken and unbroken yolks, the variously spread out albumen, and the variously colored bits of shell, the nature of the flow of eggs which previously arrived at the wringer. (Hockett, 1955, p. 210)

Although this description of speech may seem a little simplistic, it does illustrate nicely the prevailing theoretical views at the time and the very strong emphasis on abstract symbolic coding of speech into discrete idealized linguistic units. Hockett was in good company, as shown by the approach of two prominent theorists in the field of speech communication, J. C. Licklider and Morris Halle, who both endorse the same set of fundamental assumptions about the discrete symbolic nature of speech:

> There is so much evidence that speech is basically a sequence of discrete elements that it seems reasonable to limit consideration to mechanisms that break the stream of speech down into elements and identify each element as a member, or as probably a member, of one or another of a finite number of sets. (Licklider, 1952, p. 590)

> The basic problem of interest to the linguist might be formulated as follows: What are the rules that would make it possible to go from the continuous acoustic signal that impinges on the ear to the symbolization of the utterance in terms of discrete units, e.g., phonemes or the letters of our alphabet: There can be no doubt that speech is a sequence of discrete entities, since in writing we perform the kind of symbolization just mentioned, while in reading aloud we execute the inverse of this operation; that is, we go from a discrete symbolization to a continuous acoustic signal. (Halle, 1956, p. 510)

As I went back recently and thought about some of these old views in greater detail, I realized that it might be a useful intellectual exercise to review and reconsider what researchers mean by the term *normalization* in speech perception and what some of the implicit assumptions are that follow from adopting this particular approach to dealing with stimulus variability and perceptual constancy in speech. Before proceeding to this task, however, it should be pointed out here that although the most important and probably the most distinctive property of speech is its inherent physical variability (see Table I), these properties are not what are typically discussed in traditional accounts of speech perception or spoken-word recognition. Instead of encouraging research on the study of variability, most theorists have tended to emphasize the discrete symbolic nature of speech and its linguistic function in conveying meaning. Moreover, there has always been a great deal of interest in figuring out ways to eliminate variability from experiments using speech stimuli rather than studying the problem of variability directly.

TABLE I Sources of Variability in Speech Acoustics[a]

Type of variability	Sources of variability
Ambient conditions	Background noise, room reverberation, microphone/telephone characteristics
Within-speaker variability	Breathy/creaky voice quality, shifting formants, and fundamental frequencies, changing speaking rate, variable degrees of articulatory undershoot, imperfect repetition across tokens of same gesture.
Cross-speaker variability	Differences of dialect, vocal tract length and shapes, detailed articulatory habits
Segment realization variability	Coarticulatory changes, articulatory modification due to stress or duration changes, optional deletions/simplifications in fluent speech.
Word environment variability in continuous speech	Cross-word-boundary coarticulation, phonetic and phonological recoding of words in sentences, changes in word duration due to syntax, pragmatics

[a]After Klatt, 1986.

Viewed in this way, the study of variability in speech has historically taken a backseat to the formalist approach to speech derived from linguistic theory, especially the recent views of language promoted by transformational grammar with its emphasis on the linguistic competence of an idealized speaker–hearer as summarized in Chomsky's well-known passages reproduced below:

> Linguistic theory is concerned primarily with an ideal speaker-listener, in a completely homogeneous speech-community, who knows its language perfectly and is unaffected by such grammatically irrelevant conditions as memory limitations, distractions, shifts of attention and interest, and errors (random or characteristic) in applying his knowledge of the language in actual performance.
>
> We thus make a fundamental distinction between competence (the speaker-hearer's knowledge of his language) and performance (the actual use of language in concrete situations). Only under the idealization set forth in the preceding paragraph is performance a direct reflection of competence. (1965, p. 2–3)

To help in this exercise and to find a couple of good working definitions of what "normalization" means, I turned first to *Webster's New Twentieth Century Dictionary* (1983). I also consulted English and English's *Dictionary of Psychological Terms* (1958) and Reber's *Dictionary of Psychology* (1985) for definitions of several other related terms used in perception and cognition. The dictionary definitions of the words "normal," "normalization," and "normalize" are given below:

> **normal:** (adj) Conforming with or constituting an accepted standard, model, or pattern; especially, corresponding to the median or average of a large group in type, appearance, achievement, function, development, etc.; natural; standard; regular. (*Webster's*)

normal: (noun) The usual state, amount, degree, etc.; especially, the median or average. (*Webster's*)

normalization: (noun) Reduction to a normal or standard state. (*Webster's*)

normalize: (vt) To bring into conformity with a standard, pattern, model, etc. (*Webster's*)

The commonality among all three terms shown above is the proposal that some object, concept, or idea is made to conform to a "standard" or a "model" in order to produce or create equivalent forms from diverse inputs. Although not stated explicitly here, there is the further assumption of some loss or reduction of information after normalization is completed.

The definition of the closely related word "standardize," also from *Webster's* is given below:

standardize: (vt) To cause to conform to a given standard; to make standard or uniform; to cause to be without variations or irregularities. (*Webster's*)

Here we see an additional property regarding the elimination of variability added to the previous definitions of "normalization" that require conformity with a standard, pattern, or model. Thus, at least according to the dictionary definitions considered here, the process of normalization consists of at least two separate components. The first deals with bringing something into conformity with a pre-existing standard so as to produce equivalent forms, whereas the second has to do with the reduction or elimination of variability thereby creating a standard or normal state.

I believe these definitions of the word *normalization* are fairly good approximations of how this term has been used technically in speech perception over the years to deal with the problems of perceptual invariance and perceptual constancy to nonequivalent forms. Indeed, the intended meanings are consistent with the definitions of the terms *invariance* and *equivalence* given below by Reber:

invariance: (noun) Generally, characteristic of that which does not change. The term is most often used with the qualifier relative. That is, few things in this world are truly invariant but some display greater invariance, greater consistency from circumstance to circumstance than others. In general, in the study of perception and learning, those aspects of the stimulus world that display the higher invariances, relative to other aspects, are learned most quickly and easily.

equivalence: (noun) In general, any relationship between two "things" such that one may be substituted for the other in a particular setting and not alter significantly the situation. The term is often modified so that the particular form of equivalence is specified; e.g., stimulus equivalence refers to two or more stimuli that are sufficiently similar that they evoke the same or nearly the same response, response equivalence refers to similar responses made to similar stimuli, etc.

I have gone through the effort of consulting several dictionaries to make explicit several aspects of the meaning of the term normalization that most speech researchers assume more or less implicitly in their experimental and theoretical work. In considering these definitions, I believe it is reasonable to conclude that the process of "normalization" produces three consequences in perception. First, there is the generation of equivalent forms from diverse inputs. Normalization is assumed to convert physically different tokens into some common representational format and to store these "standardized" representations in some kind of memory. Second, the process of normalization entails a loss of information and, as a consequence, a reduction in stimulus variability. Finally, although not explicitly stated, I believe that normalization also entails the additional assumption that stimulus variability is an undesirable source of noise in the speech signal, which produces perturbations on abstract underlying idealized forms that are assumed to be the true objects of perceptual analysis.

The process of perceptual normalization is, of course, a key component of traditional abstractionist theories of perception, memory, and learning (Shankweiler, Strange, & Verbrugge, 1977). According to this approach, the stimulus environment is highly impoverished and, as a consequence, the perceiver must rely on top-down knowledge to recognize the intended perceptual object and recover the underlying abstract symbolic form. In the case of speech perception, these objects are the talker's intended linguistic message. Other accounts assume these objects are the talker's intended gestures (Fowler & Rosenblum, 1991; Liberman & Mattingly, 1985). In addition to these two assumptions, there is also the proposal that information processing is selective and results in substantial stimulus reduction because the nervous system cannot maintain all aspects of stimulation in the perceiver's environment. A good summary of the traditional information-processing view of perception is given by Haber (1969) below:

> The second assumption, regarding limited information-handling capacities, is also an important one. The problem of limited channel capacity has been clear in the study of perception for most of the history of experimental psychology; witness concepts such as selective attention, and immediate memory span. The nervous system is apparently just not large enough to maintain all aspects of stimulation permanently. What this suggests for information-processing analyses is that we should look for instances in which recoding of information takes place—recoding generally in such a way that some of the content is maintained more explicitly at the expense of the other aspects which are dropped out. The points in time where the recoding occurs should be particularly important ones in the study of information processing, and it is not surprising that most information-processing models refer to these points almost exclusively. (p. 4)

2.3 STIMULUS VARIABILITY IN SPEECH PERCEPTION

My colleagues and I have completed a number of experiments on the effects of different sources of variability in speech perception and spoken-word recognition (Pisoni, 1990). Instead of reducing or eliminating variability in the stimulus materials, as most speech researchers have routinely done, we deliberately introduced variability from different talkers to study the effects of these variables on perception (Pisoni, 1992). Our research on this problem began with the observations of Mullennix, Pisoni, and Martin (1989), who found that the intelligibility of isolated spoken words presented in noise was affected by the number of talkers that were used to generate the test words in the stimulus ensemble. In one condition, all the words in a test list were produced by a single talker; in another condition, the same words were produced by 15 different talkers, including male and female voices. Subjects were asked to identify the words using an open-set test format. No feedback was provided. The results were very clear. Across three different signal-to-noise ratios (SNRs), identification performance was always better for words that were produced by a single talker than for words produced by multiple talkers. Trial-to-trial variability in the speaker's voice affected recognition performance. These findings replicated results reported many years ago by Peters (1955) and Creelman (1957) and suggested that the perceptual system must engage in some form of adjustment or "recalibration" each time a novel voice is encountered during the set of trials using multiple voices.

In a second experiment, my colleagues and I measured naming latencies to the same words presented in both blocked (single-talker) and mixed (multiple-talker) test conditions (Mullennix et al., 1989). We found that subjects were not only *slower* to name words presented in multiple-talker lists but they produced *more errors* when their performance was compared to the same words from single-talker lists. Both sets of findings were surprising at the time because all the test words used in the experiment were highly intelligible when presented in isolation under quiet listening conditions. The intelligibility and naming data from these studies raised a number of additional questions about how the various perceptual dimensions of the speech signal are processed and encoded by the human listener. At the time, we naturally assumed that the acoustic attributes used to perceive voice quality were independent of the more abstract linguistic properties of the signal. However, no one had ever tested this assumption directly.

To assess whether attributes of a talker's voice were perceived independently of the phonetic form of the words, we used a speeded classification task (Mullennix & Pisoni, 1990). Subjects were required to attend selectively to one stimulus dimension (e.g., voice) while simultaneously ignoring another stimulus dimension (e.g., phoneme). Across all conditions, we found increases in interference from *both* perceptual dimensions when the subjects were required to attend selectively to only *one* of the stimulus dimensions. The pattern of results suggested that words and voices were processed as integral dimensions; that is, the perception of one dimension (e.g., phoneme) affects classification of the other dimension (e.g., voice) and vice versa, and subjects could not selectively ignore irrelevant variation on the nonattended dimension. If both perceptual dimensions were processed separately, as we originally assumed, we should have found little, if any, interference from the nonattended dimension. Not only did we find mutual interference, suggesting that the two dimensions, voice and phoneme, were perceived in a mutually dependent manner, but we also found that the pattern of interference was asymmetrical. It was easier for subjects to ignore irrelevant variation in the phoneme dimension when their task was to classify the voice dimension than it was to ignore the voice dimension when they had to classify the phonemes.

The results from these perceptual experiments were surprising given our assumption that the indexical and linguistic properties of speech are perceived independently. To study this problem further, we carried out a series of memory experiments to assess the representation of speech in long-term memory. Experiments on serial recall of lists of spoken words by Martin, Mullennix, Pisoni, and Summers (1989) and Goldinger, Pisoni, and Logan (1991) demonstrated that specific details of a talker's voice are also encoded into long-term memory. Using a continuous recognition memory procedure, Palmeri, Goldinger, and Pisoni (1993) found that detailed episodic information about a talker's voice is also encoded in memory and is available for explicit judgments even when a great deal of competition from other voices is present in the test sequence.

In another set of experiments, Goldinger (1992) found evidence that implicit memory for attributes of a talker's voice persists for a relatively long time after perceptual analysis has been completed. He also showed that the degree of perceptual similarity between voices affects the magnitude of the repetition effect in several implicit memory tasks. For example, he found that subjects identified spoken words more accurately when the words were repeated using the same voice in which they had originally been presented than when the words were repeated in a different voice. These findings suggest that the perceptual system encodes very detailed talker-specific information about spoken words in episodic memory representations.

Another series of experiments examined the effects of speaking rate on perception and memory. These studies, designed to parallel the earlier experiments on talker variability, have also shown that the perceptual details associated with differences in speaking rate are not lost as a result of perceptual analysis. In one experiment, Sommers, Nygaard, and Pisoni (1994) found that words produced at different speaking rates (i.e., fast, medium, and slow) were identified more poorly than the same words produced at only one speaking rate. These results were compared to another condition in which differences in amplitude were varied randomly from trial to trial in the test sequences. In this case, identification performance was not affected by variability in overall level.

Other experiments on serial recall have also examined the encoding and representation of speaking rate in memory. Nygaard, Sommers, and Pisoni (1995) found that subjects recall words from lists produced at a single-speaking rate better than the same words produced at several different speaking rates. Interestingly, the differences appeared in the primacy portion of the serial position curve, suggesting greater difficulty in the transfer of items into long-term memory. Differences in speaking rate, like those observed for talker variability in our earlier experiments, suggest that perceptual encoding and rehearsal processes, which are typically thought to operate on only abstract symbolic representations, are also influenced by instance-specific sources of variability. If these sources of variability were somehow "filtered out" or "normalized" by the perceptual system at relatively early stages of analysis, differences in recall performance would not be expected in memory tasks like the ones used in these experiments.

Taken together with the earlier results on talker variability, the findings on speaking rate suggest that details of the early perceptual analysis of spoken words are not lost. Instead, they become an integral part of the mental representation of spoken words in memory. In fact, in some cases, increased stimulus variability in an experiment may actually help listeners to encode items into long-term memory (Goldinger et al., 1991). Listeners encode speech signals in multiple ways along many perceptual dimensions, and the nervous system apparently preserves these perceptual details much more reliably than researchers have believed in the past.

Considering the overall pattern of results, our findings on the effects of talker variability in perception and memory tasks provide support for the proposal that detailed perceptual information about a talker's voice is preserved, and that detailed attributes of the listener's stimulus environment are encoded implicitly into long-term memory. At present, it is not clear whether there is a single "composite" representation in memory or whether these different attributes are encoded in parallel in separate representations (Eich, 1982; Hintzman, 1986). Also unclear is whether spoken words are encoded and represented in memory as a sequence of abstract symbolic phoneme-like units along with much more detailed episodic information about specific instances and the processing operations used in perceptual analysis. These are important questions for future research on the representation of speech in memory.

2.4 PERCEPTUAL LEARNING OF VOICES

Findings on talker variability have also encouraged my colleagues and me to examine the tuning or perceptual adaptation that occurs when a listener becomes familiar with the voice of a specific talker (Nygaard, Sommers, & Pisoni, 1994). This particular problem has received little attention in the speech perception literature despite the obvious relevance to problems of speaker normalization, acoustic-phonetic invariance, and the potential application to automatic speech recognition and speaker identification (Fowler, 1992; Kakehi, 1992). Our search of the research literature on talker adaptation revealed only a small number of behavioral studies with human listeners on this topic, and all of them appeared in obscure technical reports from the mid 1950s.

To determine how familiarity with a talker's voice affects the perception of spoken words, we had two groups of listeners learn to explicitly identify a set of unfamiliar voices over a 9-day period using common names (e.g., Bill, Joe, Sue, Mary). After the subjects learned to recognize the voices, we presented them with a set of novel words mixed in noise at several SNRs; one group heard the words produced by previously heard talkers, whereas the other group heard the same words produced by new talkers to whom they had not been exposed during the perceptual learning task. In this phase of the experiment, which was designed to measure speech intelligibility, subjects were required to identify the words rather

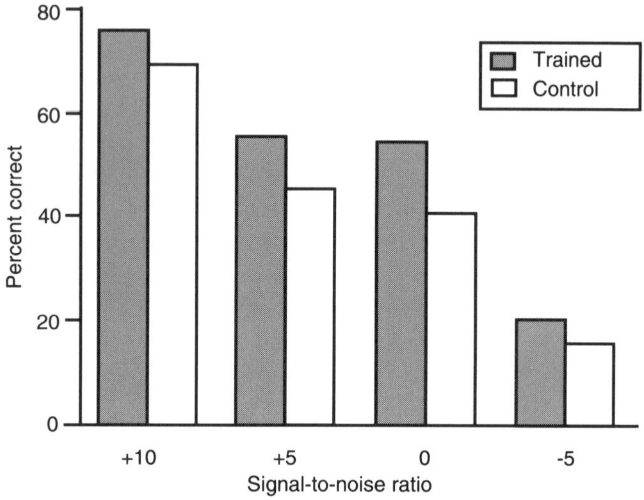

FIGURE 2 Percent correct word recognition (intelligibility) as a function of signal-to-noise ratio for trained and control subjects on the transfer task administered after voice-recognition training was completed. (From Nygaard, Sommers, & Pisoni, 1994.)

than simply recognize the voices, as they had done in the first phase of the experiment.

The results of the intelligibility experiment are shown in Figure 2 for the two groups of subjects. We found that identification performance for the trained group was reliably better than the control group at each of the SNRs tested. The subjects who had heard novel words produced by familiar voices were able to recognize words more accurately than subjects who received the same novel words produced by unfamiliar voices. Two other groups of subjects were also tested in the intelligibility experiment as controls; however, these subjects did not receive any training in recognizing the voices and were therefore not exposed to any of the stimuli prior to listening to the same set of words in noise. One control group received the set of words presented to the trained experimental group; the other control group received the words that were presented to the trained control subjects. The performance of these two control groups was not only the same, but was also equivalent to the intelligibility scores obtained by the trained control group. Thus, only the subjects in the experimental group who were explicitly trained on the voices showed an advantage in recognizing novel words produced by familiar talkers.

The findings from this perceptual learning experiment demonstrate that exposure to a talker's voice facilitates subsequent perceptual processing of novel words produced by the same talker. Thus, speech perception and spoken-word recognition draw on highly specific perceptual knowledge about a talker's voice that is obtained in an entirely different experimental task—explicit voice recognition as compared to a speech intelligibility test. Listeners show evidence of tracking changes in their listening environment, specifically, information about a talker's vocal tract transfer function and how it changes over time, and encoding this information in memory for later use when they have to process the linguistic attributes of the signal in order to identify the words in an intelligibility test.

Two additional studies were designed to assess the nature and extent of this kind of perceptual learning (Nygaard & Pisoni, 1995). Subjects in both experiments were trained to recognize a set of ten talkers from sentence-length utterances. In the first experiment, after training was completed, intelligibility was assessed using isolated words produced by familiar and unfamiliar talkers. The aim was to determine if the information learned about a talker's voice from sentences generalizes to the perception of spoken words. The assumption was that training with sentence-length utterances would focus listeners' attention on a different set of acoustic properties than training with isolated words. It was hypothesized that because sentences contain extensive prosodic and rhythmic information in addition to the specific acoustic-phonetic implementation strategies unique to individual talkers, perceptual learning of voices from sentences would require attentional and encoding demands specific to those particular test materials.

In the second experiment, after training on sentences was completed, listeners were given an intelligibility test consisting of sentence-length utterances produced by familiar and unfamiliar talkers. Two issues were addressed here. First, does specific training on sentence-length utterances generalize to similar test materials? Second, are sentence-length utterances that have higher-level semantic and syntactic constraints susceptible to the effects of familiarity with a talker's voice?

All subjects showed continuous improvement over the 3 days of training. Both groups of subjects identified talkers consistently above chance even on the first day of training, and performance rose to nearly 85% correct by the last day of training.

Surprisingly, in the first experiment we found only a small unreliable difference in the word intelligibility test for subjects who heard familiar voices during training compared to the control subjects. These results suggest that perceptual learning of talkers' voices from sentence-length utterances does not generalize to the perception of isolated words.

The results obtained in the second experiment, which assessed sentence intelligibility at three SNRs, were quite different. Figure 3 shows the total number of "key words" that were correctly identified in each sentence. Large differences were observed for the subjects who had heard novel sentences produced by *familiar* talkers. These differences became even larger as the listening conditions became poorer, demonstrating transfer of knowledge about the talker's voice from sentence-length utterances.

The results of these experiments suggest that perceptual learning of voices is both talker- and task-specific. Perceptual learning transfers in a task-specific manner, suggesting that attention must be directed to learning the specific voice attrib-

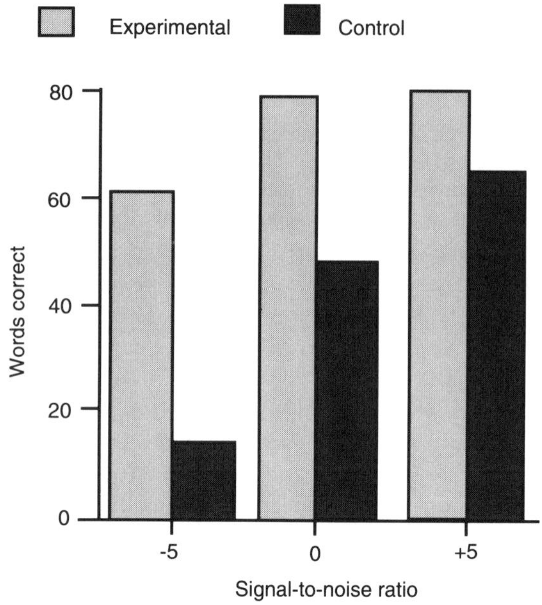

FIGURE 3 Percent correct recognition of key words in sentences as a function of signal-to-noise ratio for experimental and control groups. (From Nygaard & Pisoni, 1995.)

utes that will be relevant at test. These findings also show that talker-specific effects occur with sentence-length materials that contain higher-level semantic and syntactic constraints. Thus, talker-specific effects operate in a variety of listening situations from isolated words to sentence-length utterances, but there are both talker- and task-specific constraints on the transfer of this kind of knowledge.

Familiarity with a talker's voice involves a form of perceptual tuning and adjustment that results in modification of speech- and language-processing mechanisms. Listeners appear to retain talker-specific information about individual articulatory idiosyncrasies both at the level of acoustic-phonetic implementation in isolated words and at a more global level found in sentence-length utterances. Once again, we see close interactions and dependencies between the indexical properties of speech associated with the talker's voice and the linguistic analysis of the speech signal used in recognizing words in sentences.

What kind of perceptual knowledge does a listener acquire when he or she listens to a speaker's voice and is required to carry out an explicit name-recognition task, as our subjects did in these experiments? One possibility is that the analysis procedures or perceptual operations (Kolers, 1973) used to recognize the voices are retained in some type of "procedural" memory system and that these same processing routines are invoked again when the same voice is encountered in a subsequent intelligibility test. This kind of procedural knowledge might increase the efficiency of the perceptual analysis for novel words produced by familiar talkers because detailed analysis of the speaker's voice would not have to be carried out over and over again each time a new word was encountered. Another possibility is that the specific instances—perceptual episodes or exemplars of each talker's voice—are stored in a composite memory system and then later retrieved during the process of word recognition when new tokens from a familiar talker are presented (Estes, 1994; Jacoby & Brooks, 1984).

Whatever the exact nature of this knowledge turns out to be, the important point to emphasize here is that prior exposure to a talker's voice facilitates subsequent recognition of novel words and sentences produced by the same talker. These findings demonstrate a form of implicit memory for a talker's voice that is distinct from the retention of the individual lexical items and sentences used and the specific perceptual learning task that was employed to familiarize the listeners with the voices (Roediger, 1990). These results provide additional support for the view that the neural representation of spoken words and sentences encompasses both a symbolic description of the utterance in terms of a phonetic representation *and* additional information about the structural description of the source characteristics of the specific talker. Thus, speech perception appears to be carried out in a "talker-contingent" manner; indexical and linguistic properties of the speech signal are apparently closely interrelated and are not dissociated in perceptual analysis (Nygaard & Pisoni, 1995; Nygaard et al., 1994). One of the important discoveries of studies done within the framework of nonanalytic cognition is that many aspects of perception, learning, and categorization may not be available to conscious recollection but nevertheless will affect perceptual analysis and memory processes in a variety of ways. Thus, sweeping conclusions like those of Halle (1985) and Brown (1990) about the retention of voice-specific information in speech will obviously have to be revised in light of the present set of findings on perceptual learning of voices:

> When we learn a new word we practically never remember most of the salient acoustic properties that must have been present in the signal that struck our ears; for example, we do not remember the voice quality of the person who taught us the word or the rate at which the word was pronounced. Not only voice quality, speed of utterance, and other properties directly linked to the unique circumstances surrounding every utterance are discarded in the course of learning a new word. (Halle, 1985, p. 101)

> Clearly most of the time anyone is listening to English being spoken, he is listening for the meaning of the message—not to how the message is being pronounced. Indeed if you listen to how the words are spoken it is very unlikely that you can simultaneously understand what it is that is being said. On the whole people do not listen critically to the way the message is pronounced. The odd glottal stop or unusual pronunciation of a word may strike the listener, but most of the time he is busy abstracting the meaning of the message, and preparing his own mental comments on it. This is why most people are quite unaware of how English is actually spoken. (Brown, 1990, p. 3)

2.5 EXEMPLAR-BASED APPROACH TO SPEECH PERCEPTION

The approach to speech perception proposed here relies heavily on earlier work by Jacoby and Brooks on nonanalytic concept formation. Their studies on categorization and memory have provided evidence for the encoding and retention of episodic information and the details of perceptual analysis (Brooks, 1978; Jacoby & Brooks, 1984; Tulving & Schacter, 1990). According to this approach, stimulus variability is informative for perceptual analysis. Memory involves encoding both specific instances and the specific processing operations used during recognition (Kolers, 1973; 1976). The major emphasis of this view of cognition is on particulars, rather than abstract generalizations or symbolic coding of the stimulus input into idealized categories. I believe that the problems of variability and invariance found in speech perception can be approached in a fundamentally different way by nonanalytic or instance-based accounts of perception and memory. Moreover, this view of cognition provides insights into several long-standing theoretical issues in speech and offers a potentially useful way of dealing with findings that show that listeners encode very fine details of their stimulus environment.

The findings from studies on nonanalytic cognition are directly relevant to theoretical questions about the nature of perception and memory for speech and to assumptions about abstractionist representations based on formal linguistic analyses. When the criteria used for postulating episodic or nonanalytic representations are examined carefully, it becomes clear that speech signals display a number of distinctive properties that make them excellent candidates for this approach (Brooks, 1978; Jacoby & Brooks, 1984). These criteria are summarized in the sections below.

2.5.1 High Stimulus Variability

Speech signals display a great deal of physical variability primarily because of factors associated with the production of spoken language. Among these factors are within- and between-talker variability, changes in speaking rate and dialect, differences in social contexts, syntactic, semantic, and pragmatic effects and emotional state, as well as a variety of ambient environment effects, such as background noise, reverberation, and microphone characteristics (Klatt, 1986). These diverse sources of variability produce large changes in the acoustic-phonetic properties of speech, and they need to be accommodated in theoretical accounts of the categorization process in speech perception.

2.5.2 Complex Category Relations

The use of phonemes as perceptual units in speech perception entails a set of complex assumptions about category membership. These assumptions are based on linguistic criteria involving principles such as meaning contrast, phonetic similarity, and distributional characteristics. In traditional taxonomic linguistics, for example, the concept of a phoneme is used in a number of different ways, as shown by the definitions from Gleason (1961) given in Table II.

TABLE II Definitional Characteristics of the Phoneme[a]

- The phoneme is the minimum feature of the expression system of a spoken language by which one thing that may be said is distinguished from any other thing that might have been said.
- A phoneme is a class of sounds. There is no English phoneme that is the same in all environments, though in many phonemes the variation can easily be overlooked, particularly by a native speaker.
- A phoneme is a class of sounds that: (1) are phonetically similar and (2) show certain characteristic patterns of distribution in the language or dialect under consideration.
- A phoneme is one element in the sound system of a language having a characteristic set of interrelationships with each of the other elements in that system.
- The phoneme cannot, therefore, be acoustically defined. The phoneme is instead a feature of language structure. That is, it is an abstraction from the psychological and acoustical patterns that enables a linguist to describe the observed repetitions of things that seem to function within the system as identical in spite of obvious differences. The phonemes of a language are a set of abstractions.

[a]From Gleason, 1961

Thus, the perceptual categories used in speech display complex relations that place a number of strong constraints on the class of models that can account for these operating principles. These categories cannot be defined clearly and easily by simple rules and must be identified via a set of relations involving sound contrast and lack of contrast in meaning within a specific phonological system.

2.5.3 Incomplete Information

Spoken language is a highly redundant symbolic system that has evolved to maximize transmission of linguistic information. In the case of speech perception, research has demonstrated the existence of multiple speech cues for almost every phonetic contrast. Although these speech cues are, for the most part, highly context-dependent, they also provide reliable information that can facilitate comprehension of the intended message when the signal is presented under degraded conditions. This feature of speech perception permits very high rates of information transmission even under poor listening conditions.

2.5.4 High Analytic Difficulty

Speech is inherently multidimensional in nature. As a consequence, many quasi-independent articulatory attributes can be mapped onto the phonological categories of a specific language. Because of the complexity of speech and its high acoustic-phonetic variability, the category structure of speech is not amenable to simple hypothesis testing. As a result, it has been extremely difficult to formalize a set of explicit rules that can successfully map speech cues onto discrete phoneme categories. The perceptual units of speech are also highly automatized. The underlying category structure of a language is learned in a tacit and incidental way by young children.

2.5.5 Perceptual Spaces for Perception and Production

Among category systems, speech appears to be unique because of the close interrelations between speech production and speech perception. Speech exists simultaneously in several very different domains: the acoustic domain, the articulatory domain, and the perceptual domain. Although the relations among these domains are complex, they are not arbitrary and reflect properties of a unitary articulatory event. And, even within the domain of production and articulation, speech is encoded simultaneously in the optical display of the talker's face and the acoustic signal generated by the vocal tract. The sound contrasts used in a given language function within a common linguistic system that is shared by both production and perception. Thus, the phonetic contrasts generated in speech production by the vocal tract are precisely the same acoustic differences that are distinctive in perceptual analysis (Stevens, 1972). As a result, any theoretical account of speech perception must also take into consideration aspects of speech production and acoustics, as well as the multimodal relations between the auditory and visual correlates of speech.

In learning the sound system of a language, children not only develop abilities to discriminate and identify sounds, but they also learn to control the motor mechanisms used in articulation to generate precisely the same phonetic contrasts in speech production to which they have become attuned in perception. One reason that the developing perceptual system might preserve very fine phonetic details, as well as the specific characteristics of the talker's voice, would be to allow young children to accurately imitate and reproduce speech patterns heard in their surrounding language-learning environment (Studdert-Kennedy, 1983). This perceptuomotor skill would provide children with an enormous benefit in acquiring the phonology of the local dialect from speakers they are exposed to early in life.

In short, when properties of speech signals are examined more closely, and when the criteria for nonanalytic cognition are applied and evaluated, it becomes plausible to assume that very detailed information about specific instances in speech perception might be stored in memory. In contrast to a traditional symbolic rule-based representational approach, listeners may store a very large number of specific instances or perceptual episodes and then use them in an analogical rather than analytic way to perceive and categorize novel stimuli (Brooks, 1978; Whittlesea, 1987). Recent findings from studies on talker variability in speech perception provide support for this conclusion.

The traditional view of "normalization" assumes that perceptual constancy is achieved via a process or set of procedures involving a reduction in variability and a "loss" of detailed stimulus information. But this view is wrong. Human listeners preserve fine phonetic details and appear to encode other aspects of their listening environment, including indexical information about the talker's voice, gender, dialect, speaking rate, affect, and speaking style, among other nonlinguistic attributes in their surroundings. We believe these are important new insights into speech perception and spoken-language processing that will open up new areas of research on the study of sources of variability in speech perception.

2.6 SUMMARY AND CONCLUSIONS

This chapter began with a review and discussion of the term *normalization* as it has been used in the field of speech perception. An examination of several dictionary definitions revealed a number of distinctive properties of normalization that were generally consistent with the way this term is used technically in the field of speech perception to deal with perceptual constancy and invariance. Three consequences of normalization were addressed in greater detail. First, I discussed the assumption that normalization produces equivalent forms. Second, I examined the proposal that normalization entails a loss or reduction of information. And third, I considered the property of normalization that involves elimination of variability among specific instances. All three attributes of "normalization" are assumed in traditional abstractionist accounts of speech perception and spoken-word recognition, and all three of these attributes have played important roles in theorizing about the nature of the perceptual and neural mechanisms used in speech perception.

In the second section, I summarized findings from a series of recent experiments on the contribution of stimulus variability to speech perception and spoken-word recognition. Other results on learning novel voices and the contribution of voice information to word recognition and sentence intelligibility were also described. These studies with normal-hearing listeners demonstrate that fine details of the listener's perceptual environment are encoded and stored in memory and used at a later time during the perceptual analysis of novel stimuli. The results on the perceptual learning of voices demonstrate that the linguistic and indexical properties of speech are not maintained independently as separate channels of information by the nervous system. Interactions between these two properties of the speech signal occur early on in perceptual analysis and produce mutual dependencies that affect the efficiency of subsequent perceptual operations.

In the third section, the above-referenced observations and recent findings were considered together within the framework of recent developments in perceptual learning, memory, and categorization, specifically, the nonanalytic or instance-based approach to cognition that emphasizes the episodic encoding of specific details of the stimulus environment. The studies on talker and rate variability provide important information about speech perception and spoken-word recognition and have raised a set of new questions for future research. These findings encourage researchers to look at several of the long-standing problems in speech perception in different ways than they have been able to do in the past.

The present findings and reanalysis of the term normalization suggests several directions for research on speech perception. Exemplar-based or episodic models of categorization provide new solutions to the problems of invariance, variability, and perceptual normalization, which have been difficult to resolve with traditional models of speech perception that were motivated by formal linguistic analyses of spoken language. These problems can now be approached in quite different ways when viewed within the general framework of nonanalytic or instance-based models of cognition, which provide novel ways of dealing with stimulus variability—one of the most difficult problems in the field of speech perception and spoken-language processing.

ACKNOWLEDGMENTS

This research was supported in part by National Institutes of Health (NIH) Research Grant DC-00111 and in part by National Institute on Deafness and Other Communication Disorders (NIDCD) Research Training Grant DC00012 to Indiana University in Bloomington, Indiana. I thank Steve Chin for his editorial help and Darla Sallee for her assistance in preparing the manuscript.

REFERENCES

Brooks, L. (1978). Non-analytic concept formation and memory for instances. In E. Rosch & B. Lloyd (Eds.), *Cognition and categorization* (pp. 169–211). Hillsdale, NJ: Erlbaum.

Brown, G. (1990). *Listening to spoken English* (2nd ed.). New York: Longmans.

Bryd, D. (1992). Sex, dialects, and reduction. *ICSLP 92 Proceedings,* pp. 827–830.

Chomsky, N. (1965). *Aspects of the theory of syntax.* Cambridge, MA: MIT Press.

Creelman, C. D. (1957). Case of the unknown talker. *Journal of the Acoustical Society of America, 29,* 655.

Eich, J. E. (1982). A composite holographic associative memory model. *Psychological Review, 89,* 627–661.

English, H. B., & English, A. C. (1958). *A comprehensive dictionary of psychological and psychoanalytical terms: A guide to usage.* New York: Longmans, Green.

Estes, W. K. (1994). *Classification and cognition.* New York: Oxford University Press.

Fowler, C. A. (1990). Listener-talker attunements in speech. *Haskins Laboratories Status Report on Speech Research, SR-101/102,* 110–129.

Fowler, C. A., & Rosenblum, L. D. (1991). The perception of phonetic gestures. In I. G. Mattingly & M. Studdert-Kennedy (Eds.), *Modularity and the motor theory of speech perception* (pp. 33–59). Hillsdale, NJ: Erlbaum.

Gleason, H. A. (1961). *An introduction to descriptive linguistics.* New York: Holt, Rinehart & Winston.

Goldinger, S. D. (1992). *Words and voices: Implicit and explicit memory for spoken words. Research on Speech Perception* (Tech. Rep. No. 7). Bloomington: Indiana University.

Goldinger, S. D., Pisoni, D. B., & Logan, J. S. (1991). On the locus of talker variability effects in recall of spoken word lists. *Journal of Experimental Psychology: Learning, Memory, and Cognition, 17,* 152–162.

Haber, R. N. (1969). *Information-processing approaches to visual perception.* New York: Holt, Rinehart & Winston.

Halle, M. (1956). *For Roman Jakobson: Essays on the occasion of his sixtieth birthday, 11 October 1956.* The Hague: Mouton.

Halle, M. (1985). Speculations about the representation of words in memory. In V. A. Fromkin (Ed.), *Phonetic linguistics* (pp. 101–104). New York: Academic Press.

Hintzman, D. L. (1986). Schema abstraction in a multiple-trace memory model. *Psychological Review, 93,* 411–423.

Hirahara, T., & Kato, H. (1992). The effect of FO on vowel identification. In Y. Tohkura, E. Vatikiotis-Bateson, & Y. Sagisaka (Eds.), *Speech perception, production and linguistic structure* (pp. 89–112). Tokyo: Ohmsha Publishing.

Hockett, C. F. (1955). *A manual of phonology.* Baltimore: Waverly Press.

Huttenlocher, D. P., & Zue, V. W. (1984). A model of lexical access based on partial phonetic information. *Proceedings ICASSP-84,* pp. 1–4.

Jacoby, L. L., & Brooks, L. R. (1984). Nonanalytic cognition: Memory, perception, and concept learning. In G. Bower (Ed.), *The psychology of learning and motivation,* (pp. 1–47). New York: Academic Press.

Kakehi, K. (1992). Adaptability to differences between talkers in Japanese monosyllabic perception. In Y. Tohkura, E. Vatikiotis-Bateson, & Y. Sagisaka (Eds.), *Speech perception, production and linguistic structure* (pp. 135–142). Tokyo: Ohmsha Publishing.

Klatt, D. H. (1979). Speech perception: A model of acoustic-phonetic analysis and lexical access. *Journal of Phonetics, 7,* 279–312.

Klatt, D. H. (1986). The problem of variability in speech recognition and in models of speech perception. In J. S. Perkell & D. H. Klatt (Eds.), *Invariance and variability in speech processes* (pp. 300–319). Hillsdale, NJ: Erlbaum.

Klatt, D. H. (1989). Review of selected models of speech perception. In W. Marslen-Wilson (Ed.), *Lexical representation and process* (pp. 169–226). Cambridge, MA: MIT Press.

Kolers, P. A. (1973). Remembering operations. *Memory & Cognition, 1,* 347–355.

Kolers, P. A. (1976). Pattern analyzing memory. *Science, 191,* 1280–1281.

Liberman, A. M., & Mattingly, I. G. (1985). The motor theory of speech perception revised. *Cognition, 21,* 1–36.

Licklider, J. C. R. (1952). On the process of speech perception. *Journal of the Acoustical Society of America, 24,* 590–594.

Martin, C. S., Mullennix, J. W., Pisoni, D. B., & Summers, W. V. (1989). Effects of talker variability on recall of spoken word lists. *Journal of Experimental Psychology: Learning, Memory, and Cognition, 15,* 676–684.

Mullennix, J. W., & Pisoni, D. B. (1990). Stimulus variability and processing dependencies in speech perception. *Perception & Psychophysics, 47,* 379–390.

Mullennix, J. W., Pisoni, D. B., & Martin, C. S. (1989). Some effects of talker variability on spoken word recognition. *Journal of the Acoustical Society of America, 85,* 365–378.

Nygaard, L. C., & Pisoni, D. B. (1995). Talker- and task-specific perceptual learning in speech perception. *Proceedings of the XIIIth International Congress of Phonetic Sciences, Stockholm, Sweden,* pp. 194–197.

Nygaard, L. C., Sommers, M. S., & Pisoni, D. B. (1994). Speech perception as a talker-contingent process. *Psychological Science, 5,* 42–46.

Nygaard, L. C., Sommers, M. S., & Pisoni, D. B. (1995). Effects of stimulus variability on perception and representation of spoken words in memory. *Perception & Psychophysics, 57,* 989–1001.

Palmeri, T. J., Goldinger, S. D., & Pisoni, D. B. (1993). Episodic encoding of voice attributes and recognition memory for spoken words. *Journal of Experimental Psychology: Learning, Memory, and Cognition, 19,* 1–20.

Peters, R. W. (1955). *The relative intelligibility of single-voice and multiple-voice messages under various conditions of noise* (Joint Project Report No. 56, pp. 1–9). Pensacola, FL: U.S. Naval School of Aviation Medicine.

Pisoni, D. B. (1990). Effects of talker variability on speech perception: Implications for current research and theory. *Proceedings of the 1990 International Conference on Spoken Language Processing, Kobe, Japan,* pp. 1399–1407.

Pisoni, D. B. (1992). Some comments on invariance, variability and perceptual normalization in speech perception. *Proceedings of the 1992 International Conference on Spoken Language Processing, Banff, Canada,* pp. 587–590.

Pisoni, D. B., Nusbaum, H. C., Luce, P. A., & Slowiaczek, L. M. (1985). Speech perception, word recognition and the structure of the lexicon. *Speech Communication, 4,* 75–95.

Reber, A. S. (1985). *The Penguin dictionary of psychology.* Harmondsworth, UK: Penguin Books.

Roediger, H. L. (1990). Implicit memory: Retention without remembering. *American Psychologist, 45,* 1043–1056.

Shankweiler, D., Strange, W., & Verbrugge, R. (1977). Speech and the problem of perceptual constancy. In R. Shaw & J. Bransford (Eds.), *Perceiving, acting, and knowing: Toward an ecological psychology* (pp. 315–345). Hillsdale, NJ: Erlbaum.

Shipman, D. W., & Zue, V. W. (1982). Properties of large lexicons: Implications for advanced isolated word recognition systems. *Proceedings ICASSP-82,* pp. 546–549.

Sommers, M. S., Nygaard, L. C., & Pisoni, D. B. (1994). Stimulus variability and spoken word recognition: I. Effects of variability in speaking rate and overall amplitude. *Journal of the Acoustical Society of America, 96,* 1314–1324.

Stevens, K. N. (1972). The quantal nature of speech: Evidence from articulatory acoustic data. In E. E. David, Jr., & P. B. Denes (Eds.), *Human communication: A unified view* (pp. 51–66). New York: McGraw-Hill.

Studdert-Kennedy, M. (1974). The perception of speech. In T. A. Sebeok (Ed.), *Current trends in linguistics* (pp. 2349–2385). The Hague: Mouton.

Studdert-Kennedy, M. (1983). On learning to speak. *Human Neurobiology, 2,* 191–195.

Tulving, E., & Schacter, D. L. (1990). Priming and human memory systems. *Science, 247,* 301–306.

Webster's new twentieth century dictionary. (1983). New York: Simon & Schuster.

Whittlesea, B. W. A. (1987). Preservation of specific experiences in the representation of general knowledge. *Journal of Experimental Psychology: Learning, Memory, and Cognition, 13,* 3–17.

Zue, V. W. (1985). The use of speech knowledge in automatic speech recognition. *Proceedings of the IEEE, 73*(11), 1602–1615.

3

Words and Voices

Perception and Production in an Episodic Lexicon

STEPHEN D. GOLDINGER

3.1 INTRODUCTION

In the first decade of the twentieth century, a German scientist named Richard Semon described a theory of memory that anticipated many aspects of contemporary theories (Schacter, Eich, & Tulving, 1978; Semon, 1909/1923). In modern parlance, we would call Semon's view an "episodic," "exemplar," or "multiple-trace" theory, because it assumed that every stimulus, such as a spoken word, leaves a unique trace in memory. Upon presentation of a new stimulus, all traces are activated in proportion to their similarity to the stimulus. The most activated traces come to consciousness and the stimulus is thus "recognized." The assumption of unique traces allowed Semon's theory to explain the permanence of specific memories; the challenge was to also create *abstraction* from a collection of idiosyncratic traces. The resolution apparently derived from Galton, who discovered that blending many faces into a photographic composite creates the image of a "generic" face. Galton applied this phenomenon as a memory metaphor: "Whenever a single cause throws different groups of brain elements simultaneously into excitement, the result must be a blended memory" (1883, p. 229; cited in Hintzman, 1986). Semon used this idea, assuming that abstraction occurs at *retrieval* as countless partially redundant traces respond to an input.

Talker Variability in Speech Processing

For a variety of reasons, including the behaviorist movement, Semon's ideas were lost from mainstream psychology (see Schacter et al., 1978). When cognitive science had a resurgence in the late 1950s, most theories emphasized minimalist, symbolic representations. Perception was theorized to entail *information reduction,* such that successive stages of information processing derive progressively more abstract representations of analog inputs (Posner, 1964). Whereas Semon's theory emphasized a proliferation of partially redundant traces, later theories emphasized representational economy. Especially in theories of language, the recoding of specific episodes (tokens) into canonical representations (types) remains a basic assumption (see Pisoni, Chap. 2, this volume).

In speech perception and spoken-word recognition, this view is motivated by the extreme variability of the signal (see Goldinger, Pisoni, & Luce, 1996; Klatt, 1979, 1989). The acoustic properties of speech are affected by many factors, including phonetic contexts, prosodic contours, speaking rates, and speakers. Decades of speech research have failed to reveal invariant patterns that automatic recognition systems can reliably identify. Thus, variability in speech is considered a perceptual "problem" to be solved by listeners, just as it must be solved in speech-recognition systems (Gerstman, 1968). Consider *speaker variability:* Speakers differ in the sizes and shapes of their vocal tracts (Fant, 1973; Joos, 1948; Peterson & Barney, 1952), glottal characteristics (Monsen & Engebretson, 1977), strategies for producing phonemes (Ladefoged, 1980), and native dialects. As such, there is great acoustic variability in nominally identical words across individuals. Nevertheless, we recognize most words across most speakers without difficulty.

Abstractionist theories of word recognition assume that special processes match variable stimuli to canonical representations in memory (Forster, 1976; McClelland & Elman, 1986; Morton, 1969; Oden & Massaro, 1978; Pisoni & Sawusch, 1975; Studdert-Kennedy, 1976). For example, speech is presumably *normalized* with respect to lexical entries. Following Neisser (1967), the term implies that speech is filtered with respect to "phonetically irrelevant" information, such as voice details. Speaker normalization presumably allows the listener to follow the lexical and semantic content of speech; superficial details are exploited by the perceptual machinery and are then discarded (Krulee, Tondo, & Wightman, 1983). Together, the assumptions of speaker normalization and an abstract lexicon suggest that long-term memory for spoken words should reflect elements of meaning; elements of perception, such as voice details, should be lost. Indeed, most theories treat voice details as "noise" that the speech processor must resolve to derive phonetic or lexical percepts. The speaker's voice is merely a noisy vehicle for abstract information. For example, Halle (1985) claimed that

> when we learn a new word we practically never remember most of the salient acoustic properties that must have been present in the signal that struck our ears; for example, we do not remember the voice quality, speed of utterance, and other properties directly linked to the unique circumstances surrounding every utterance. (p. 101).

Unfortunately, the speaker normalization hypothesis is generally unfalsifiable, at least via perceptual tests. Consider speaker variability effects in word recognition: Mullennix, Pisoni, and Martin (1989) examined listeners' perceptual performance to words spoken by 1 or 10 speakers. They found that speaker variability reduced identification of words in noise, and slowed shadowing of words in the clear. Given these data, they concluded that a *capacity-demanding* normalization process usurps resources needed for primary task performance (see also Nusbaum & Morin, 1992). But, had they found no effect of speaker variability, they may have reasonably concluded that *automatic* normalization supports fluent performance. Null effects of speaker (and font) variability are commonly interpreted in this manner (Brown & Carr, 1993; Green, Kuhl, Meltzoff, & Stevens, 1991; Jackson & Morton, 1984; Krulee et al., 1983). Apparently, both positive and null effects of speaker variability reflect normalization. The speaker normalization hypothesis is necessitated by a priori assumptions of abstract lexical representation. If one assumes that variable signals are mapped onto ideal templates or prototypes, perception implies normalization by fiat. We can study how the process works: Is it automatic or capacity demanding? But for researchers hoping to *test* the normalization hypothesis, this circularity is a frustrating barrier.

Most theories of speech perception must assume speaker normalization, but different representational assumptions could alleviate this "logical necessity." For example, in a lexicon of countless perceptual episodes, spoken words could be compared directly to prior traces, without intervening normalization. Questioning such basic representational assumptions allows us to consider speaker normalization a *testable hypothesis,* rather than an assumed process, equally evidenced by the presence or absence of effects.

Many contemporary theories of memory and categorization resemble Semon's forgotten theory. Global memory models assume parallel access to countless memory traces (Eich, 1982; Gillund & Shiffrin, 1984; Hintzman, 1986, 1988; Medin & Schaffer, 1978; Murdock, 1982; Nosofsky, 1984, 1986; Underwood, 1969). Connectionist models also embody a multiple-trace assumption (Knapp & Anderson, 1984; McClelland & Rumelhart, 1985). These theories are all partially motivated by common findings of accurate memories for "irrelevant" details of experience. Memory for detail is evident for nonlinguistic stimuli, such as faces (Bahrick, Bahrick, & Wittlinger, 1975; Bruce, 1988), pictures (Roediger & Srinivas, 1992; Shepard, 1967; Standing, Conezio, & Haber, 1970), musical pitch (Halpern, 1989), social interactions (Lewicki, 1986; Smith & Zarate, 1992), and physical dynamics (Cutting & Kozlowski, 1977).

Contrary to traditional views, *linguistic* information processing also leaves detailed memories. Subjects spontaneously remember the presentation modalities of words (Hintzman, Block, & Inskeep, 1972; Hintzman, Block, & Summers, 1973; Kirsner, 1974; Lehman, 1982; Light, Stansbury, Rubin, & Linde, 1973), the location of information on text pages (Lovelace & Southall, 1983; Rothkopf, 1971), and the exact wording of sentences (Begg, 1971; Keenan, MacWhinney,

& Mayhew, 1977). Experiments on *transformed text* demonstrate persistence of visual details in memory after reading (Kolers, 1976; Kolers & Ostry, 1974). Similar findings occur with isolated printed words. Hintzman et al. (1972) showed subjects words in uppercase block letters and lowercase script letters. In a recognition memory test, half of the "old" words were repeated in their original format and half were switched. Hit rates were higher for words repeated in their original format (see also Hintzman & Summers, 1973; Kirsner, 1973; Roediger & Blaxton, 1987). Jacoby and Hayman (1987) found that changing the typeface of words between study and test reduced accuracy of perceptual identification. They concluded that visual details of words persist in memory, and they suggested that visual word *perception* relies on episodic memory. Given these data, it would be surprising if spoken-word perception operated differently. Indeed, relative to visual words, there are *better* reasons to assume that surface details of spoken words persist in memory.

The human voice conveys "personal information" about a speaker, including age, gender, emotional state, regional origin, and social status. These *indexical aspects* of speech (Abercrombie, 1967; Ladefoged & Broadbent, 1957) are typically ignored in theories of phonetic perception, but are clearly important. For example, changes in "tone of voice" are pervasive and readily understood in conversation (e.g., sarcasm). Introspection suggests that voice memory is accurate; we recognize friends on the telephone, and so on. More formally, although early research (McGehee, 1937) indicated that long-term memory for voices is poor, later experiments found reliable voice memory (Carterette & Barneby, 1975; Hollien, Majewski, & Doherty, 1982; Papcun, Kreiman, & Davis, 1989). Van Lancker, Kreiman, and Emmorey (1985; Van Lancker, Kreiman, & Wickens, 1985) reported that famous voices are recognized quite well, even when played backwards or at abnormal speaking rates.

3.2 MEMORY FOR WORDS AND VOICES

As with printed words, several studies have assessed the persistence of voice details in memory for isolated spoken words. Hintzman et al. (1972) played subjects words spoken by a male and a female. In a surprise recognition memory test, half the words were repeated in their original voice and half were repeated in the opposite voice. Listeners discriminated old and new voices well above chance (see Cole, Coltheart, & Allard, 1974; Geiselman & Belleza, 1976, 1977). Schacter and Church (1992; Church & Schacter, 1994) reported that *implicit memory* for spoken words includes voice details. Indeed, the details retained in implicit memory are quite specific, including intonation contour and vocal pitch.

As noted above, Mullennix et al. (1989; Summerfield & Haggard, 1973) found detrimental effects of speaker variability on identification of words in noise, and speeded shadowing of words in the clear. In a follow-up study, Martin, Mullennix, Pisoni, and Summers (1989) investigated serial recall of word lists pro-

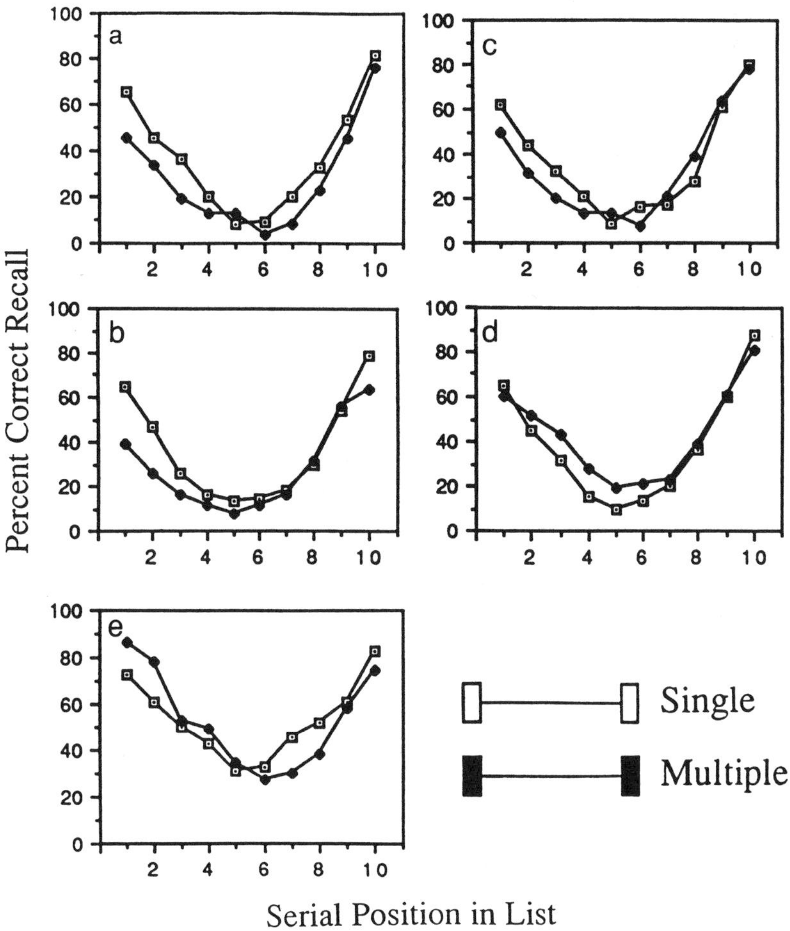

FIGURE 1 Serial recall data from Goldinger et al. (1991). Open symbols denote recall of speaker lists; closed symbols denote recall of 10-speaker lists. Words were presented at rates of one word every (a) 250 ms; (b) 500 ms; (c) 1000 ms; (d) 2000 ms; (e) 4000 ms.

duced by 1 or 10 speakers. Primacy recall was less accurate from 10-speaker lists than from 1-speaker lists. Also, recall of digits shown *before* the spoken lists was reduced when followed by 10-speaker lists, relative to 1-speaker lists. Martin et al. suggested that speaker variability induces a mandatory normalization process, usurping attention needed for rehearsal. However, this was challenged by Goldinger, Pisoni, and Logan (1991), who found that speaker variability interacts with presentation rate. Figure 1 displays our results: At fast presentation rates, recall from 1-speaker lists was superior to recall from 10-speaker lists, as Martin et al. found. But at slower rates, recall from 10-speaker lists was actually *more* accurate than recall from 1-speaker lists (see Lightfoot, 1989; Nygaard, Sommers, & Pisoni, 1992, for replications).

Presentation rate is assumed to affect rehearsal (Murdock, 1962; Rundus, 1971), so these results also suggest that speaker variability usurps attention, but the deeper implication is different. Although speaker variability increases processing load, voice information is clearly encoded in long-term memory. Indeed, lexical and voice information are processed as integral dimensions of spoken words (Mullennix & Pisoni, 1990); neither dimension can be ignored in favor of the other. Apparently, word and voice processing are interdependent, sharing a limited-capacity system (Cutting & Pisoni, 1978; Nusbaum & Morin, 1992). Thus, attending to spoken words implies attending to voice. Speaker variability may reduce recall at faster rates by mere distraction (Aldridge, Garcia, & Mena, 1987).

In a similar experiment, Goldinger (1990) examined *self-paced* serial recall of single- and multiple-speaker word lists. In this procedure, subjects are given dynamic control of presentation rate. They press a button to play each word, pausing as long as they wish between words. This procedure provides two forms of data, allowing examination of self-determined presentation rates and subsequent recall. The results of the single- and multiple-speaker comparisons are shown in Figure 2. The left panel shows mean listening times as a function of serial position; the right panel shows corresponding recall. The recall data closely resemble the slow presentation rate data of Goldinger et al. (1991). More important, the self-determined listening times corroborate the interpretation above: Speaker variability motivates listeners to pause longer between words, allowing for increased rehearsal.

Of course, earlier studies had established that voice details are encoded in memory during word recognition (Cole et al., 1974; Geiselman & Belleza, 1976; Hintzman et al., 1972; Light et al., 1973). Unfortunately, most prior studies were limited in scope, using only two stimulus voices, usually a male and a female. Thus, memory for voice could reflect analog episodes, as in MINERVA 2, or abstract "gender tags" (Geiselman & Crawley, 1983). To address this issue, Palmeri, Goldinger, and Pisoni (1993) investigated "continuous recognition memory" for words and voices. In this task, words are continuously presented, minimizing rehearsal. All words are presented twice; subjects classify each as "new" on its first presentation, and "old" on its repetition (Shepard & Teghtsoonian, 1961). The primary independent variable is the number of intervening words, or *lag,* between the words' first and second presentations. Typically, as lag increases, recognition decreases.

Our study extended research by Craik and Kirsner (1974). In their study, words were first spoken by either a male or female; when repeated, half the words retained their original voice and half switched voices. Craik and Kirsner found that same-voice repetitions were recognized more accurately than different-voice repetitions at all lags, up to 32 intervening words. They concluded that perceptual details of spoken words persist in memory for at least 2–3 min. Unlike Craik and

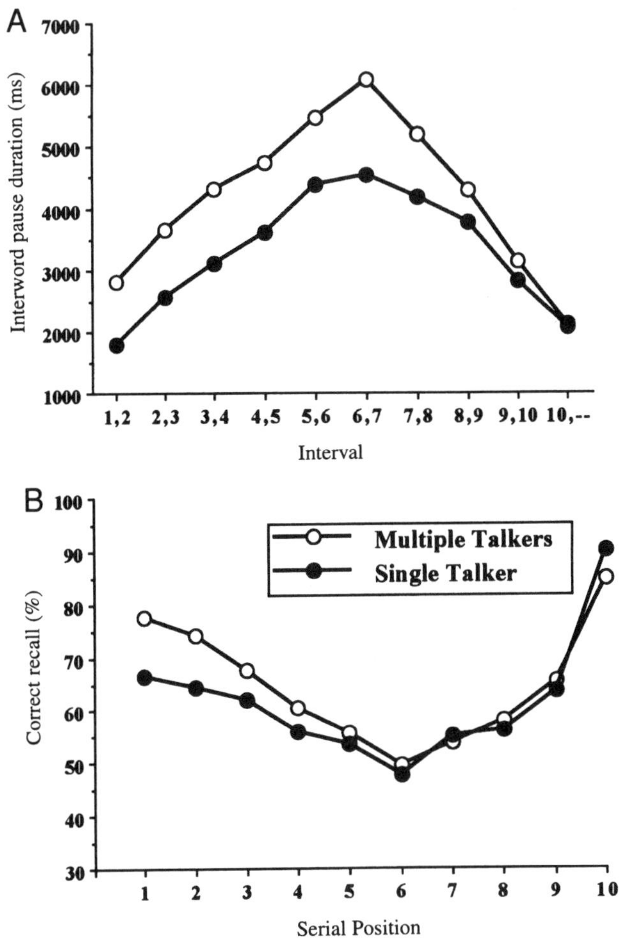

FIGURE 2 Self-paced serial recall data from Goldinger (1990). (A) Self-determined presentation rates as a function of serial position; (B) Subsequent recall.

Kirsner, we used several levels of speaker variability. Subjects heard 2, 6, 12, or 20 voices; half the speakers were male and half were female. This change let us evaluate two hypotheses that a two-voice, male–female design would not. First, we could evaluate the *automaticity* of voice encoding: If subjects intentionally encode voices, increasing from 2 to 20 speakers should impair their ability to do so. Second, including multiple speakers of both genders let us evaluate Geiselman and Crawley's (1983) *voice connotation* hypothesis. By this view, male and female voices invoke different connotations of words, like the idea of abstract "gender tags" mentioned above. Thus, recognition should be *gender-dependent,* rather than *voice-dependent:* Same-voice repetitions and different-voice/same-

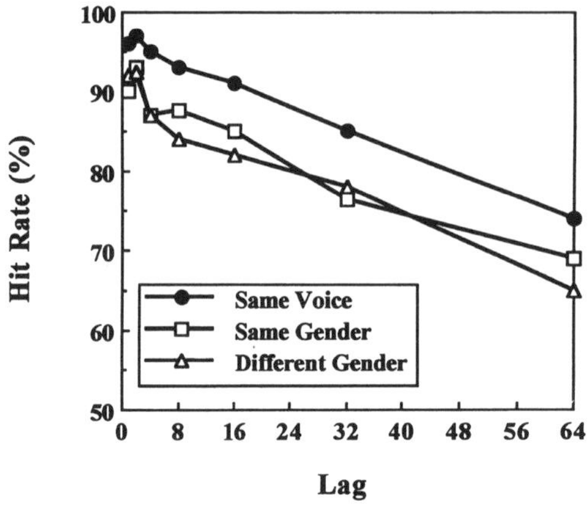

FIGURE 3 Continuous recognition memory data from Palmeri et al. (1993). Hit rates are shown as a function of lag between first and second presentations of words. Separate functions denote same-voice, different-voice/same-gender, and different-voice/different-gender repetitions.

gender repetitions should yield equivalent recognition; both should be superior to different-voice/different-gender repetitions. Third, whereas Craik and Kirsner used lags up to 32 intervening trials, we tested lags up to 64 intervening trials.

Figure 3 shows recognition hit rates for words as a function of repetition voice and lag, averaged across number of speakers. (Only results from 6-, 12-, and 20-voice lists are shown, because 2-voice lists cannot include different-voice/different-gender repetitions.) Although it is not shown, recognition accuracy and voice effects were equivalent across all levels of speaker variability. Increasing from 2 to 20 speakers had no effect on word or voice encoding, suggesting that voice encoding is automatic. Figure 3 shows that recognition of same-voice repetitions was superior to recognition of different-voice repetitions, regardless of gender. This pattern was consistent at all levels of speaker variability, suggesting that detailed word + voice traces are encoded during perception; only repetition of an exact stimulus facilitates later recognition. Thus, an interpretation based on abstraction, such as the voice connotation hypothesis, was not supported. The same-voice advantage was equivalent across all lags, suggesting that coherent word + voice traces may last indefinitely. Sheffert and Fowler (1995) recently replicated these results.

Palmeri et al. found that voice details are retained in episodic memory for 4–5 min, but a robust voice effect at maximum lag suggested that episodic traces may last far longer than we assessed. Recently, Goldinger (1996) extended this study in several important respects: Episodic retention was assessed over longer time periods, using both *explicit* and *implicit* memory measures. Whereas explicit measures entail conscious recollection, implicit measures entail facilitation of task performance, possibly without conscious recollection (Musen & Treisman, 1990;

Tulving & Schacter, 1990; Tulving, Schacter, & Stark, 1982). Moreover, the perceptual similarities among all 10 voices in the stimulus set were discovered using a multidimensional scaling (MDS) procedure (Carterette & Barneby, 1975; Kruskal & Wish, 1978; Shepard, 1980). If traces of spoken words retain fine perceptual details, then memory for an "old" word in a new voice should be affected by the perceptual similarity of the voices, even within genders.

There were many conditions in this research, so I only review several major findings (see Goldinger, 1996, for complete explication). In an explicit recognition memory experiment, listeners identified 150 words presented in the clear. In later test sessions, they classified 300 words as "old" or "new." Subjects heard either 2, 6, or 10 stimulus voices and, between sessions, they waited either 5 min, 1 day, or 1 week. In all conditions, the voices of half the "old" words were changed between study and test.

Figure 4 displays recognition memory hit rates in all conditions. As all panels show, hit rates decreased steadily over time. As in continuous recognition, no effect of total variability was observed; hit rates were equivalent with 2, 6, and 10 voices in the stimulus set. Of primary interest were *voice effects:* At the 5-min and 1-day delays, same-voice repetitions were recognized more accurately than different-voice repetitions. The voice effect diminished over time, and was absent at the 1-week delay. Apparently, episodic traces of spoken words are available to explicit memory for at least a day, but either the traces or their availability diminishes over the course of a week.

Figure 5 shows the effects of *perceptual similarity* on recognition memory in the six-voice conditions. Data from "different-voice" trials were divided into categories corresponding to all pairwise combinations of speakers. In six-voice conditions, there were 15 unique combinations of two speakers. Hit rates for all voice pairings were correlated with their corresponding perceptual distances, determined by MDS. Figure 5 shows results as a function of delay between study and test: Open circles represent the 5-min delay; filled circles represent the 1-day delay; open squares represent the 1-week delay. The best-fitting lines through each data set are drawn and labeled on the figure. (Results for the 10-voice condition were qualitatively similar to the data shown here.)

In general, as the perceptual distance between study and test voices increased, recognition memory hit rates decreased. If the study and test tokens of a word are similar, the test word apparently accesses an episodic trace of the study word, leading to a correct "old" response. The probability or "strength" of such access decreases steadily with decreased similarity. This suggests that episodic traces created during study retain perceptual details with *great precision.* However, the traces (or their availability) decay over time, and the correlation diminishes to insignificance after 1 week.

In a conceptually similar implicit memory experiment, listeners identified 300 words presented in noise during study sessions. In later test sessions, they again identified 300 words in noise. In both sessions, subjects heard either 2, 6, or 10 stimulus voices. Between sessions, they waited either 5 min, 1 day, or 1 week.

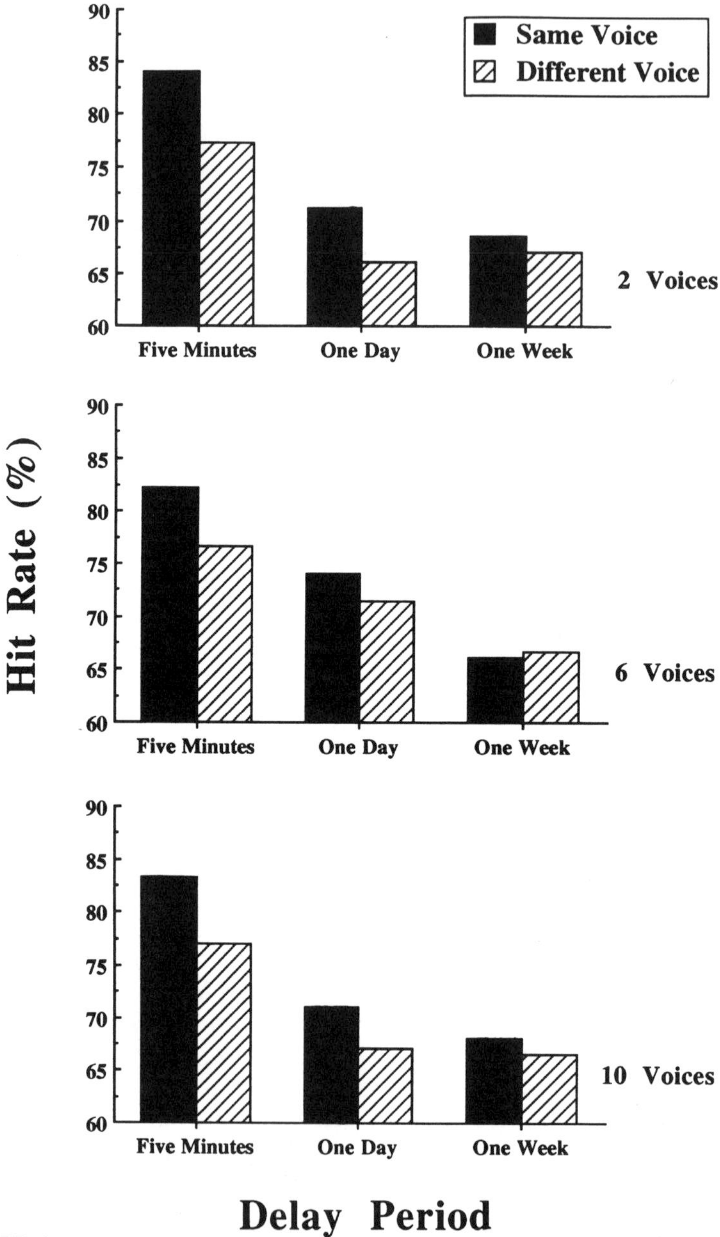

FIGURE 4 Recognition memory data from Goldinger (1996). Hit rates are shown in separate panels as a function of number of voices (2, 6, or 10), and in dark and light bars for same- and different-voice repetitions, respectively.

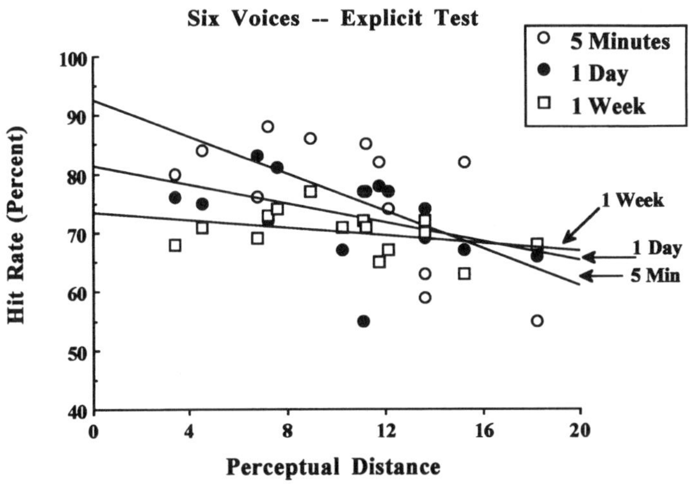

FIGURE 5 Correlations of intervoice perceptual distances and hit rates from six-voice conditions of Goldinger (1996). Hit rates are shown as a function of delay between study and test sessions (three correlation slopes are labeled) and perceptual distance between speakers' voices (determined via multidimensional scaling).

All study words were repeated during test, but half of the voices were changed between sessions.

Figure 6 displays the perceptual identification data from test sessions, in terms of repetition effects across study and test. Positive numbers indicate that identification accuracy improved during test, relative to study. Of primary interest were voice effects: At all delays, same-voice repetitions were identified more accurately than different-voice repetitions. (This pattern was consistent across the 2-, 6-, and 10-voice conditions.) In contrast to the explicit recognition memory data, these results show that episodic traces of spoken words are available to implicit memory for as long as a week.

Figure 7 shows the correlations of perceptual similarity and repetition effects in the six-voice conditions. (Results for the 10-voice condition were qualitatively similar to the data shown here.) In general, as the perceptual distance between study and test voices increased, identification rates decreased, suggesting that episodic traces retain voice details with great precision. Moreover, these details influence perceptual performance for a full week.

Given these results, a logical question arises for theories of word recognition: If episodic traces of words persist in memory and affect perception, why not assume they constitute the mental lexicon? Several theories propose word recognition based on episodic representations. Jacoby (1983a, 1983b; Jacoby & Brooks, 1984; Jacoby & Dallas, 1981; Jacoby & Hayman, 1987; Jacoby & Witherspoon, 1982) has suggested that word recognition occurs via "nonanalytic" means—stimuli are recognized by direct comparison to prior episodes, rather than transla-

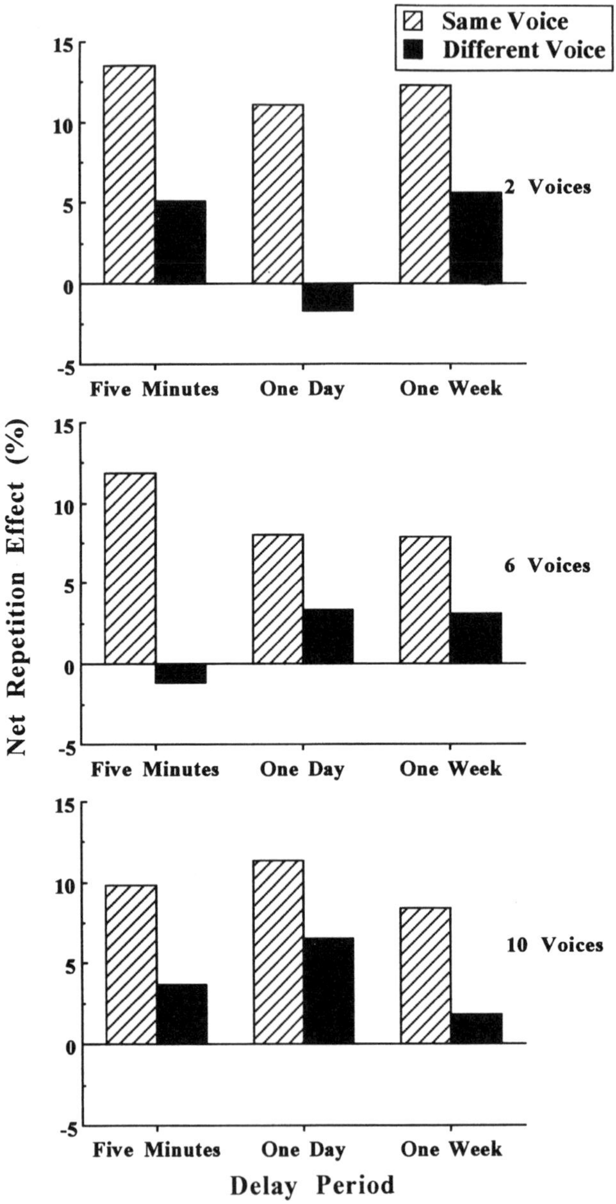

FIGURE 6 Perceptual identification data from Goldinger (1996). Hit rates are shown in separate panels as a function of number of voices (2, 6, or 10), and in dark and light bars for same- and different-voice repetitions, respectively.

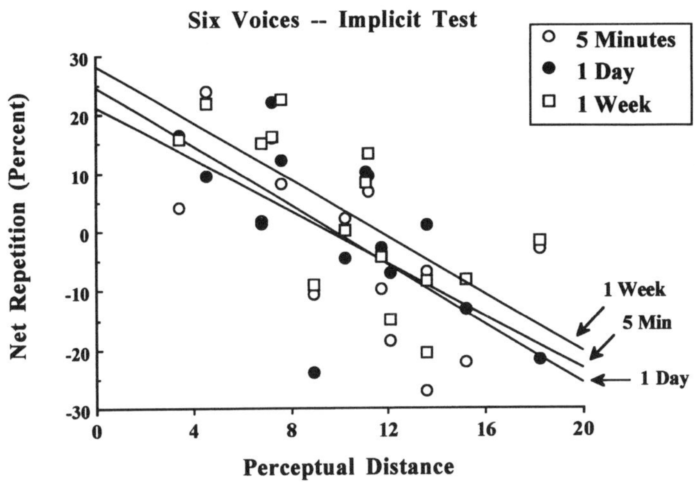

FIGURE 7 Correlations of intervoice perceptual distances and hit rates, from six-voice conditions of Goldinger (1996). Hit rates are shown as a function of delay between study and test sessions (three correlation slopes are labeled) and perceptual distance between speakers' voices (determined via multidimensional scaling).

tion into abstract features. Feustel, Shiffrin, and Salasoo (1983; Monsell, 1991; Salasoo, Shiffrin, & Feustel, 1985) proposed a hybrid model of visual word recognition, including episodic and abstract representations. Kirsner and Dunn (1985; Kirsner, Dunn, & Standen, 1987) proposed a theory of word recognition based on episodic *procedural records,* in the sense of Kolers (1976). Jusczyk's WRAPSA model of speech perception development (Jusczyk, 1993; Jusczyk, Pisoni, & Mullennix, 1992) incorporates episodic storage and on-line abstraction in a manner reminiscent of Semon's theory. In all these theories, episodic memory traces retain the perceptual details typically considered "noise" in abstractionist theories. Strangely, although the benefits of episodic theories have been noted, little formal modeling has occurred (although see Salasoo et al., 1985).

3.3 HINTZMAN'S MINERVA 2 MEMORY MODEL

The theories cited above are all hybrids, compromising between abstractionist and episodic views. However, the best way to assess the viability of an episodic view is to test a pure model. If a purely episodic model fails, we can always retreat to less extreme versions. The particular model I have been testing is Hintzman's (1986, 1988) MINERVA 2. This model takes the idea of exemplar storage to a logical extreme, assuming that every experience creates an independent memory trace, including all perceptual details, context, and so on. Despite their separate storage and idiosyncratic attributes, *aggregates* of traces activated at retrieval create conscious experience. Thus, as in Semon's theory, MINERVA 2 accounts for the specificity and generality of memory with one set of exemplar traces. Computer simulations of MINERVA 2 (Hintzman, 1986, 1988; Hintzman & Ludlam, 1980) show behaviors typically considered hallmarks of abstract representations, such as deriving long-lasting prototypes from random dot patterns (Posner & Keele, 1968, 1970; Shin & Nosofsky, 1992).

Word recognition in MINERVA 2 occurs as follows: For every known word, a potentially vast collection of partially redundant traces resides in memory. When a stimulus word is presented, an analog probe is communicated to all traces in parallel. Traces are activated by the probe in proportion to their mutual similarity. An aggregate of all activated traces constitutes an *echo* sent to consciousness from long-term memory. The echo may contain information not present in the probe itself (such as the word's name), thus associating the probe to past information in memory. Echoes have two important properties in MINERVA 2: *Echo intensity* reflects the total activation in memory created by the probe. With greater similarity of traces to the probe, and with greater numbers of such traces, echo intensity increases. Thus, echo intensity provides an index of stimulus familiarity, and can be used to simulate recognition memory judgments. *Echo content* is the "net response" of long-term memory to the probe. Because all traces respond in parallel, each in proportion to its similarity to the probe, echo content is determined by a unique combination of the probe and the activated traces. This is clarified by a relevant example, as follows.

Assume that detailed traces of spoken words reside in memory. If a common word is presented in a familiar voice, many traces will strongly respond. Thus, even if an *exact match* to the probe exists in memory, all the similar activated traces create a "generic echo," regressing toward the mean of the activated set. If a rare word is presented in an unfamiliar voice, fewer traces will respond, and they will respond weakly. Thus, an exact match to the probe will contribute significantly to the echo content. Therefore, effects of specific token repetition should be greater for unusual stimuli, or for stimuli presented in unusual contexts. [In general, for any model to predict repetition effects with common English words, contextual encoding must be assumed (see Gillund & Shiffrin, 1984; Hintzman, 1988). Presumably, voice effects are observable in experiments because the words are experienced in a unique setting for relatively unique purposes.]

I have recently conducted simulations of MINERVA 2 that qualitatively replicate the explicit recognition memory data above. In the model, memory traces ("spoken words") are represented as vectors of binary elements. Using vector representations has several advantages, including computational simplicity and theoretical transparency (Hintzman, 1986). If the model mimics data patterns without assuming complex representations (Klatt, 1979; McClelland & Elman, 1986), it allows a focus on the model's *central processes,* rather than peripheral details. The vectors were divided into segments corresponding to major dimensions: Each word was represented by a 100-element vector, 50 elements corresponding to its name and meaning, 25 corresponding to voice properties, and 25 corresponding to the context of its presentation. (The model, of course, must "discover" these dimensions.) Every input creates a new trace in memory. Some forgetting occurs over time, simulated by random elements reverting to zero.

The simulations were designed to mimic the six-voice condition. An initial "lexicon" was created for the model: 144 "words" were generated and stored 20 times each. The name elements were identical for all 20 tokens of each word; the voice and context elements were randomly generated. To test the model, 144 new vectors were generated (analogous to words presented at study and test); each had name elements corresponding to stored words, and all had identical context elements. Six configurations of voice elements denoted six different "speakers." These "voice subvectors" were designed to approximate the similarity relations among the voices used in the real experiment. All words were created in all voices, and all pairwise combinations of voices were tested in the simulation, as in the experiment.

The study session was simulated by presenting the model with 72 words, 12 in each voice. The model simply categorized and stored each trace. Intuitively, this phase allows the model to associate words in its lexicon with the specific context of the study phase, as would be necessary for a human subject. In the test phase, the model was presented with all 144 words. The 72 "new" words contained 12 tokens in each voice. The 72 "old" words had voice assignments to mimic the real experiment; 36 words retained their original voice, and 36 had new voices. Between study and test, the model completed 1, 3, or 10 forgetting cycles, to represent three delay periods. The dependent variable was *echo intensity;* these are analogous to hit rates, reflecting the model's familiarity with each test word (Hintzman, 1986). Results are shown in Figure 8. The upper panel shows echo intensities as a function of "voice" and "delay period." As in the human data, "hit rates" were higher for "same-voice" trials, and this difference vanished as forgetting cycles increased. The lower panel displays results for "different-voice" trials, in terms of similarity between study and test voices. Like human subjects, the model was sensitive to the magnitude of "voice" changes, and this sensitivity to detail diminished over forgetting cycles. In sum, MINERVA 2 accurately predicts the qualitative patterns of the human data.

Tests of the simulation model also motivated post hoc analyses of word-frequency effects in the original data. In the simulations above, all words had equal frequencies (20 traces each). To ensure the results were not due to this arbitrary decision, I randomly increased the frequencies of some words and decreased the frequencies of others. When the simulations were repeated, the same-voice advantage was *smaller* for high-frequency words than for low-frequency words. The source of this behavior in the model is transparent. High-frequency words are represented by many traces. When a new token is presented, so many traces respond that idiosyncratic details of any particular trace, even a perfect

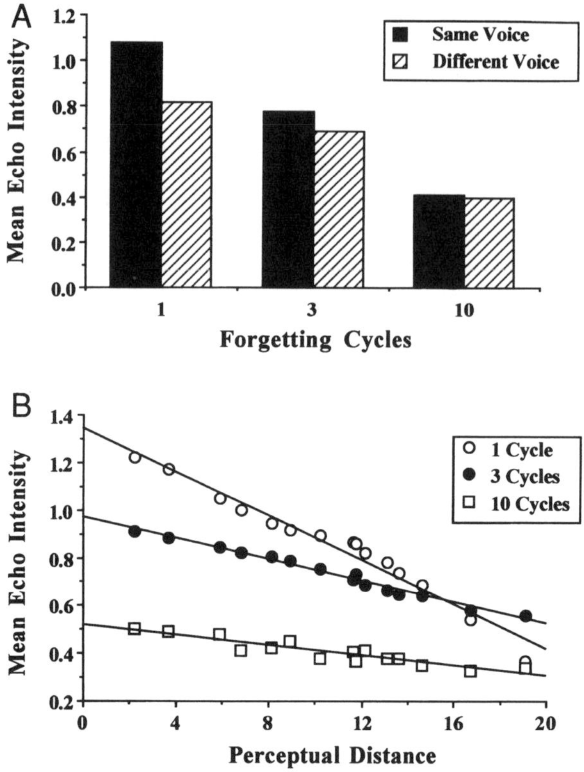

FIGURE 8 Simulation of the recognition memory experiment by Goldinger (1996). (A) Echo intensities (analogous to hit rates) to same-voice and different-voice trials, as a function of forgetting cycles. (B) Mean echo intensities for different-voice trials, as a function of perceptual distances between voices.

match to the new token, are obscured in the aggregate echo (Hintzman, 1986; see also Gillund & Shiffrin, 1984). High-frequency words thus inspire "generic" representations in consciousness, but abstraction occurs *dynamically* in perception, rather than at storage. When an "old" high-frequency word is presented for recognition memory, context elements of the study trace that are essential to the task are obscured, reducing accuracy relative to low-frequency words.

Given these predictions from the model, I returned to the data to conduct several post hoc analyses. Observed hit rates were first correlated with word frequency (using the Kucera & Francis, 1967, norms). As predicted by the model and previous research (Glanzer & Adams, 1985), hit rates were higher for lower frequency words ($p < .01$). Second, the magnitudes of voice effects for all words ("same-voice" minus "different-voice" hit rates) were correlated with word frequencies. Voice effects were also stronger for lower frequency words ($p < .05$).

3.4 EPISODES IN PERCEPTION AND PRODUCTION

The research summarized previously examined basic issues of lexical representation by investigating perception and memory of spoken words. In current research, researchers are further investigating these issues via speech *production.* A common task in word-recognition research is *single-word shadowing* (or naming), in which subjects hear words and repeat them as quickly as possible. The typical dependent measure is the latency between stimulus and response onsets, reflecting the speed of word recognition (Radeau, Morais, & Dewier, 1989; Slowiaczek & Hamburger, 1992). An alternative measure is the speech output itself. The original motor theory (Liberman, Cooper, Shankweiler, & Studdert-Kennedy, 1967) proposed that "speech is perceived by processes that are also involved in its production" (p. 452). Research by Porter supports this claim, showing that listeners can shadow random syllables faster than they can say the same syllables without shadowing (Porter & Castellanos, 1980; Porter & Lubker, 1980). This finding suggests that shadowers may be able to "drive" their articulators directly from speech input. (Although Marslen-Wilson, 1985, showed that even extremely fast shadowers conduct full lexical, syntactic and semantic analysis of input speech. Porter's results may be unique to meaningless syllabic input.).

Acoustic measures of speech are typically used as dependent variables in applied research, such as testing the effects of alcohol or noise on speech (Johnson, Pisoni, & Bernacki, 1990; Summers, Pisoni, Bernacki, Pedlow, & Stokes, 1988), and the intelligibility of disordered speech (Geschwind, 1975). Few studies on basic perception have examined speech acoustics, but there are several precedents, all using word durations. Wright (1979; also Geffen & Luszcz, 1983; Geffen, Stierman, & Tildesley, 1979) had subjects read word lists aloud, finding longer durations of, and longer pauses between, low-frequency words. This suggests that less familiar articulations take longer to prepare and execute (see Balota, Boland, & Shields, 1989). Whalen and Wenk (1993) reported that when subjects read homophones (e.g., time–thyme) aloud, the lower frequency spelling leads to longer word durations. These findings suggest that psychological aspects of lexical representation can affect acoustic-phonetic aspects of speech.

3.4.1 A Pilot Study

Several years ago, I conducted a pilot experiment to examine this idea. Listeners heard words produced by multiple speakers and shadowed the words as quickly as possible. The hypothesis was that subjects' vocal characteristics would change to approximate stimulus speakers' voices—*spontaneous vocal imitation.* "Changes" in voice were determined by comparing subjects' speech in shadowing to a baseline condition, in which they read words from a computer. Indeed, subjects tended to imitate the stimulus speakers. For example, Figure 9 shows results on pitch tracking—a tendency for shadowers to mimic pitch. Each panel shows pitch tracking for a single subject; three men and three women participated.

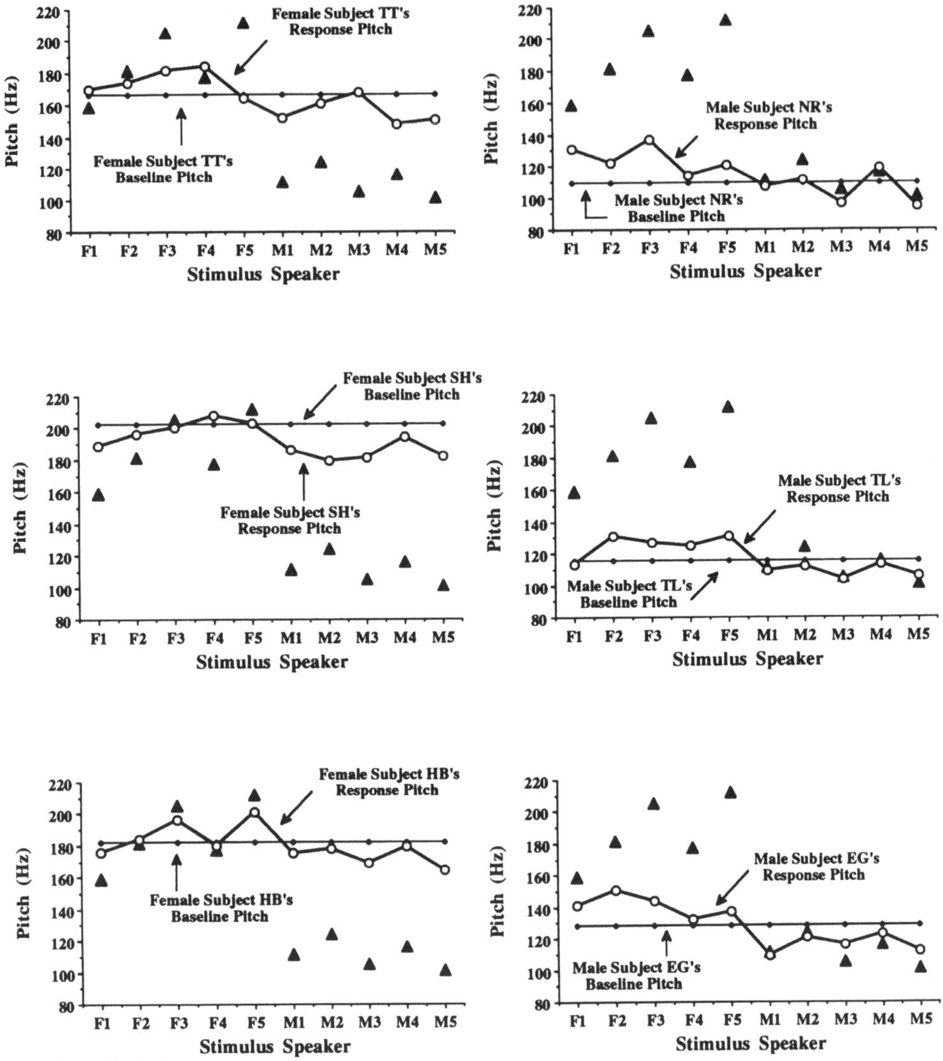

FIGURE 9 Pilot data on pitch tracking. Each panel shows pitch tracking for a single subject. Black triangles represent the pitches of the 10 stimulus speakers. Each subject's baseline pitch and response pitches to each stimulus speaker are shown.

The constant triangles in each panel represent the vocal pitches of the 10 stimulus speakers. Each subject's baseline pitch, and response pitches to each stimulus speaker, are shown. All subjects tended to mimic the stimulus speakers (this was statistically reliable for each subject). These data are corroborated by Oliver (1990), who had 3-, 4-, and 5-year-old children shadow words produced by 10 speakers. All children tended to match *durations* of the stimulus words.

By itself, spontaneous vocal imitation is not particularly revealing with respect to word recognition. But, given Hintzman's model, more interesting predictions are possible. Recall the hypothesized differences in echo content for high- and low-frequency words. High-frequency words create "generic" echoes; they excite so many traces that the idiosyncracies of any particular trace are obscured. Conversely, echoes for low-frequency words are more influenced by old traces that resemble the new stimulus. If we assume that shadowing responses are based on echoes (which constitute the conscious recognition of input words), we can predict that spontaneous imitation will be *stronger* for lower frequency words. Fortunately, in the pilot experiment, all words were presented twice in the baseline condition and twice in the shadowing condition. By examining imitation in the second presentation of each word, this prediction was testable. (This analysis presumes the first shadowing trial creates the idiosyncratic memory trace necessary to influence later echo content.)

I conducted a post hoc analysis on the pilot data, correlating word frequencies with "imitation scores," which reflected the degree of vocal imitation (comparing the shadowing and baseline conditions) in terms of pitch tracking, intonation tracking (pitch tracking *within* words), and duration matching. As predicted, lower frequency words yielded stronger imitation ($p < .05$). Naturally, shadowing latencies were also faster for higher frequency words. Apparently, speech production in shadowing is affected by episodic aspects of lexical representation.

From the perspective of testing MINERVA 2, a benefit of this paradigm is simultaneous assessment of echo intensity and content. Stronger echoes should yield faster responses, as observed. If the subjects' speech is a "readout" of the echo, we can estimate echo content. Previous theories have related speech perception to production, usually positing relations via modular structures or abstract nodes (Cooper, 1979; Liberman et al., 1967; MacKay, Wulf, Yin, & Abrams, 1993). Such models cannot make predictions regarding speech acoustics. In current research, we are now extending the basic method of the pilot experiment, using more motivated stimuli and manipulations. Partial data from our first experiment is available for a progress report; these data represent four completed shadowing subjects.

3.5 EPISODIC EFFECTS IN SINGLE-WORD SHADOWING

Our ongoing experiment conceptually replicates the pilot experiment above, but also improves it in several key respects. First, the stimuli were changed; to test MINERVA 2, a key diagnostic attribute is word frequency. The words in the pilot experiment were taken from the Modified Rhyme Test (House, Williams, Hecker, & Kryter, 1965) and did not have an ideal range or balance of frequencies. New words were selected to cover a wide range and balance of word frequencies. All words were again recorded by multiple speakers, but we increased the experimental power by selecting speakers with a considerable "perceptual range" of voices. Toward this end, we recorded 20 volunteers reading short lists of nonwords. Undergraduate subjects rated the similarities between all pairs of voices, creating a full similarity matrix to analyze via MDS (Kruskal & Wish, 1978). With the scaling solution, we selected the 10 speakers that maximized interspeaker perceptual distances. These 10 speakers then recorded our full stimulus set.

Our new experiment also improves the pilot experiment in terms of design. The pilot experiment did not support any comparisons, other than shadowing versus baseline. Our current experiment manipulates word frequency, number of repetitions, and response timing. Also, the shadowing data are now analyzed by perceptual analysis. The rationale for examining word frequency has already been explained; the rationales for the latter factors are as follows.

3.5.1 Number of Repetitions

In our current experiment, words are shadowed either 2, 6, or 12 times. In theory, the first presentation of each word creates an episodic memory trace with relevant voice and contextual details. Later presentations of each word can then be tested for imitation. If the initial trace constitutes a prominent aspect of the echo for the second presentation (as predicted for low-frequency words), imitation should be observed. This logic, used in the post hoc analysis of frequency effects in the pilot data, creates three new predictions regarding repeated words: First, as is typically observed, subjects should *respond faster* as words are repeated more often (Jackson & Morton, 1984; Masson & Freedman, 1990; Scarborough, Cortese, & Scarborough, 1977). This is because echo intensity will increase as more perfect matches to the stimulus token are compiled in memory. Second, imitation should *increase* as repetitions increase, as a memory trace resembling the stimulus token is added to the echo with each repetition. Third, frequency effects should *diminish* with increasing repetitions. This occurs (in response times) when subjects name printed words aloud (Scarborough et al., 1977). Abstractionist models explain this interaction by short-term priming of canonical units, like logogens (Morton, 1969); low-frequency words show greater repetition effects because high-frequency words are already "near ceiling." In MINERVA 2, with each repetition, echoes become increasingly characterized by context-specific traces created in the experiment. Thus, MINERVA 2 predicts an interaction of Frequency $\times$ Number of Repetitions in vocal imitation, not just response times.

3.5.2 Response Timing

One difficulty of interpretation arises with respect to imitation observed in the pilot experiment. The imitation data are theoretically relevant only if they reflect the *spontaneous* response from memory to spoken words (i.e., imitation reflects on-line word recognition). But, subjects may simply have a "frivolous tendency" to imitate speech in shadowing, regardless of word-recognition processes or the nature of lexical representations. Perhaps imitating the speaker makes the task easier or more interesting. Of course, the pilot data cast doubt on this atheoretic account: If subjects simply imitate the speaker for amusement, it is difficult to explain why word frequency influences the likelihood of imitation. Nevertheless, the possibility merits further examination.

Our current experiment includes an *immediate shadowing* condition, in which subjects shadow words as quickly as possible. In this condition, an optimal subject may use echo content to help "drive" their articulation (although see Marslen-Wilson, 1985). It also includes a *delayed shadowing* condition (Balota & Chumbley, 1985), in which subjects hear words, but do not speak until shown a visual cue. The cue is given after variable delays ranging from 2–4 sec. Presumably, if subjects frivolously imitate the speaker while shadowing, they should continue to do so, even when required to wait a few seconds. However, MINERVA 2 predicts that imitation will *decrease* over delays: The stimulus word should be recognized immediately. But as the subject holds that word in working memory, waiting to speak, there is *continuous interaction* between working memory and long-term memory. This is the model's fundamental behavior; it simulates communication between these memory systems. These continual interactions will force a "regression toward the mean" of the lexical category, as each successive echo "drifts" closer to the central tendency of all prior traces in memory. Thus, idiosyncratic details of the original shadowing stimulus will be attenuated in the eventual echo used at output.

Note that this is a progressive cycle—the first echo from long-term memory to the shadowing word contains some idiosyncracies of the stimulus, but is already more "abstract" than the input, as other traces contribute to echo content. If this echo is held in working memory, and is communicated to long-term memory again, the next echo will move still closer to the central tendency (prototype) of the lexical category. After several seconds, the echo in working memory—the basis of a delayed shadowing response—will be a totally generic member of the lexical category (this prototype may be the speaker's own voice). Thus, observed vocal imitation should decline with increasing response delays.

3.5.3 Perceptual Analysis

Our primary dependent measure is imitation of the speaker by the subject. But "imitation" is difficult to operationally define. In the pilot study, I compared acoustic parameters of the subject's utterance to the same acoustic parameters in the stimulus. This process required a series of binary questions: Which of the subject's two utterances (baseline or shadowing) is closer in duration to the stimulus token? Which has the closer pitch, formant-frequency values, and intraword intonation? By tallying these results, I compiled total "imitation scores." This approach to data analysis has at least two drawbacks: First, conducting acoustic analyses on a token-by-token basis is extremely time-consuming. Second, the psychological validity of the imitation scores is unknown. Clearly, many acoustic properties can be catalogued and compared, but do they actually reflect *perceptual* similarity between tokens? Computing imitation scores also requires arbitrary decisions (e.g., should duration and pitch tracking receive equal weight?). In sum, it is unclear that imitation scores actually estimate the experience of a listener.

Because piecemeal collections of acoustic parameters can only approximate the perceptual gestalt, a more valid measure of imitation comes from perceptual tests (Summers et al., 1988). Thus, each subjects' shadowing speech is now used in an adjunct perceptual experiment. Groups of naive listeners are asked to perform an *AXB classification task.* On every trial, listeners hear two tokens of a word, produced by a shadowing subject in the baseline and experimental conditions. These *A* and *B* stimuli surround the *X* stimulus—the original token that the shadowing subject shadowed. Subjects judge which stimulus, the first (*A*) or the third (*B*), sounds like a "better imitation" of the second (*X*). The percentage of subjects who correctly choose the shadowed stimulus is used as a dependent measure of "imitation" for the original shadowing experiment.

To summarize, the ongoing shadowing experiment carefully extends the pilot experiment reported above. The expected results are (a) stronger imitation for lower frequency words, (b) stronger imitation with more repetitions, (c) an interaction of these factors, and (d) decreased imitation across delays. I plan to include 8–10 shadowing subjects in the experiment; each shadowing subjects' tokens are digitized and presented in an AXB experiment with about 30 listeners. To date, I have completed this entire process for four shadowers–two men and two women. The combined AXB results for these four shadowers are shown in Figure 10. The upper panels show imitation judgments for the immediate shadowing tokens; the lower panels show judgments for the delayed shadowing tokens. The left panels show results for low-frequency words; the right panels show high-frequency words. In each panel, separate bars indicate the 2nd, 6th, and 12th repetition of each word.

Evidence for imitation in shadowing is constituted by listeners choosing the shadowed stimulus as a better imitation of *X* than the control stimulus. As Figure 10 shows, the data collected thus far support the predictions above. Imitation is clearly more detectable in immediate shadowing than in delayed shadowing. It is also more detectable with low-frequency words and with increased repetitions (all $p < .05$) To this point, we cannot determine whether Frequency and Number of Repetitions reliably interact (in the immediate shadowing conditions), but a trend in the predicted direction is evident. Although preliminary in nature, these data suggest that the acoustic content of shadowers' speech may reflect underlying processes of lexical access. Moreover, those lexical access processes seem to be fundamentally influenced by detailed episodic memory traces.

3.6 THEORIES OF SPEAKER NORMALIZATION

As noted in the introduction, most theories of speech perception assume the signal is perceptually converted to a series of phonemes and words, via processes

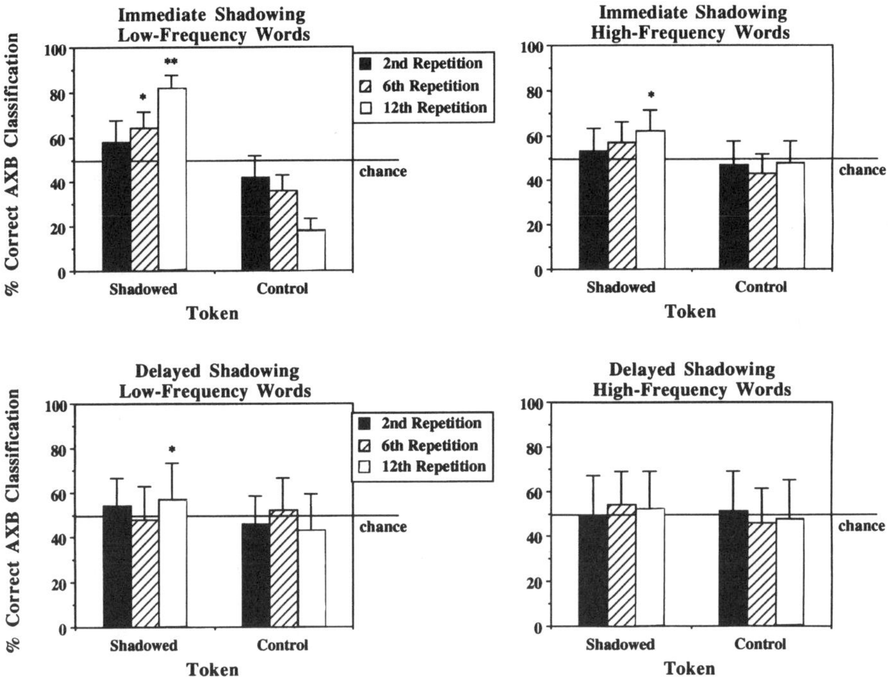

FIGURE 10 Combined AXB classification data for four shadowing subjects. Upper panels show AXB imitation judgments for the immediate shadowing conditions; lower panels show delayed shadowing conditions. Each panel shows data as a function of word frequency and number of repetitions.

of information reduction and memory matching (Oden & Massaro, 1978; Pisoni & Sawusch, 1975; Studdert-Kennedy, 1976). Inherent to this view is perceptual normalization: Speech is "filtered" with respect to surface information, such as voice details. This reduces the stimulus to essential elements for comparison to abstract lexical representations in long-term memory. Joos (1948) noted that speakers vary widely in vocal tract dimensions, dialects, and other factors that influence speech acoustics. Nevertheless, listeners easily recognize messages across speakers. Joos suggested that listeners use small speech samples to estimate speakers' vowel spaces. Subsequent perception makes reference to this constructed representation. Although Joos never stated that information is lost via normalization, the notion is certainly consistent with later information-processing models (Pisoni, 1992). Most theories treat voice details as "noise" the speech processor must bypass en route to deriving phonetic percepts. For example, Nusbaum and Morin (1992) wrote,

> The acoustic pattern of a segment must be interpreted in the context of the talker who produced the segment. In other words, the listener must normalize talker differences in order to recognize the phonetic structure of speech. (p. 114)

Although Nusbaum and Morin (1992) never stated that voice information is discarded after normalization, their quote implies that voices are merely vehicles of abstract information. This certainly contains an element of truth—abstract entities (e.g., words) are recognized in speech. However, the data reviewed in this chapter all suggest that speaker normalization does not imply information reduction. The data all show long-term memory for surface details of spoken words. Similar data arise in other tasks: Jusczyk et al. (1992) found that 2-month-old infants recognize phonetic constancy across voices, but they *also* remember voice information for several minutes. Green et al. (1991) examined a "cross-gender McGurk illusion" (McGurk & MacDonald, 1976). In trials that paired female faces with male voices (or vice-versa), the inconguous sources of information fluently combined to yield the illusion. This suggests that perception normalizes the signal early in processing, allowing fusion of abstract representations. Nevertheless, Green et al. noted that surface information remains available to the subject:

> The results of the present study . . . demonstrate that differences in the gender of the talker producing the auditory and visual signals had no impact on the integration of phonetic information. Thus, by the time the phonetic information was integrated from the auditory and visual modalities, it was sufficiently abstract as to be neutral with respect to the talker differences. Nonetheless . . . observers are very aware of an incompatibility between the cross-gender face-voice pairs. This suggests that the neutralization of talker differences for the purposes of phonetic categorization does not result in a loss of detailed information about the talker. (p. 533)

Indeed, there is *no evidence* in the literature that normalization reduces information. To respect the data, normalization must be construed only as perceptual compensation, not filtering. Notably, several computational models of vowel normalization posit such compensation without information loss (Johnson, 1990; Miller, 1989; Nearey, 1989; Syrdal & Gopal, 1986). Thus, concepts of speaker normalization and data on voice memory can peacefully coexist. However, two questions remain: First, is normalization a sound theoretical construct? Second, is it a real phenomenon? With respect to the first question, most theories view normalization as a logical necessity. This reflects the common assumption of an abstract mental lexicon. The variable signal must be converted to a "normal" form prior to comparison with memory. Clearly, different representational assumptions could remove this "logical necessity." An episodic lexicon could support direct matching of spoken words to detailed traces, without normalization.

With respect to the second question, the available data do not support normalization. Consider vowel perception: Research by Verbrugge and Rakerd (1986) suggested that speech contains sufficient information to specify vowel identity without reference to vocal tract dimensions. Verbrugge and Rakerd presented "silent-center" syllables to listeners for identification. These were /bVb/ syllables with the central 60% removed, leaving only initial and final consonants, with partial transitions. Listeners easily identified the missing vowels. In another test, the transitional portions of syllables produced by male and female speakers were spliced together, creating cross-gender, silent-center stimuli. Although the vowel spaces of combined speakers differed widely, the missing vowels were still easily identified. Verbrugge and Rakerd concluded that vowels need not be identified from center frequencies, as most theories assume. Speaker-independent, dynamic information is sufficient for vowel perception, suggesting that perception may not require normalization.

Taken together, research and theory do not create a compelling argument for speaker normalization. The hypothesis stems from theories assuming abstract lexical representations. Once the representations are questioned, the access processes must also be questioned. The circularity of the normalization hypothesis was noted in the introduction, and the data are equivocal. Episodic theories of the lexicon may provide an important new direction. All theories assume that speech perception involves categorization, but there is no reason that the implied categories must entail abstract units. The data indicate that detailed episodes are automatically created in perception, and they affect later perception. Thus, it is parsimonious to assume they constitute the basic substrate of the lexicon.

3.7 THE EPISODIC LEXICON

The introduction began with Richard Semon's theory of memory (1909/1923; Schacter et al., 1978), which assumed all stimuli leave unique traces in memory. These traces support memory of specific experiences, and they collectively support abstract cognition. We have now come full circle, returning to the concepts Semon introduced at the turn of the century. With recent findings in implicit memory, interest in episodic models has increased dramatically. Smith and Zarate (1992) recently proposed a theory of social judgment based on MINERVA 2 (Hintzman, 1986). Logan (1988) proposed that attentional automaticity requires the collection of multiple instances in memory. With respect to memory for visual patterns, Musen and Treisman (1990) concluded the following:

> To account for implicit memory performance, we suggest that . . . a separate episodic token or exemplar is laid down for each particular occurrence of each pattern. (p. 136)

As Jacoby and Brooks (1984) argued, the available data suggest that episodes subserve perception. Indeed, several episodic models have been previously described. For example, Klatt's (1979) Lexical Access From Spectra (LAFS) model assumes a lexicon of spectral templates, representing the acoustic correlates of speech sounds in different phonetic environments (Wickelgren, 1969). Multiple templates are used to resolve variability: LAFS precompiles variability directly into memory. Thus, the normalization requirement is relaxed, and potentially useful information is not discarded. Similarly, Tulving and Schacter (1990; Schacter, 1990) proposed a memory system called the Perceptual Representation System (PRS), which is used to identify perceptual objects, including words. PRS contains long-lasting representations of perceptual forms, with all details intact.

By virtue of its strong assumptions, Hintzman's MINERVA 2 may be the "gold standard" of exemplar theories. Like Semon's theory, MINERVA 2 accounts for specificity and generality of memory with one set of exemplar traces. With minor modifications, MINERVA 2 could serve as a model of the lexicon, and would certainly predict frequency, neighborhood, and priming effects. Simulations confirm that MINERVA 2 predicts the results of Goldinger (1996) and the results of my new shadowing experiments. However, MINERVA 2 is clearly not the only episodic model that predicts such results. The context model (Nosofsky, 1986) and the Search of Associative Memory (SAM) model (Gillund & Shiffrin, 1984) both incorporate the necessary assumptions. In addition, several less extreme models also predict the key results.

3.7.1 Hybrid Models

Feustel et al. (1983; Salasoo et al., 1985) described a hybrid model of the lexicon, in which both abstract lexical codes and episodic traces contribute to perception. By this view, words become *codified* via repetition; multiple episodes coalesce into unitary codes, similar to logogens. Episodes mediate token-specific repetition effects, but abstract codes provide the lexicon stability and permanence. Similarly, Kirsner and Dunn (1985; Kirsner et al., 1987) proposed a lexicon of abstract representations and episodic *procedural records.* By this view, word identification entails processes that match stimuli to lexical entries. Records of these processes are stored as episodic traces, and surface details, such as voice, shape the record. Upon later word identification, past records are reapplied to the degree they resemble new inputs. Regarding repetition effects, Kirsner et al. (1987) wrote the following:

> The essence of our account is that word identification is achieved by reference to a record. Similarity is the critical parameter. If the record collection includes an example that is similar to the current stimulus description, identification will be achieved easily and quickly. . . . The character of the record collection can be determined by repetition priming. (p. 151).

The record-based model borrows logic from Kolers (1976; Kolers & Ostry, 1974), who suggested that fluent rereading of transformed text reflects memory for perceptual operations applied when subjects originally decoded the passages. When identical transformed text is presented, the visual patterns activate records of previous operations, leading to fluent reprocessing and savings in reading time. Of course, Kolers studied only conscious, strategic processes applied to a difficult perceptual problem. Kirsner and Dunn (1985) applied the notion of procedural records to *all* perceptual processes, regardless of difficulty or salience. Recognizing a word in an unfamiliar voice entails normalization and matching procedures, stored in a record. Later identification of the same stimulus will use the record, creating a strong repetition effect. Or, if a similar stimulus is presented, its perceptual operations will partially overlap the previous record, creating residual savings. With increased exposure to a speaker's voice (or handwriting, rotated text, foreign accent, etc.), the increasing episode collection will support asymptotic (totally "normalized") performance. This prediction was recently supported by Nygaard, Sommers, and Pisoni (1994), who made listeners familiar with speakers' voices and found facilitated identification of *new* words produced by those speakers.

3.7.2 Distributed Memory Models

Another alternative to strict exemplar models are distributed memory models (Eich, 1982; Knapp & Anderson, 1984; McClelland & Rumelhart, 1985). In McClelland and Rumelhart's (1985) model, memory traces are created by patterns of activation in a connectionist network. The trace for any given stimulus is unique, and can be retrieved via repetition of its original pattern. The model develops abstract categories by superimposing countless traces, but its storage is far more economical than the localist MINERVA 2 model. As McClelland and Rumelhart (1985) wrote,

> Our theme will be to show that distributed models provide a way to resolve the abstraction–representation of specifics dilemma. With a distributed model, the superposition of traces automatically results in abstraction though it can still preserve to some extent the idiosyncracies of specific events and experiences. (p. 160)

It is easy to imagine how a distributed network derives a central tendency from a set of exemplars. With all memory traces superimposed, however, a natural question is whether repetition effects in a distributed memory model could display adequate sensitivity to perceptual details (as in Goldinger, 1996). Could the repetition of an old stimulus have a "special" effect after several similar patterns are combined into a common substrate? Presumably, as in MINERVA 2, if contextual encoding sufficiently delimits the traces activated during test, such results are possible.

3.8 CONCLUSION

Jacoby (1983b) noted that "[t]here is a great deal of unexploited similarity between theories of episodic memory and theories of perception. . . . The difference . . . is largely removed if it is assumed both types of task involve parallel access to a large population of memories for prior episodes" (pp. 35–36). The data reviewed in this chapter, taken together with related findings, support an episodic view of the mental lexicon (see Tenpenny, 1995). By an abstractionist view, perceptual idiosyncracies of words are normalized, allowing listeners to identify tokens as types. By an episodic view, words are recognized against a background of countless, detailed episodes. The speech signal is not a noisy vehicle of linguistic content; the signal itself is an integral aspect of later representation. Perhaps the episodic view should be called "Richard Semon's theory of the lexicon."

ACKNOWLEDGMENTS

This research summarized in this chapter was supported by several sources: National Institutes of Health (NIH) Research Grant DC-00111-16 and National Institute for Deafness and Communicative Disorders (NIDCD) Training Grant DC-00012-13 to Indiana University, and NIDCD FIRST Award R29-DC02629-01 to Arizona State University. Preparation of this chapter was supported entirely by the FIRST award. I thank David Pisoni for invaluable help with all phases of this research.
Correspondence: S. D. Goldinger, Department of Psychology, Arizona State University, Box 871104, Tempe, Arizona 85287-1104. Internet: goldinger@asu.edu

REFERENCES

Abercrombie, D. (1967). *Elements of general phonetics.* Chicago: University of Chicago Press.

Aldridge, J. W., Garcia, H. R., & Mena, G. (1987). Habituation as a necessary condition for maintenance rehearsal. *Journal of Memory and Language, 26,* 632–637.

Bahrick, H., Bahrick, P., & Wittlinger, R. (1975). Fifty years of memory for names and faces: A cross-sectional approach. *Journal of Experimental Psychology: General, 104,* 54–75.

Balota, D., Boland, J., & Shields, L. (1989). Priming in pronunciation: Beyond pattern recognition and onset latency. *Journal of Memory and Language, 28,* 14–36.

Balota, D., & Chumbley, J. (1985). The locus of word-frequency effects in the pronunciation task: Lexical access and/or production? *Journal of Memory and Language, 24,* 89–106.

Begg, I. (1971). Recognition memory for sentence meaning and wording. *Journal of Verbal Learning and Verbal Behavior, 10,* 176–181.

Brown, J., & Carr, T. (1993). Limits on perceptual abstraction in reading: Asymmetric transfer between surface forms differing in typicality. *Journal of Experimental Psychology: Learning, Memory, and Cognition, 19,* 1277–1296.

Bruce, V. (1988). *Recognizing faces.* Hillsdale, NJ: Erlbaum.

Carterette, E., & Barnebey, A. (1975). Recognition memory for voices. In A. Cohen & S. G. Nooteboom (Eds.), *Structure and process in speech perception* (pp. 246–265). New York: Springer-Verlag.

Church, B., & Schacter, D. L. (1994). Perceptual specificity of auditory priming: Memory for voice intonation and fundamental frequency. *Journal of Experimental Psychology: Learning, Memory, and Cognition, 20,* 521–533.

Cole, R. A., Coltheart, M., & Allard, F. (1974). Memory of a speaker's voice: Reaction time to same- or different-voiced letters. *Quarterly Journal of Experimental Psychology, 26,* 1–7.

Cooper, W. (1979). *Speech perception and production.* Norwood, NJ: Ablex.

Craik, F. I. M., & Kirsner, K. (1974). The effect of speaker's voice on word recognition. *Quarterly Journal of Experimental Psychology, 26,* 274–284.

Cutting, J., & Kozlowski, L. (1977). Recognizing friends by their walk: Gait perception without familiarity cues. *Bulletin of the Psychonomic Society, 9,* 353–356.

Cutting, J., & Pisoni, D. (1978). An information-processing approach to speech perception. In J. Kavanagh & W. Strange (Eds.), *Speech and language in the laboratory, school, and clinic* (pp. 38–72). Cambridge, MA: MIT Press.

Eich, J. M. (1982). A composite holographic associative recall model. *Psychological Review, 89,* 627–661.

Fant, G. (1973). *Speech sounds and features.* Cambridge, MA: MIT Press.

Feustel, T., Shiffrin, R., & Salasoo, A. (1983). Episodic and lexical contributions to the repetition effect in word recognition. *Journal of Experimental Psychology: General, 112,* 309–346.

Forster, K. I. (1976). Accessing the mental lexicon. In R. Wales & E. Walker (Eds.), *New approaches to language mechanisms* (pp. 257–287). Amsterdam: North-Holland.

Galton, F. (1883). *Inquiries into human faculty and its development.* London: Macmillan.

Geffen, G., & Luszcz, M. (1983). Are the spoken durations of rare words longer than those of common words? *Memory & Cognition, 11,* 13–15.

Geffen, G., Stierman, I., & Tildesley, P. (1979). The effect of word length and frequency on articulation and pausing during delayed auditory feedback. *Language and Speech, 22,* 191–199.

Geiselman, R., & Bellezza, F. (1976). Long-term memory for speaker's voice and source location. *Memory & Cognition, 4,* 483–489.

Geiselman, R., & Bellezza, F. (1977). Incidental retention of speaker's voice. *Memory & Cognition, 5,* 658–665.

Geiselman, R., & Crawley, J. (1983). Incidental processing of speaker characteristics: Voice as connotative information. *Journal of Verbal Learning and Verbal Behavior, 22,* 15–23.

Gerstman, L. H. (1968). Classification of self-normalized vowels. *IEEE Transactions on Audio and Electroacoustics, AU-16,* 78–80.

Geschwind, N. (1975). The apraxias: Neural mechanisms of disorders of learned movement. *American Scientist, 63,* 188–195.

Gillund, G., & Shiffrin, R. (1984). A retrieval model for both recognition and recall. *Psychological Review, 91,* 1–67.

Glanzer, M., & Adams, J. (1985). The mirror effect in recognition memory. *Memory & Cognition, 13,* 8–20.

Goldinger, S. D. (1990). *Effects of Talker Variability on Self-paced Serial Recall. Research on speech perception* (Progress Report no. 16, pp. 313–326). Bloomington: Indiana University Press.

Goldinger, S. D. (1996). Words and voices: Episodic traces in spoken word identification and recognition memory. *Journal of Experimental Psychology: Learning, Memory, and Cognition, 22,* 1166–1183.

Goldinger, S. D., Pisoni, D. B., & Logan, J. (1991). On the nature of talker variability effects on serial recall of spoken word lists. *Journal of Experimental Psychology: Learning, Memory, and Cognition, 17,* 152–162.

Goldinger, S. D., Pisoni, D. B., & Luce, P. A. (1996). Speech perception and spoken word recognition: Research and theory. In N. J. Lass (Ed.), *Principles of experimental phonetics* (pp. 277–327). St. Louis, MO: Mosby.

Green, K., Kuhl, P., Meltzoff, A., & Stevens, E. (1991). Integrating speech information across talkers, gender, and sensory modality: Female faces and male voices in the McGurk effect. *Perception & Psychophysics, 50,* 524–536.

Halle, M. (1985). Speculation about the representation of words in memory. In V. Fromkin (Ed.), *Phonetic linguistics* (pp. 101–114). New York: Academic Press.

Halpern, A. (1989). Memory for the absolute pitch of familiar songs. *Memory & Cognition, 17,* 572–581.

Hintzman, D. L. (1986). "Schema abstraction" in a multiple-trace memory model. *Psychological Review, 93,* 411–428.

Hintzman, D. L. (1988). Judgments of frequency and recognition memory in a multiple-trace memory model. *Psychological Review, 95,* 528–551.

Hintzman, D. L., Block, R., & Inskeep, N. (1972). Memory for mode of input. *Journal of Verbal Learning and Verbal Behavior, 11,* 741–749.

Hintzman, D. L., Block, R., & Summers, J. (1973). Modality tags and memory for repetitions: Locus of the spacing effect. *Journal of Verbal Learning and Verbal Behavior, 12,* 229–238.

Hintzman, D. L., & Ludlam, G. (1980). Differential forgetting of prototypes and old instances: Simulation by an exemplar-based classification model. *Memory & Cognition, 8,* 378–382.

Hintzman, D. L., & Summers, J. (1973). Long-term visual traces of visually presented words. *Bulletin of the Psychonomic Society, 1,* 325–327.

Hollien, H., Majewski, W., & Doherty, E. (1982). Perceptual identification of voices under normal, stress, and disguise speaking conditions. *Journal of Phonetics, 10,* 139–148.

House, A., Williams, C., Hecker, M., & Kryter, K. (1965). Articulation-testing methods: Consonantal differentiation with a closed-response set. *Journal of the Acoustical Society of America, 37,* 158–166.

Jackson, A., & Morton, J. (1984). Facilitation of auditory word recognition. *Memory & Cognition, 12,* 568–574.

Jacoby, L. (1983a). Perceptual enhancement: Persistent effects of an experience. *Journal of Experimental Psychology: Learning, Memory, and Cognition, 9,* 21–38.

Jacoby, L. (1983b). Remembering the data: Analyzing interactive processes in reading. *Journal of Verbal Learning and Verbal Behavior, 22,* 485–508.

Jacoby, L., & Brooks, L. R. (1984). Nonanalytic cognition: Memory, perception, and concept learning. In G. Bower (Ed.), *The psychology of learning and motivation,* (Vol 18, pp. 1–47). New York: Academic Press.

Jacoby, L., & Dallas, M. (1981). On the relationship between autobiographical memory and perceptual learning. *Journal of Experimental Psychology: General, 110,* 306–340.

Jacoby, L., & Hayman, C. (1987). Specific visual transfer in word identification. *Journal of Experimental Psychology: Learning, Memory, and Cognition, 13,* 456–463.

Jacoby, L., & Witherspoon, D. (1982). Remembering without awareness. *Canadian Journal of Psychology, 36,* 300–324.

Johnson, K. (1990). The role of perceived speaker identity in FO normalization of vowels. *Journal of the Acoustical Society of America, 88,* 642–654.

Johnson, K., Pisoni, D., & Bernacki, R. (1990). Do voice recordings reveal whether a person is intoxicated? A case study. *Phonetica, 47,* 215–237.

Joos, M. A. (1948). Acoustic phonetics. *Language, 24,* (Suppl. 2), 1–136.

Jusczyk, P. W. (1993). From general to language-specific capacities: The WRAPSA model of how speech perception develops. *Journal of Phonetics, 21,* 3–28.

Jusczyck, P. W., Pisoni, D. B., & Mullennix, J. (1992). Some consequences of stimulus variability on speech processing by 2-month-old infants. *Cognition, 43,* 253–291.

Keenan, J., MacWhinney, B., & Mayhew, D. (1977). Pragmatics in memory: A study in natural conversation. *Journal of Verbal Learning and Verbal Behavior, 16,* 549–560.

Kirsner, K. (1973). An analysis of the visual component in recognition memory for verbal stimuli. *Memory & Cognition, 1,* 449–453.

Kirsner, K. (1974). Modality differences in recognition memory for words and their attributes. *Journal of Experimental Psychology, 102,* 579–584.

Kirsner, K., & Dunn, J. C. (1985). The perceptual record: A common factor in repetition priming and attribute retention? In M. I. Posner & O. M. Marin (Eds.), *Attention and performance XI* (pp. 547–565). Hillsdale, NJ: Erlbaum.

Kirsner, K., Dunn, J. C., & Standen, P. (1987). Record-based word recognition. In M. Coltheart (Ed.), *Attention and performance XII* (pp. 147–167). Hillsdale, NJ: Erlbaum.

Klatt, D. H. (1979). Speech perception: A model of acoustic-phonetic analysis and lexical access. *Journal of Phonetics, 7,* 279–312.

Klatt, D. H. (1989). Review of selected models of speech perception. In W. Marslen-Wilson, (Ed.), *Lexical representation and process* (pp. 169–226). Cambridge, MA: MIT Press.

Knapp, A., & Anderson, J. (1984). Theory of categorization based on distributed memory storage. *Journal of Experimental Psychology: Learning, Memory, and Cognition, 10,* 616–637.

Kolers, P. A. (1976). Reading a year later. *Journal of Experimental Psychology: Human Learning and Memory, 2,* 554–565.

Kolers, P. A., & Ostry, D. (1974). Time course of loss of information regarding pattern analyzing operations. *Journal of Verbal Learning and Verbal Behavior, 13,* 599–612.

Krulee, G., Tondo, D., & Wightman, F. (1983). Speech perception as a multilevel processing system. *Journal of Psycholinguistic Research, 12,* 531–554.

Kruskal, J. B., & Wish, M. (1978). *Multidimensional scaling.* London: Sage University Press.

Kucera, H., & Francis, W. (1967). *Computational analysis of present-day American English.* Providence: Brown University Press.

Ladefoged, P. (1980). What are linguistic sounds made of? *Language, 56,* 485–502.

Ladefoged, P., & Broadbent, D. E. (1957). Information conveyed by vowels. *Journal of the Acoustical Society of America, 29,* 98–104.

Lehman, E. B. (1982). Memory for modality: Evidence for an automatic process. *Memory & Cognition, 10,* 554–564.

Lewicki, P. (1986). *Nonconscious social information processing.* San Diego, CA: Academic Press.

Liberman, A., Cooper, F., Shankweiler, D., & Studdert-Kennedy, M. (1967). Perception of the speech code. *Psychological Review, 74,* 431–461.

Light, L. L., Stansbury, C., Rubin, C., & Linde, S. (1973). Memory for modality of presentation: Within-modality discrimination. *Memory & Cognition, 1,* 395–400.

Lightfoot, N. (1989). *Effects of talker familiarity on serial recall of spoken word lists. Research on speech perception* (Progress Report no. 15, pp. 419–443). Bloomington: Indiana University Press.

Logan, G. D. (1988). Toward an instance theory of automatization. *Psychological Review, 95,* 492–527.

Lovelace, E. A., & Southall, S. D. (1983). Memory for words in prose and their locations on the page. *Memory & Cognition, 11,* 429–434.

MacKay, D., Wulf, G., Yin, C., & Abrams, L. (1993). Relations between word perception and production: New theory and data on the verbal transformation effect. *Journal of Memory and Language, 32,* 624–646.

Marslen-Wilson, W. (1985). Speech shadowing and speech comprehension. *Speech Communication, 4,* 55–73.

Martin, C., Mullennix, J., Pisoni, D., & Summers, W. (1989). Effects of talker variability on recall of spoken word lists. *Journal of Experimental Psychology: Learning, Memory, and Cognition, 15,* 676–684.

Masson, M. E. J., & Freedman, L. (1990). Fluent identification of repeated words. *Journal of Experimental Psychology: Learning, Memory, and Cognition, 16,* 355–373.

McClelland, J., & Elman, J. (1986). The TRACE model of speech perception. *Cognitive Psychology, 18,* 1–86.

McClelland, J., & Rumelhart, D. (1985). Distributed memory and the representation of general and specific information. *Journal of Experimental Psychology: General, 114,* 159–188.

McGehee, F. (1937). The reliability of the identification of the human voice. *Journal of General Psychology, 17,* 249–271.

McGurk, H., & MacDonald, J. (1976). Hearing lips and seeing voices. *Nature (London), 264,* 746–748.

Medin, D., & Schaffer, M. (1978). Context theory of classification. *Psychological Review, 85,* 207–238.

Miller, J. D. (1989). Auditory-perceptual interpretation of the vowel. *Journal of the Acoustical Society of America, 85,* 2114–2134.

Monsell, S. (1991). The nature and locus of word frequency effects in reading. In D. Besner & G. W. Humphreys (Eds.), *Basic processes in reading* (pp. 148–197). Hillsdale, NJ: Erlbaum.

Monsen, R. B., & Engebretson, A. M. (1977). Study of variations in the male and female glottal wave. *Journal of the Acoustical Society of America, 62,* 981–993.

Morton, J. (1969). Interaction of information in word recognition. *Psychological Review, 76,* 165–178.

Mullennix, J. W., & Pisoni, D. B. (1990). Stimulus variability and processing dependencies in speech perception. *Perception & Psychophysics, 47,* 379–390.

Mullennix, J. W., Pisoni, D. B., & Martin, C. S. (1989). Some effects of talker variability on spoken word recognition. *Journal of the Acoustical Society of America, 85,* 365–378.

Murdock, B. (1962). Serial position effect of free recall. *Journal of Experimental Psychology, 64,* 482–488.

Murdock, B. (1982). A theory for the storage and retrieval of item and associative information. *Psychological Review, 89,* 609–626.

Musen, G., & Treisman, A. (1990). Implicit and explicit memory for visual patterns. *Journal of Experimental Psychology: Learning, Memory, and Cognition, 16,* 127–137.

Nearey, T. M. (1989). Static, dynamic, and relational properties in vowel perception. *Journal of the Acoustical Society of America, 85,* 2088–2113.

Neisser, U. (1967). *Cognitive psychology.* New York: Appleton-Century-Crofts.

Nosofsky, R. M. (1984). Choice, similarity, and the context theory of classification. *Journal of Experimental Psychology: Learning, Memory, and Cognition, 10,* 104–114.

Nosofsky, R. M. (1986). Attention, similarity, and the identification-categorization relationship. *Journal of Experimental Psychology: General, 115,* 39–57.

Nusbaum, H., & Morin, T. (1992). Paying attention to differences among talkers. In Y. Tohkura, E. Bateson, & Y. Sagisaka (Eds.), *Speech perception, production, and linguistic structure* (pp. 33–61). Tokyo: IOS Press.

Nygaard, L., Sommers, M., & Pisoni, D. (1992). Effects of speaking rate and talker variability on the representation of spoken words in memory. In J. Ohala (Ed.), *Proceedings of the International Conference on Spoken Language Processing.* (pp. 591–594). Edmonton: University of Alberta Press.

Nygaard, L. C., Sommers, M. S., & Pisoni, D. B. (1994). Speech perception as a talker-contingent process. *Psychological Science, 5,* 42–46.

Oden, G., & Massaro, D. (1978). Integration of featural information in speech perception. *Psychological Review, 85,* 172–191.

Oliver, B. (1990). *Talker normalization and word recognition in preschool children. Research on speech perception* (Progress Report no. 16, pp. 379–390). Bloomington: Indiana University Press.

Palmeri, T. J., Goldinger, S. D., & Pisoni, D. B. (1993). Episodic encoding of voice attributes and recognition memory for spoken words. *Journal of Experimental Psychology: Learning, Memory, and Cognition, 19,* 309–328.

Papcun, G., Kreiman, J., & Davis, A. (1989). Long-term memory for unfamiliar voices. *Journal of the Acoustical Society of America, 85,* 913–925.

Peterson, G. E., & Barney, H. L. (1952). Control methods used in a study of the vowels. *Journal of the Acoustical Society of America, 24,* 175–184.

Pisoni, D. B. (1992). Some comments on talker normalization in speech perception. In Y. Tohkura (Ed.), *Speech perception, production, and linguistic structure* (pp. 143–151). Tokyo: Ohmsha Publishing.

Pisoni, D. B., & Sawusch, J. R. (1975). Some stages of processing in speech perception. In A. Cohen & S. Nooteboom (Eds.), *Structure and process in speech perception* (pp. 16–34). Heidelberg: Springer-Verlag.

Porter, R. J., & Castellanos, F. X. (1980). Speech-production measures of speech perception: Rapid shadowing of VCV syllables. *Journal of the Acoustical Society of America, 67,* 1349–1356.

Porter, R. J., & Lubker, J. F. (1980). Rapid reproduction of vowel-vowel sequences: Evidence for a fast and direct acoustic-motoric linkage in speech. *Journal of Speech and Hearing Research, 23,* 593–602.

Posner, M. (1964). Information reduction in analysis of sequential tasks. *Psychological Review, 71,* 491–503.

Posner, M., & Keele, S. (1968). Genesis of abstract ideas. *Journal of Experimental Psychology, 77,* 353–363.

Posner, M., & Keele, S. (1970). Retention of abstract ideas. *Journal of Experimental Psychology, 83,* 304–308.

Radeau, M., Morais, J., & Dewier, A. (1989). Phonological priming in spoken word recognition: Task effects. *Memory & Cognition, 17,* 525–535.

Roediger, H., & Blaxton, T. (1987). Effects of varying modality, surface features, and retention interval on priming in word-fragment completion. *Memory & Cognition, 15,* 379–388.

Roediger, H., & Srinivas, K. (1992). Specificity of operations in perceptual priming. In P. Graf & M. Masson (Eds.), *Implicit memory: New directions* (pp. 17–48). Hillsdale, NJ: Erlbaum.

Rothkopf, E. (1971). Incidental memory for location of information in text. *Journal of Verbal Learning and Verbal Behavior, 10,* 608–613.

Rundus, D. (1971). Analysis of rehearsal in free recall. *Journal of Experimental Psychology, 89,* 43–50.

Salasoo, A., Shiffrin, R., & Feustel, T. (1985). Building permanent memory codes: Codification and repetition effects in word identification. *Journal of Experimental Psychology: General, 114,* 50–77.

Scarborough, D. L., Cortese, C., & Scarborough, H. S. (1977). Frequency and repetition effects in lexical memory. *Journal of Experimental Psychology: Human Perception and Performance, 3,* 1–17.

Schacter, D. (1990). Perceptual representation systems and implicit memory: Toward a resolution of the multiple memory systems debate. *Annals of the New York Academy of Sciences, 608,* 543–571.

Schacter, D., & Church, B. (1992). Auditory priming: Implicit and explicit memory for words and voices. *Journal of Experimental Psychology: Learning, Memory, and Cognition, 18,* 915–930.

Schacter, D., Eich, J., & Tulving, E. (1978). Richard Semon's theory of memory. *Journal of Verbal Learning and Verbal Behavior, 17,* 721–743.

Semon, R. (1923). *Mnemic psychology* (B. Duffy, Trans.). London: Allen & Unwin. (Original work published 1909)

Sheffert, S. M., & Fowler, C. A. (1995). The effects of voice and visible speaker change on memory for spoken words. *Journal of Memory and Language, 34,* 665–685.

Shepard, R. N. (1967). Recognition memory for words, sentences, and pictures. *Journal of Verbal Learning and Verbal Behavior, 6,* 156–163.

Shepard, R. N. (1980). Multidimensional scaling, tree-fitting and clustering. *Science, 210,* 390–398.

Shepard, R. N., & Teghtsoonian, M. (1961). Retention of information under conditions approaching a steady state. *Journal of Experimental Psychology, 62,* 302–309.

Shin, H., & Nosofsky, R. (1992). Similarity-scaling studies of dot-pattern classification and recognition. *Journal of Experimental Psychology: General, 121,* 278–304.

Slowiaczek, L., & Hamburger, M. (1992). Prelexical facilitation and lexical interference in auditory word recognition. *Journal of Experimental Psychology: Learning, Memory, and Cognition, 6,* 1239–1250.

Smith, E., & Zarate, M. (1992). Exemplar-based model of social judgment. *Psychological Review, 99,* 3–21.

Standing, L., Conezio, J., & Haber, R. (1970). Perception and memory for pictures: Single-trial learning of 2560 visual stimuli. *Psychonomic Science, 19,* 73–74.

Studdert-Kennedy, M. (1976). Speech perception. In N. J. Lass (Ed.), *Contemporary issues in experimental phonetics* (pp. 243–293). New York: Academic Press.

Summerfield, Q., & Haggard, M. (1973). *Vocal tract normalization as demonstrated by reaction times. Report on research in progress in speech perception,* (no. 2). Belfast, Ireland: Queen's University of Belfast.

Summers, W., Pisoni, D. B., Bernacki, R., Pedlow, R., & Stokes, M. (1988). Effects of noise on speech production: Acoustic and perceptual analyses. *Journal of the Acoustical Society of America, 84,* 917–928.

Syrdal, A. K., & Gopal, H. S. (1986). A perceptual model of vowel recognition based on the auditory representation of American English vowels. *Journal of the Acoustical Society of America, 79,* 1086–1100.

Tenpenny, P. L. (1995). Abstractionist versus episodic theories of repetition priming and word identification. *Psychonomic Bulletin & Review, 2,* 339–363.

Tulving, E., & Schacter, D. (1990). Priming and human memory systems. *Science, 247,* 301–306.

Tulving, E., Schacter, D., & Stark, H. (1982). Priming effects in word fragment completion are independent of recognition memory. *Journal of Experimental Psychology: Learning, Memory, & Cognition, 8,* 336–342.

Underwood, B. J. (1969). Attributes of memory. *Psychological Review, 76,* 559–573.

Van Lancker, D., Kreiman, J., & Emmorey, K. (1985). Familiar voice recognition: Patterns and parameters. Part I: Recognition of backward voices. *Journal of Phonetics, 13,* 19–38.

Van Lancker, D., Kreiman, J., & Wickens, T. (1985). Familiar voice recognition: Patterns and parameters. Part II: Recognition of rate-altered voices. *Journal of Phonetics, 13,* 39–52.

Verbrugge, R., & Rakerd, B. (1986). Evidence of talker-independent information for vowels. *Language and Speech, 29,* 39–57.

Whalen, D., & Wenk, H. (1993). *Effect of the proper/common distinction on duration.* Presented at the 34th annual meeting of the Psychonomic Society, Washington, DC.

Wickelgren, W. A. (1969). Context-sensitive coding, associative memory, and serial order in (speech) behavior. *Psychological Review, 76,* 1–15.

Wright, C. (1979). Duration differences between rare and common words and their implications for the interpretation of word frequency effects. *Memory & Cognition, 7,* 411–419.

4

On the Nature of Perceptual Adjustments to Voice

JOHN W. MULLENNIX

4.1 INTRODUCTION

Much of the traditional research in speech perception has examined how linguistically based sound units (e.g., acoustic-phonetic units) emerge out of the speech waveform. In recent years, this research has moved from investigations of the acoustic cues to various phoneme contrasts to examinations of the problems of perceptual normalization and perceptual constancy. In speech perception, perceptual constancy means that, despite variations in the speech waveform caused by factors such as speech rate fluctuations and voice differences between individual talkers, normal-hearing subjects have little trouble perceiving speech sounds under a variety of different conditions. In order to fully understand speech perception, the problem of perceptual constancy must be solved. The key to the solution is to view the problem in terms of adjustments that the perceptual system makes to speech rate and voice (Fourcin, 1968; Joos, 1948; Rand, 1971; Summerfield & Haggard, 1973).

In this chapter, I will focus on one aspect of this problem: perceptual adjustments to voice. The primary theme of this chapter is the necessity of developing a sophisticated picture of the processes that handle voice information during speech perception in order to properly understand the mechanism responsible for perceptual adjustments to voice. There are two major issues to be considered.

Talker Variability in Speech Processing

First, the relationship of perceptual adjustments to voice to phonetic processing must be examined. Do perceptual adjustments to voice occur independently of phonetic processing? Or are the processes that perform adjustments to voice inexorably intertwined with phonetic processes? Is voice information extracted from the speech signal processed in the same manner as acoustic-phonetic information, or is voice processed in a substantially different manner? The second issue considers the relationship of perceptual adjustments to voice to attention. Do these adjustments to voice require selective attention or processing capacity? Or are these adjustments automatic, requiring no capacity? Below, recent research relevant to each of these two major issues is reviewed. In addition, a few tentative answers and conclusions are offered in response to the questions that fall under each issue.

4.2 THE RELATIONSHIP OF PERCEPTUAL ADJUSTMENTS TO VOICE TO PHONETIC PROCESSING

In order to assess how perceptual adjustments to voice occur, the similarities and differences between the processing of voice and the processing of phonetic information during speech perception need to be studied. Why? Researchers know a great deal about how acoustic-phonetic information in the speech waveform is processed, but they know much less about how voice information is extracted from the speech signal. If one can set up situations where voice processing is compared to phonetic processing, then one can gain some insight into the way that voice is handled and, as a result, perhaps clarify the way that perceptual adjustments to voice are performed. One way to attack this issue is to conduct perceptual studies on voice that are similar in approach to studies conducted on phonetic processing. Studies of this sort can be directed toward assessing whether perceptual processes operating on voice information behave as phonetic processes do.

One study that fits into this particular niche was conducted recently by myself and colleagues (Mullennix, Johnson, Topcu-Durgun, & Farnsworth, 1995). The purpose of this study was to (a) determine whether voice-based stimuli are perceived categorically, much as phonetic-based stimuli are, and (b) determine whether the processing of voice-based stimuli occurs at an early, auditory level in the perceptual system or at a higher, more abstract level. For this study, a male–female synthetic voice continuum was generated, with all speech utterances consisting of the vowel /i/. In one experiment, categorical perception was investigated. Subjects were presented with male–female voice continuum stimuli and were run through standard perceptual identification and ABX discrimination procedures. The results are presented in Figure 1.

As shown in this figure, the shallow identification function and the high overall discrimination with the absence of a discrimination peak indicate that the voice stimuli were not perceived categorically. In addition, the discrimination

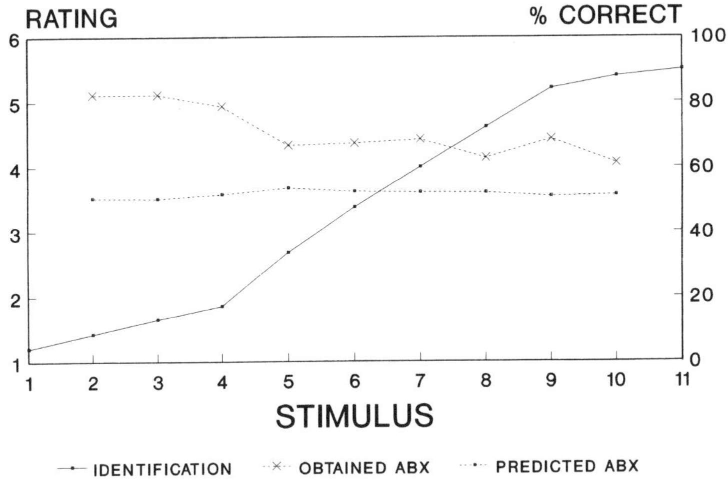

FIGURE 1 Identification and ABX discrimination data. The identification data are indexed by the rating scale on the left *y*-axis. The obtained versus predicted discrimination performance in terms of percent correct discrimination is indexed by the percent correct scale on the right *y*-axis. (From Mullennix et. al, 1995)

function resembled a Weber-like psychophysical function typical of the types of functions derived for low-level auditory sounds like tones. These results suggest that the synthetic voice stimuli were perceived in a manner more like simple auditory sounds and less like complex speech sounds. The tentative conclusion offered for these findings was that there exists a significant difference in the way that voice information and phonetic information are processed during speech perception.

In the same study, we also examined the perceptual effects of selective adaptation on the continuum. In a series of experiments, a number of voice-based adaptors that varied in their acoustic composition were used. The results indicated that adaptation of the continuum was driven by the auditory overlap of adaptor to continuum endpoint. Following the logic by which selective adaptation of phonetically based speech sounds has been explained (see Samuel, 1986), it was concluded that the processing of voice-based stimuli occurs at an early, auditory level of perceptual processing. When considering the Mullennix et al. (1995) results for categorical perception and selective adaptation, the conclusion is that voice processing is not categorical and occurs at an early auditory level of processing. This suggests that voice processing during perception does not occur in quite the same way as phonetic analysis does.

Additional evidence suggesting that the processing of voice involves low-level auditory processes during perception comes from another recent study in our laboratory examining the short-duration time course of voice processing (Mullennix & Howe, 1993). In previous research, Cole, Coltheart, and Allard

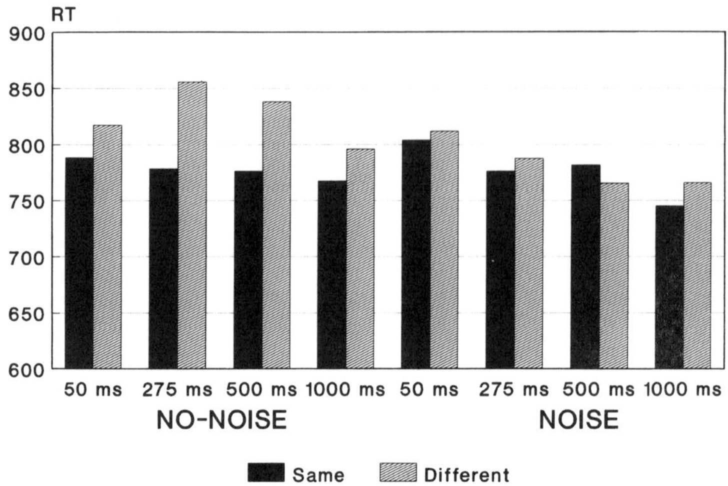

FIGURE 2 Response latency performance (RT) (in ms) for same-voice and different-voice trials across interstimulus intervals (ISI) for noise-filled conditions and no-noise (silent interval) conditions.

(1974; see also Allard & Henderson, 1975) examined same–different decisions for pairs of spoken words presented in the same voice or in different voices. They found that responses to word pairs that mismatched in voice (e.g., different-voice word pairs) were slower than responses to same-voice pairs. These effects were observed over interstimulus intervals (ISI) ranging from 500 ms to 8 s. Similar effects were observed by Mullennix and Pisoni (1988) for shorter time intervals from 100 ms to 2 s. One way to interpret these results is to say that voice information must be available for a brief period of time during or subsequent to perceptual processing in order for these voice mismatch effects to occur. These results are not unexpected, because it is obvious that voice information must pass through some intermediate stage of processing between initial encoding and long-term memory in order to be retained for later retrieval. In order to provide another perspective from which to examine the nature of voice processing, Mullennix and Howe (1993) conducted a study similar in flavor to those cited above. In our study, we also tested the effects of voice mismatches on same–different decisions to spoken words. However, we included two manipulations designed to elucidate the nature of voice processing under these conditions. First of all, same–different decisions to voice were assessed, instead of same–different decisions to words, with subjects specifically attending to voice information and deciding whether the two voices they heard for a given word pair were the "same voice" or "different voices." In previous studies, voice information was more "incidental," whereas in our study, selective attention was focused on voice. Secondly, stimuli were presented under two conditions. In one condition, the ISI was silent, as in all previous studies. But in another condition, the ISI was filled with noise, with the noise acting as an auditory backward mask. Our hypothesis was that if the voice information available for same–different voice decisions over very short time intervals (from 50 ms to 1000 ms) is "low-level" and relatively unprocessed, then the introduction of a noise mask should interfere with the processing or retention of the voice information. Under this scenario, one would expect that the voice mismatch effect observed in previous research would be smaller in magnitude or obliterated. However, if the voice information is more elaborately encoded into a "higher level" format during this time, then the noise mask should have little effect, and the voice mismatch effect should be about the same as for the silent ISI condition. The results are plotted in Figure 2.

Under the "no-noise" silent interval conditions, there is a substantial and significant voice mismatch effect, with responses slowed to different-voice word pairs. This result mirrors previous findings. However, under noise mask conditions, the voice mismatch effect was absent, with no reliable differences in responses between different-voice pairs and same-voice pairs. Thus, the introduction of the noise-filled interval mask resulted in the elimination of the voice mismatch effect. This result provides additional insight into the nature of voice processing, at least during time intervals up to 1000 ms. It appears that voice information that becomes available to other processes during this time period is veridical and relatively unprocessed, unlike phonetic information, which appears to be highly encoded after a time lapse of 250 ms (e.g., see Massaro, 1974).

Additional information that the processing of voice and phonetic analysis differ was obtained by Mullennix and Pisoni (1990). In this study, we used a variant of the Garner (1974) speeded-classification paradigm to examine the processing relationship between voice and phoneme. In brief, we found that "voice" and "phoneme" stimulus dimensions are processed as integral stimulus dimensions. However, the processing relationship between the voice dimension and the phonetic dimension was asymmetric, with variations in voice causing greater interference on phonetic classifications than vice versa. These results are important for many reasons, some of which are discussed below, but of special consideration here is the processing asymmetry. Processing asymmetries of this sort are typically interpreted within hybrid serial/parallel or parallel-contingent modes of processing (McClelland, 1979; Turvey, 1973; Wood, 1974, 1975). Applying this logic to our situation, it appears that the analysis of phonetic information is partially contingent on the analysis of voice information. In layman's terms, phonetic processes "wait" for at least partial voice processing to occur before they proceed. Going back to the integrality result, the finding of integrality suggests that processing of voice and phonetic analysis are tied together very closely. Either voice and phoneme information are extracted at different rates, or else the outputs from voice analysis and phonetic analysis processes interfere with each other in asymmetric fashion. This result constitutes another small piece of evidence, suggesting that voice processing and phonetic analysis during speech perception do not proceed in the same fashion.

In my discussion so far, I have attempted to highlight differences between the ways that voice information and phonetic information are recovered from the signal. An important point to make is that if there are qualitative (or perhaps just quantitative) differences in the way that voice information and phonetic information are extracted from the speech waveform, this does not necessarily mean that these processes are separate from one another or occur independently. In fact, our finding of integrality (Mullennix & Pisoni, 1990) argues against independent processes. There is now an extensive literature of research in speech perception that strongly suggests that perceptual adjustments to voice directly affect phonetic processing. This literature suggests that here is a good possibility that a distinction between voice processing and phonetic analysis is simply artificial, with both processes reflecting different facets of a more holistic processing mechanism that operates on the totality of information contained in the speech waveform.

The largest amount of research suggesting that perceptual adjustments to voice affect phonetic processing appears in studies that examine the perceptual consequences of talker variability on speech perception (Assmann, Nearey, & Hogan, 1982; Creelman, 1957; Fourcin, 1968; Mullennix, Pisoni, & Martin, 1989; Peters, 1955; Strange, Verbrugge, Shankweiler, & Edman, 1976; Verbrugge, Strange, Shankweiler, & Edman, 1976; Weenink, 1986). The common approach in these studies is to introduce talker variability across trials and observe its impact on perception of speech sounds or spoken words. Talker variability is usually defined as the comparison of performance for multiple-talker stimuli versus single-talker stimuli. The main finding from these studies is that perception of spoken utterances is impaired in conditions with talker variability, relative to conditions where items are spoken by a single talker. This impairment is usually interpreted as the consequence of a perceptual mechanism that is making adjustments or compensations for changes in talker voice. One study that illustrates talker variability effects was conducted by Mullennix et al. (1989). Mullennix et al. examined listeners' perceptual identification and naming performance to lists of words spoken by one talker or by multiple talkers. Two major results were observed in this study: First, for word naming, responses to words produced by multiple talkers were substantially slower than responses to words produced by a single talker. This increase in processing time under multiple-talker conditions appeared to reflect perceptual adjustments to voice performed on each trial. Second, talker variability also affected perceptual word identification, with identification rate being worse under multiple-talker conditions. Both of these results suggest that voice processing, in terms of making perceptual adjustments to voice over trials, had a direct or indirect effect on phonetic processing, as perception of speech became worse or slowed as perceptual adjustments to voice were invoked. Moreover, when spoken words were distorted by envelope-shaped noise, an interaction occurred between talker variability and distortion level, with the detrimental effects of talker variability increased as distortion level increased. Because distortion of the signal interferes with auditory coding processes, this result suggests that the perceptual mechanism that adjusts for different talkers is related to early auditory coding processes. These findings are important in two respects. One, they indicate that there is a strong relationship between perceptual adjustments to voice and phonetic processing. And two, they provide evidence that the processing of voice during speech perception is accomplished at a relatively low level in the system.

A slightly different approach showing that perceptual adjustments to voice affect phonetic analysis was taken by Nygaard, Sommers, and Pisoni (1994). Nygaard et al. familiarized listeners with a set of unfamiliar voices. After listeners learned to reliably recognize the voices, they were presented with a perceptual word-identification task. Some listeners were presented with words produced by the talkers familiar to them; other listeners were presented with words produced by unfamiliar talkers. The results indicated that word identification was superior for words produced by familiar talkers, as reflected by speech intelligibility scores. In this situation familiarity with a talker's voice appears to facilitate phonetic analysis. Whether this facilitation is direct or indirect is unclear. The fact that speech intelligibility was affected is important, because this suggests that any relationship between voice processing and phonetic processing that occurs takes place at an early level of perception. This result has important implications for the nature of the relationship of perceptual adjustments to voice to phonetic processing.

Given that perceptual adjustments to voice processing affect phonetic processing, then the next step in characterizing this relationship is to begin examining the microstructure of the interactions between these respective processes. As we considered this issue, we decided that one way to address the problem was to go back and examine the time course of the effects of voice on phonetic processing in greater detail. Thus, we decided to investigate whether the short-duration processing relationship between voice and speech is dependent on a fixed time window that occurs during perceptual analysis of the speech signal (Mullennix & Howe, 1996). The study was set up as follows. First, a primed word-identification task was used. Spoken target words were presented at low-amplitude sound levels, with the listeners' task to identify the words. The target word was "primed" by the occurrence of a neutral "voice prime" word spoken in the same voice or different voice as the target word. Priming was examined in both forward and backward temporal priming paradigms. In forward priming, a voice prime occurred first followed by the target word. In backward priming, the target word occurred first followed by a voice prime. All target words were spoken by one male speaker (JM), with the voice prime spoken by JM or by a female speaker (DRW). The time course was examined by manipulating the ISI between prime and target word (50 ms to 500 ms), providing a means to test whether time elapse (up to 500 ms) affects the efficacy of voice information on spoken-word identification.

A number of hypotheses were entertained. If voice information is processed or retained over the short duration and affects the perception of subsequent speech targets, one would expect forward-priming effects for voice. However, the situation for backward priming is different. If perceptual processing for the speech target is already completed by the time the voice prime is encountered, then

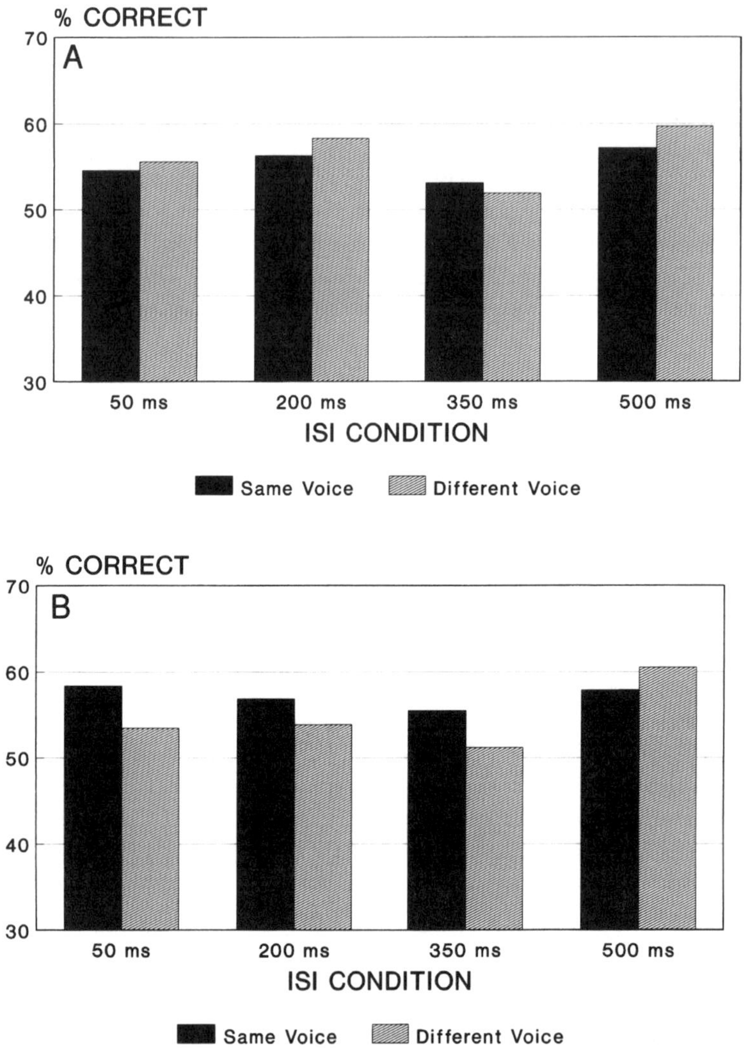

FIGURE 3 Percent correct word identification as a function of voice (same or different), ISI interval, and priming condition (A, forward or B, backward).

backward voice priming effects may not occur. However, if backward voice primes have an effect, this would suggest that there is a time window that remains open after stimulus offset during which voice information can still affect perceptual analysis of the word. The comparison of forward versus backward priming provides further information about the time course of information extraction for speech sounds and whether those processes are affected by voice information that remains available for a period of time. We felt that the results from such an experiment would provide useful information to help delineate the relationship between perceptual adjustments to voice and phonetic processing.

Figure 3 shows the percent correct word-identification data collapsed across subject for both forward and backward priming conditions as a function of voice prime type and ISI.

For the forward-priming condition, we found no significant difference in identification of words for same-voice trials versus different-voice trials. However, for the backward-priming condition, same-voice trial target words were identified reliably better than different-voice trial target words (57.2% vs. 54.8%, respectively). Although the absolute difference in identification was not that large, the task was very difficult, probably explaining the small but reliable difference. When considering these results, they did not conform to our a priori expectations. A same-voice word-identification advantage was observed for backward priming only, meaning that voice information encountered after the target word only affected word identification. Although this pattern of results was puzzling, the backward-priming effect did provide some evidence that voice information removed in time from a speech utterance affects phonetic processing of that utterance. However, any interpretation of this finding is complicated by the lack of a forward voice-priming effect. Why did voice priming only occur in the backward temporal priming condition? After reflecting upon the results of this experiment, one possibility emerged. We thought it conceivable that the arrangement of the stimulus sequences across forward- and backward-priming conditions may have affected selective attention to the voice primes. In forward priming, for each trial, subjects heard the voice prime first, followed by the target word and the response interval. Subjects in this condition had to focus their attentional resources on the second stimulus target word in order to identify it. However, the first stimulus voice prime could have been selectively ignored on each trial, as processing of the prime was irrelevant to the subjects' task. In backward priming, subjects heard the target word first, followed by the prime and the response interval. In this situation, it is much less likely that subjects selectively ignored the voice prime. These subjects had to focus their attention on the first stimulus target, but also had to focus their attention on retaining word-identity information throughout the second stimulus voice prime interval while awaiting the response interval. So, the backward voice prime may have been attended to just because it was interspersed between two trial-related events (stimulus target and initiation of the response interval) that subjects had to monitor and as a result actively attend to.

To test our hypothesis, we repeated the experiment but with one additional change: We also required listeners to attend to the neutral voice prime and to report whether the prime was spoken by the male speaker or the female speaker at the end of each trial. The results of this second experiment are shown in Figure 4.

For forward-priming, same-voice trial words were identified reliably better than different-voice trial words (58.5 vs. 56.9%). For backward-priming, same-voice trial words were also identified reliably better than different-voice words

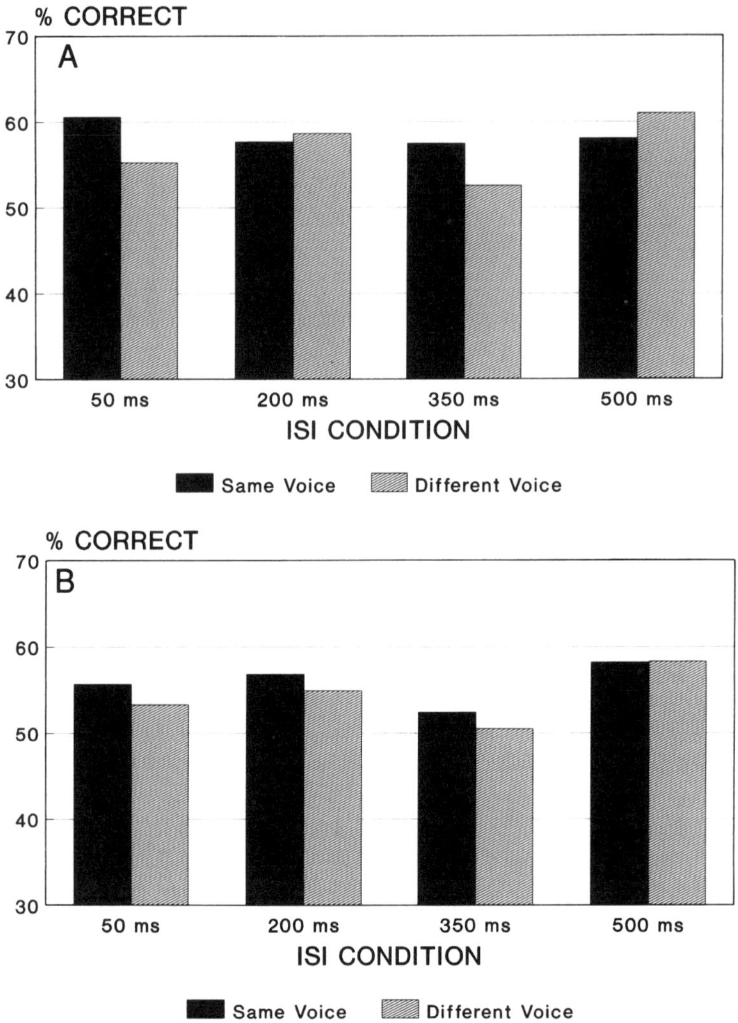

FIGURE 4 Percent correct word identification as a function of voice (same or different), interstimulus interval (ISI), and priming condition (A, forward or B, backward).

(55.8 vs. 54.3%, respectively). Thus, the backward-priming results of our first experiment were replicated, and an effect of voice in forward priming was also obtained. The results of the second experiment suggest that selective attention to voice appears to be an important factor in obtaining voice-priming effects. This issue is taken up again in the next section and discussed in further detail.

The main finding from this study is that perceptual adjustments to voice affect perceptual word identification. This study provides further evidence that these adjustments are closely related to phonetic processing. Upon inspecting the time course of the voice-priming effects, it appears that there may be a 350-ms time window before phonetic processing of a target word begins and after the cessation of target word presentation where voice information can affect acoustic-phonetic processing. However, the results over ISI were somewhat variable, so we did not place a great deal of confidence in this 350-ms value. However, if this result is replicated, the finding would be at odds with the same–different studies that showed voice mismatch effects at ISIs up to 8 s. One possible explanation for this discrepancy could be that, in the same/different task, the emphasis is on decision-level processes, whereas in the identification task, the emphasis is on perceptual-level processes. On the other hand, it may turn out that any issues of the availability of voice information to phonetic processes is simply a task-dependent phenomenon that deserves further research.

To summarize the findings discussed so far, a clear picture begins to emerge concerning the nature of the processes that adjust for voice-related variation in the speech waveform. The evidence is consistent with the idea that extraction of voice information occurs at a fairly low level in the auditory system. These processes appear to be highly related to psychophysical processes that extract basic information about auditory sounds. In addition, the information about voice produced by these processes seems to be relatively unprocessed, as compared to more highly encoded phonetic sounds. There is overwhelming evidence from talker variability experiments and others indicating that the operation of the processes that adjust for voice interfere significantly with phonetic processing, though it is unclear whether this interference is direct or indirect. Future studies should examine more closely the microstructure of interactions between voice and phonetic processing.

4.3 VOICE, ATTENTION, AND AUTOMATICITY

Another issue regarding perceptual adjustments to voice involves whether these adjustments are "automatic," meaning that they are not under attentional control and capacity-free, or whether these adjustments require attention and processing capacity. A number of studies would appear consistent with the hypothesis that voice processing in general is automatic, given that when the processing of voice information is "incidental" to the task at hand, voice is retained in memory and exerts an effect on memory recognition and recall for spoken words. For example, results from implicit memory tasks (Church & Schacter, 1994; Schacter & Church, 1992), recognition memory tasks (Craik & Kirsner, 1974; Goldinger, 1992; Lively, 1994; Palmeri, Goldinger, & Pisoni, 1993), explicit memory word-recall tasks (Goldinger, Pisoni, & Logan, 1991; Martin, Mullennix, Pisoni, & Summers, 1989), and incidental learning tasks (Geiselman & Bellezza, 1976, 1977; Geiselman & Crawley, 1983) show that voice information appears to be automatically (and without intention) carried into memory (see also Goldinger, Chap. 3, this volume). But one question about these findings is whether incidental processing means automatic processing. Although voice information may be incidentally carried into episodic memory, is this process automatic and capacity-free?

Mullennix et al. (1989) suggested that perceptual adjustments to voice involved a capacity-limited process, with attention allocated to the processing of each new talker voice encountered. But, their experiments did not test this assumption directly. On the other hand, Martin et al. (1989) found some evidence that a digit preload task interfered more with encoding multiple-talker stimuli into memory compared to single-talker stimuli. Martin et al. (1989) examined the effects of talker variability and processing load on serial recall. Words within a list were spoken by either one or ten talkers; processing load was manipulated via a digit preload task. Recall of early-list items was better in single-talker lists than in multiple-talker lists. Also, recall of digits presented before the spoken lists was better when followed by single-talker lists than by multiple-talker lists. Their findings suggest that talker variability increases perceptual processing load, thus interfering with rehearsal and transfer of words to long-term memory (LTM). These results are consistent with the idea that perceptual adjustments to voice require processing capacity and decrease recall from LTM.

One study designed specifically to test assumptions about capacity and perceptual adjustments to voice was conducted by Nusbaum and Morin (1989; see also 1992). They conducted a dual-task speech monitoring experiment with vowels and CV syllables presented under single-talker and multiple-talker conditions. Processing load was manipulated by giving listeners a digit preload task to perform (either one or three two-digit numbers) while they performed the monitoring task. Their results indicated that monitoring performance for single-talker conditions did not differ much as a function of load; however, load had a substantial effect on monitoring under the multiple-talker conditions. The straightforward interpretation of this result is that the perceptual adjustments to voice necessitated in the multiple-talker conditions required a significant amount of processing capacity, thus competing for the capacity required by the preload task. Thus, in this study, the conclusion is that perceptual adjustments to voice require capacity.

The issue of capacity was explored further in a recent preliminary study in our laboratory. Farnsworth and Mullennix (1995) conducted a speech-classification study where assessments were made about the nature of the capacity used for adjustments to voice. In previous research on selective attention and phoneme processing (Pitt & Samuel, 1990), evidence was found indicating that subjects had the ability to focus an attentional "spotlight" on phonemes that occur in various temporal locations in speech. Pitt and Samuel (1990) found that listeners who were given prior information about the temporal location of a target phoneme were able to perceive the phoneme more efficiently, suggesting that one can focus selective attention (or processing capacity) on temporal phoneme location. Farnsworth and Mullennix (1995) designed a situation where the capacity required by perceptual adjustments to voice and the capacity required to selectively attend to phoneme location were pitted against one another. In our experiment, listeners participated in a speeded classification task for speech consonants (C) (or vowels

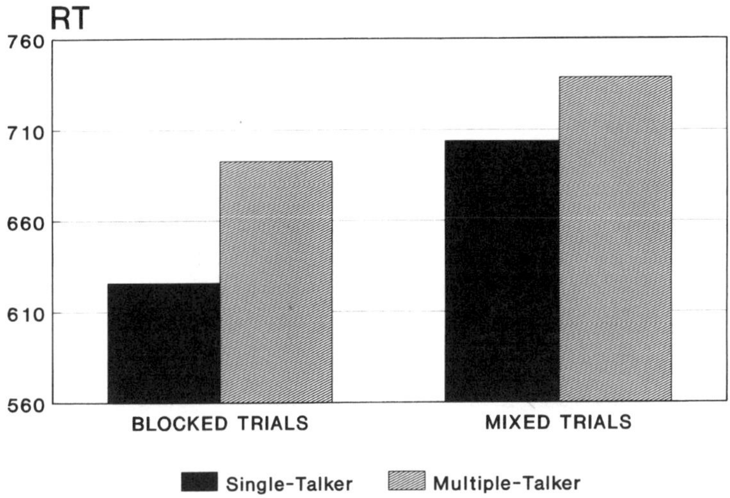

FIGURE 5 Response latency performance (RT) (in ms) for single-talker and multiple-talker conditions across phoneme location conditions (blocked trials versus mixed trials) for consonants.

[V]) with two variables manipulated: talker variability and phoneme location variability. Talker variability was manipulated by presenting stimuli under single-talker or multiple-talker conditions, whereas phoneme location variability was manipulated by presenting the target phoneme in blocked conditions (e.g., a target consonant always appeared in a CV) or mixed conditions (e.g., a target consonant could appear in a CV or VC from trial to trial). The logic behind these manipulations was as follows. If the processing capacity required for perceptual adjustments to voice comes from the same pool as the processing capacity required to selectively attend to phoneme location, then there should be an interaction between talker variability and phoneme location variability, with the effect of talker variability greater under mixed location conditions. However, if the processing capacity required for each respective variable originates from separate, independent resource pools, then there should be no interaction between the two variables.

The results for the first experiment for speech consonant classification are shown in Figure 5.

Both talker variability and phoneme location variability had detrimental effects on performance. An interaction between the two variables was observed, but in the opposite direction predicted. That is, the effect of talker variability was greater under conditions where phoneme location over syllables remained constant. This unexpected result left us in a quandary. One possible explanation of the pattern we observed is that there was an overpowering negative effect of phoneme location variability. It is possible that the talker variability effect was "washed out" by the dominance of the capacity requirements produced by uncertainty in phoneme location. Overall, the interaction suggests that there is some relationship between capacity used for adjustments to voice and capacity used for

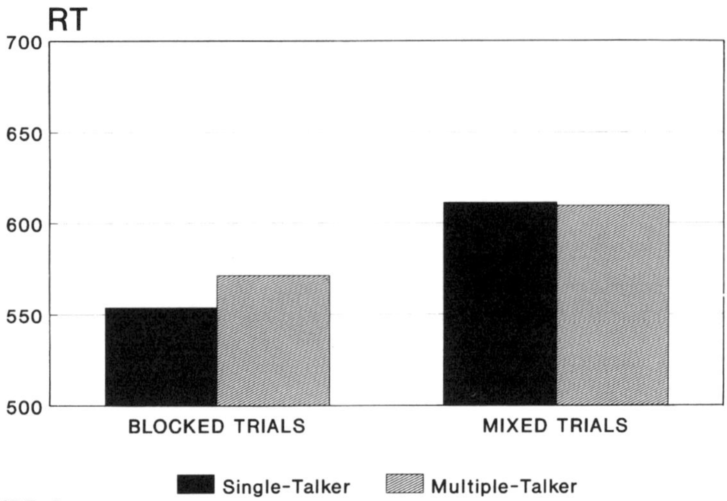

FIGURE 6 Response latency performance (RT) (in ms) for single-talker and multiple-talker conditions across phoneme location conditions (blocked trials versus mixed trials) for vowels.

attending to phoneme location, but the nature of this relationship is unclear, with respect to positing common or independent pools of processing capacity.

A second experiment was conducted that was similar to the first, except that listeners classified vowels. The results are shown in Figure 6. The results of the second experiment were also unexpected. Overall, there was no significant effect of talker variability. This result was puzzling, because it was the first perceptual experiment using a talker variability manipulation that I had ever encountered in our laboratory where an effect of talker variability was absent! At any rate, the lack of the talker variability effect precluded any interpretations of the data relevant to our hypotheses. So, overall, the results of the study were equivocal. Another possible reason for the pattern of results observed may have been due to the speech consonants and vowels chosen for the task. In our first experiment, listeners classified /b/ and /p/ stimuli. In the second experiment, they classified /i/ and /u/ stimuli. After going back and examining the response latency data for these classifications, we noted that vowel classification was much faster and apparently much easier than consonant classification. It is possible that the vowel classification was so easy (and at ceiling) that processing capacity was not taxed. Currently, we are in the midst of calibrating the difficulty of different speech classifications and are repeating the experiments with classification pairs that vary in difficulty and presumably the amount of resources that are required. At any rate, the results of this study do not provide any evidence supporting the idea that the capacity used for perceptual adjustments to voice is separate from the capacity used for selective attention to phoneme location. But, these data are difficult to interpret and are suggestive at best.

The discussion so far has focused on the issue of capacity requirements. The research pertaining to this issue appears to support the idea that perceptual adjustments to voice require capacity, suggesting that these processes are not capacity-free and that they are mediated by attention (Nusbaum & Morin, 1992). But what of the issue of automaticity? One characteristic of automaticity is that the processes are capacity-free, so on this point, I would conclude that perceptual adjustments to voice are not automatic. However, another characteristic of automaticity is that the allocation of processing to the stimulus is not under conscious, attentional control by the individual. On this point, there is some suggestion that perceptual adjustments to voice may be *mandatory,* but not automatic. To revisit Mullennix and Pisoni (1990), we found that voice-based and phonetic-based stimulus dimensions were processed integrally. One interpretation of this finding is that the voice dimension cannot be selectively ignored when phonetic classifications are required. So, if voice cannot be selectively ignored, then it appears that the allocation of attention to voice is mandatory (in the sense of Fodor, 1983), thus acting to reduce the available processing resources for phonetic coding.

However, the issue of capacity and automaticity may not be completely solved. As previously discussed, Mullennix and Howe (1996) found that forward priming of spoken word identification seemed to be contingent on selective attention being allocated to the voice prime stimulus. In this case, it appeared that, even if voice had been mandatorily processed, when additional focused attention resources are allocated to the voice stimulus, further processing occurs, resulting in a "voice-priming" effect on phonetic processing. So, in terms of the effect of voice information removed in time on phonetic processing and word identification, focused attention may be necessary to produce this effect. However, the relationship between the manner in which attention is allocated to voice in this situation and the manner in which attention is allocated to voice in order to perform a perceptual adjustment is not clear.

To summarize, when considering all of the available evidence pertaining to this issue, it appears that perceptual adjustments to voice involve a mandatory, attention-demanding process. The involuntary allocation of selective attention to voice usurps processing capacity that would normally be devoted to phonetic coding. Thus, although perceptual adjustments to voice may be mandatory, clearly they are not capacity-free. However, further research needs to be performed in order to ascertain the conditions under which focused selective attention to voice affects processing.

4.4 CONCLUSION

Based on the issues addressed in the present chapter, it is clear that researchers have made significant progress in understanding one aspect of the perceptual normalization problem in speech perception, that is, perceptual adjustments to talker voice. Regardless of the term used for this phenomenon (see Pisoni,

Chap. 2, this volume) much work has demonstrated that the processing and extraction of voice information during speech perception has a significant influence on how acoustic-phonetic information is processed. It is possible that the detrimental effects observed for talker variability on phonetic processing may have a relatively uninteresting explanation based on processing capacity trade-offs between perceptual voice adjustments and phonetic analysis. However, other findings suggest that even if this is true, the story is probably more complex. There is strong evidence to suggest that the extraction of voice information from the speech waveform occurs differently than extraction of acoustic-phonetic information. Voice processing is not categorical, appears to occur at an early, auditory level of processing, and is available for a longer amount of time in an unprocessed format than phonetic information is. These findings bring up an interesting question that has not received much attention. Is the extraction of voice information from the speech waveform *qualitatively* or *quantitatively* different than the extraction of acoustic-phonetic information? When considering all the research, it turns out that the answer is not clear. The finding of integrality by Mullennix and Pisoni (1990) suggested that the processing of voice and phoneme are highly related, yet differ in the rate at which each type of information becomes available to the system. One possibility that deserves some serious consideration is that any distinction made between voice processing and phonetic processing is an artificial distinction that does not reflect the actual process at work during speech perception. Perhaps one holistic perceptual process is at work on the signal, with information about different parameters related to voice and phonetic units extracted at different processing rates. Recent work indicating that voice information and acoustic-phonetic information are automatically encoded into episodic memory is certainly consistent with a holistic viewpoint (see Goldinger, Chap. 3, this volume; Pisoni, Chap. 2, this volume). On the other hand, perhaps a distinction between voice processing and phonetic processing is warranted, with two mechanisms working in parallel on the signal. But if this latter assertion is correct, then does one need to posit another additional mechanism for perceptual adjustments to speech rate? Speech timing? In the name of parsimony, I would say no. Then again, parsimony does not always reflect how the real world operates! At any rate, one direction for future research that should prove fruitful is to investigate the microstructure of the relationship between perceptual adjustments to voice and phonetic analysis. By eliciting specific details about how voice affects phonetic analysis, perhaps some insights can be gleaned that will help to answer some of these major issues. These, in turn, will provide valuable information that will be relevant to constructing an appropriate theory of speech processing and recognition.

REFERENCES

Allard, F., & Henderson, L. (1975). Physical and name codes in auditory memory: The pursuit of an analogy. *Quarterly Journal of Experimental Psychology, 28,* 475–482.

Assmann, P., Nearey, T. M., & Hogan, J. (1982). Vowel identification: Orthographic, perceptual, and acoustic aspects. *Journal of the Acoustical Society of America, 71,* 975–989.

Church, B. A., & Schacter, D. L. (1994). Perceptual specificity of auditory priming: Implicit memory for voice intonation and fundamental frequency. *Journal of Experimental Psychology: Learning, Memory, and Cognition, 20,* 521–533.

Cole, R. A., Coltheart, M., & Allard, F. (1974). Memory for a speaker's voice: Reaction time to same- or different-voiced letters. *Quarterly Journal of Experimental Psychology, 26,* 1–7.

Craik, F. I. M., & Kirsner, K. (1974). The effect of speaker's voice on word recognition. *Quarterly Journal of Experimental Psychology, 26,* 274–284.

Creelman, C. D. (1957). Case of the unknown talker. *Journal of the Acoustical Society of America, 29,* 655.

Farnsworth, L. M., & Mullennix, J. W. (1995, May). *The effects of talker variability across CV and VC environments.* Paper presented at the 129th meeting of the Acoustical Society of America, Washington, DC.

Fodor, J. A. (1983). *Modularity of mind.* Cambridge, MA: MIT Press.

Fourcin, A. (1968). Speech-source interference. *IEEE Transactions on Audio and Electroacoustics, AU-16,* 65–67.

Garner, W. R. (1974). *The processing of information and structure.* Hillsdale, NJ: Erlbaum.

Geiselman, R. E., & Bellezza, F. S. (1976). Long-term memory for speaker's voice and source location. *Memory & Cognition, 4,* 483–489.

Geiselman, R. E., & Bellezza, F. S. (1977). Incidental retention of speaker's voice. *Memory & Cognition, 5,* 658–665.

Geiselman, R. E., & Crawley, J. M. (1983). Incidental processing of speaker characteristics: Voice as connotative information. *Journal of Verbal Learning and Verbal Behavior, 22,* 15–23.

Goldinger, S. D. (1992). *Words and voices: Implicit and explicit memory for spoken words. Research on speech perception* (Tech. Rep. No. 7). Bloomington: Indiana University.

Goldinger, S. D., Pisoni, D. B., & Logan, J. S. (1991). On the nature of talker variability effects on recall of spoken word lists. *Journal of Experimental Psychology: Learning, Memory, and Cognition, 17,* 152–162.

Joos, M. A. (1948). Acoustic phonetics. *Language, 24,* (Suppl. 2), 1–136.

Lively, S. E. (1994). *Preserving the perceptual record: Retention of talker-specific information in long-term memory. Research on speech perception* (Tech. Rep. No. 9). Bloomington: Indiana University Press.

Martin, C. S., Mullennix, J. W., Pisoni, D. B., & Summers, W. V. (1989). Effects of talker variability on recall of spoken word lists. *Journal of Experimental Psychology: Learning, Memory, and Cognition, 15,* 676–684.

Massaro, D. W. (1974). Perceptual units in speech perception. *Journal of Experimental Psychology, 102,* 199–208.

McClelland, J. L. (1979). On the time-relations of mental processes: An examination of processes in cascade. *Psychological Review, 86,* 287–330.

Mullennix, J. W., & Howe, J. N. (1993, November). *Auditory memory and voice perception.* Paper presented at the 34th annual meeting of the Psychonomic Society, Washington DC.

Mullennix, J. W., & Howe, J. N. (1996). *The effects of short-duration voice processing on spoken word identification.* Manuscript submitted for review.

Mullennix, J. W., Johnson, K. A., Topcu-Durgun, M., & Farnsworth, L. M. (1995). The perceptual representation of voice gender. *Journal of the Acoustical Society of America, 98,* 3080–3095.

Mullennix, J. W., & Pisoni, D. B. (1988). *Detailing the nature of talker normalization in speech perception. Research on speech perception* (Progress Report No. 13, pp. 289–305). Bloomington: Indiana University Press.

Mullennix, J. W., & Pisoni, D. B. (1990). Stimulus variability and processing dependencies in speech perception. *Perception & Psychophysics, 47,* 379–390.

Mullennix, J. W., Pisoni, D. B., & Martin, C. S. (1989). Some effects of talker variability on spoken word recognition. *Journal of the Acoustical Society of America, 85,* 365–378.

Nusbaum, H., & Morin, T. (1989, May). *Perceptual normalization of talker differences.* Paper presented at the 117th meeting of the Acoustical Society of America, Syracuse, NY.

Nusbaum, H., & Morin, T. (1992). Paying attention to differences among talkers. In Y. Tohkura, E. Vatikiotis-Bateson, & Y. Sagisaka (Eds.), *Speech perception, production, and linguistic structure* (pp. 113–134). Tokyo: IOS Press.

Nygaard, L. C., Sommers, M. S., & Pisoni, D. B. (1994). Speech perception as a talker-contingent process. *Psychological Science, 5,* 42–46.

Palmeri, T. J., Goldinger, S. D., & Pisoni, D. B. (1993). Episodic encoding of voice attributes and recognition memory for spoken words. *Journal of Experimental Psychology: Learning, Memory, and Cognition, 19,* 1–20.

Peters, R. W. (1955). *The relative intelligibility of single-voice and multiple-voice messages under various conditions of noise* (Joint Project Report No. 56, pp. 1–9). Pensacola, FL: U.S. Naval School of Aviation Medicine.

Pitt, M. A., & Samuel, A. G. (1990). Attentional allocation during speech perception: How fine is the focus? *Journal of Memory and Language, 29,* 611–632.

Rand, T. (1971). Vocal tract size normalization in the perception of stop consonants. *Haskins Laboratories Status Report on Speech Research, SR-25/26,* 141–146.

Samuel, A. (1986). Red herring detectors and speech perception: In defense of selective adaptation. *Cognitive Psychology, 18,* 452–499.

Schacter, D., & Church, B. (1992). Auditory priming: Implicit and explicit memory for words and voices. *Journal of Experimental Psychology: Learning, Memory, and Cognition, 18,* 915–930.

Strange, W., Verbrugge, R. R., Shankweiler, D. P., & Edman, T. R. (1976). Consonant environment specifies vowel identity. *Journal of the Acoustical Society of America, 60,* 213–224.

Summerfield, Q., & Haggard, M. (1973). *Vocal tract normalization as demonstrated by reaction times. Report of speech research in progress* (No. 2, pp. 1–12). Belfast, Ireland: Queen's University of Belfast.

Turvey, M. T. (1973). On peripheral and central processes in vision: Inferences from an information-processing analysis of masking with patterned stimuli. *Psychological Review, 80,* 1–52.

Verbrugge, R., Strange, W., Shankweiler, D., & Edman, T. (1976). What information enables a listener to map a talker's vowel space? *Journal of the Acoustical Society of America, 60,* 198–212.

Weenink, D. J. M. (1986). The identification of vowel stimuli from men, women, and children. *Proceedings 10 from the Institute of Phonetic Sciences of the University of Amsterdam,* pp. 41–54.

Wood, C. C. (1974). Parallel processing of auditory and phonetic information in speech discrimination. *Perception & Psychophysics, 15,* 501–508.

Wood, C. C. (1975). A normative model for redundancy gains in speeded classification: Application to auditory and phonetic dimensions in speech discrimination. In F. Restle, R. M. Shiffrin, N. J. Castellan, H. Lindman, & D. B. Pisoni (Eds.), *Cognitive theory* (Vol. 1, p. 55–77). Hillsdale, NJ: Erlbaum.

5

Listening to Voices

Theory and Practice in Voice Perception Research

JODY KREIMAN

The study of voice production and perception has a long history in many disciplines (Laver, 1981). What makes two speech samples sound like the same voice? What must they have in common, and what can vary without altering personal quality? How do listeners discriminate among or recognize voices, and how accurate is "earwitness" testimony? Questions like these have long engaged researchers in disciplines ranging from performing arts to police science, from engineering to biomedicine.

Traditionally, linguists and speech perception researchers have treated speaker information as an "extra message" in the acoustic signal that must be normalized or factored away so that the semantic message may be recovered (Peters, 1954). However, recent research (e.g., Nygaard, Sommers, & Pisoni, 1994, and the references contained therein, and the other chapters in this volume) suggests that speaker-specific aspects of the signal are not "noise," but instead provide information critical to extracting the semantic message. Thus interest in voice perception has increased among speech perception researchers.

A large literature exists describing the study of voice perception, and a number of reviews have appeared (Bricker & Pruzansky, 1976; Bull & Clifford, 1984; Hecker, 1971; Hollien, 1990; Kreiman, 1987; Laver, 1981; Siegman, 1987; Yarmey, 1995). (The general term *voice perception* will be used throughout this chapter to denote any task where a listener hears a voice and makes a response, including recognition, discrimination, and evaluation tasks, as described below.)

Talker Variability in Speech Processing

In this chapter I review some recent work, and argue that researchers have not in fact answered any of the long-standing fundamental questions about voice perception. Furthermore, I argue that the approaches traditionally used in voice perception research will in fact never provide answers to the fundamental questions of how listeners recognize voices, discriminate among speakers, or even of how accurately listeners can identify speakers.

The point of this discussion is *not* that previous research is invalid or without interest. The focus of this chapter on voice perception also means that several research areas where substantial progress is being made, including laryngeal biomechanics (e.g., Berke & Gerratt, 1993) and voice synthesis (e.g., Childers & Lee, 1991; Granström, 1992; Karlsson, 1992; Klatt & Klatt, 1990) are excluded from discussion.[1] My goal in this chapter is rather to suggest that current approaches to voice perception research have been exhausted, and that a new approach is necessary if the questions of interest are ever to be answered.

5.1 REVIEW OF THE LITERATURE ON VOICE PERCEPTION

5.1.1 Overview of Voice Perception Tasks

Following the classic speech chain model (Denes & Pinson, 1993), voice perception is traditionally viewed as a succession of stages that transmit information from a speaker to a listener (Bricker & Pruzansky, 1976). Perceived vocal quality reflects the contribution of all the stages in Figure 1.

Within a given study, differences among speakers are generally assumed to contribute the majority of variance in voice perception tasks. That is, when recognition accuracy varies from target to target, the differences are assumed to be due mostly to differences in the similarity of the target and test voices. Similarly, differences in ratings in evaluative tasks are assumed to be due largely to differences in the extent to which the voices being rated possess the quality being rated (Kreiman & Gerratt, 1996). Differences among speakers (*interspeaker* variability in quality) may be due to innate factors (anatomy, age, gender, and so on) and/or to learned (dialectal and idiolectal) aspects of speech (Garvin & Ladefoged, 1963; Ladefoged, 1956). Speakers also differ from occasion to occasion in the precise way they produce utterances (*intraspeaker* variability in quality). Thus the task for listeners in discrimination studies is traditionally described as determining whether observed differences in quality are due to within- or between-speaker factors. In recognition tasks, listeners compare a stored representation to a newly presented probe voice and make a similar decision.

[1] Most studies of pathological voice quality, machine recognition, recognition via spectrogram, and voice production have also been excluded. For reviews of these areas, see, for example, Bricker and Pruzansky (1976), Hollien (1990), Kreiman, Gerratt, Kempster, Erman, and Berke (1993), and Titze (1994).

Speaker → Utterance → Transmitted Acoustic Signal → Listener → Listener Response

FIGURE 1 Stages of transmitting information from a speaker to a listener.

The amount and kind of information available about who is speaking also depends on the utterance produced. For example, limited information about articulation is available from steady state vowels, and whisper does not provide information about the vocal source. The amount and kind of information available to listeners may also be affected by filtering, masking, or other characteristics of the transmission system used to present signals. Listeners also contribute to voice perception through their experience with different classes of voice, perceptual habits, attention to the task, and so on (Kreiman, Gerratt, Kempster, Erman, & Berke, 1993).

Finally, the output of the voice perception process is a decision, the precise form of which depends on the listener's task. Two broad classes of task are generally distinguished: voice evaluation tasks, and voice identification (discrimination or recognition) tasks (Bricker & Pruzansky, 1976). In evaluation tasks, stimuli are rated on some scale, or are compared with respect to some attribute. For example, listeners may estimate a speaker's age, or rate the breathiness of a voice, or compare two samples to determine which is rougher. Such tasks are particularly common in the literature on perception of pathological voice quality (see Kreiman et al., 1993, for review). Performance may be evaluated by counting the number of correct responses when "correct" is defined (for example, when age is estimated), by correlating responses with measures from some other domain (the correlation between estimates of personality and the results of a psychological inventory, or the correlation between scalar ratings and acoustic measures, for example), or by the extent to which listeners agree in their ratings. Identification tasks involve associating a voice sample with the speaker who produced it by naming the speaker, by selecting another sample (believed to have been) produced by the same speaker, or by determining whether two voice samples were produced by the same or different speakers. Performance in these tasks is usually measured by the number of correct responses.

The majority of voice perception studies have investigated the effects of changes in one or more of the cells in Figure 1 on voice ratings or recognition scores. Studies have examined the perception of speaker characteristics (including the relative contributions of the source and vocal tract to personal quality; disguise; mimicry; perception and recognition of gender, height, weight, and race from voice; and so on), effects of changes in the speech presented (sample duration, content, and different conditions of distortion), effects of changes in tasks (for example, including a face during learning, or varying retention intervals), effects of altering the transmission system (e.g., presenting voices over the telephone), and finally, the contributions of listeners to voice perception (differences between populations of listeners in perceptual strategy or accuracy, confidence in responses, effects of experience or training, and so on). The review of these areas that appears next focuses on work that has appeared since Bricker and Pruzansky's (1976) review article (see also Hecker, 1971).

5.1.2 Studies Focusing on Speaker Characteristics

Many studies have examined the extent to which listeners can judge a speaker's personal characteristics from voice. Gender is accurately judged, although mistakes do occur (Lass, Almerino, Jordan, & Walsh, 1980; Lass, Hughes, Bowyer, Waters, & Bourne, 1976; see also Mullennix, Johnson, Topcu-Durgun, & Farnsworth, 1995). Estimates of age are generally accurate within a decade (Hartman & Danauer, 1976; Jacques & Rastatter, 1990; Linville & Fisher, 1985; Ptacek & Sander, 1966; Shipp, Qi, Huntley, & Hollien, 1992; see Helfrich, 1979, for review). Listeners apparently can also judge whether a speaker is sober or intoxicated with better than chance accuracy (Pisoni & Martin, 1989). The large literature concerning the perception of stress, mood, and emotional state from voice has been reviewed by Disner (1982), Scherer (1986; Pittam & Scherer, 1993), and Siegman (1987).

Studies of other personal characteristics have produced mixed or negative results. For example, it is unclear whether a speaker's race can be accurately evaluated from voice samples (cf. Lass, Almerino et al., 1980; Lass, Mertz, & Kimmel, 1978; Walton & Orlikoff, 1994). Judgments of a speaker's height and weight have generated particular controversy. Lass and colleagues (e.g., Lass, Barry, Reed, Walsh, & Amuso, 1979; Lass, Beverly, Nicosia, & Simpson, 1978; Lass & Davis, 1976; Lass, Phillips, & Bruchey, 1980) originally reported that listeners were accurate in their assessments of height and weight, under a variety of conditions of signal distortion. Subsequent studies from other laboratories reported negative results (Gunter & Manning, 1982; Kunzel, 1989). Most recently, Van Dommelen (1993) reanalyzed the data from Lass, Beverly, et al. (1978), and found that listeners' judgments, though wrong, were highly consistent. He concluded that significant vocal stereotypes exist for these characteristics, as they do for judgments of personality from speech (e.g., Apple, Streeter, & Krauss, 1979; Aronovitch, 1976; Hunt & Lin, 1967; Kramer, 1963; Scherer, 1979; Taylor, 1934).

Accuracy of identification varies widely by speaker, and some voices (whether familiar or unfamiliar) are more confusable than others (Bricker & Pruzansky, 1966; Nygaard & Pisoni, 1996; Papcun, Kreiman, & Davis, 1989; Thompson, 1985a, 1985b; Williams, 1964; Yarmey & Matthys, 1992; cf. Clifford, Rathborn, & Bull, 1981, who found differences among voices with short, but not long, retention intervals). Thompson (1985a) reported that after 7 days hit rates (the percentage of correct "same" or "heard previously" responses) ranged from

15–90% for a set of 12 "nondistinctive" voices; false alarm rates (the percentage of incorrect "heard previously" responses) ranged from 15–50%. Clifford (1980; Clifford et al., 1981) reported differential effects of voice distinctiveness at short delays (10–130 min) between presentation and test: The number of correct responses declined over time for "hard-to-recognize" voices, but not for easy-to-recognize voices. Papcun et al. (1989) reported no differences in hit rates for easy-to-remember versus hard-to-remember voices at delays of 1, 2, or 4 weeks, but did find increases in the number of false alarms attributed to less distinctive targets as delay increased. Yarmey (1993) found that recognition of stereotypical "bad guy" voices was significantly worse than that of "good guy" voices. Differences in recognizability among speakers may be related in part to the speaker's gender: two studies reported that male voices were recognized at better rates than were female voices, although large differences in recognizability were observed within both groups of speakers (Nygaard & Pisoni, 1996; Thompson, 1985a). However, little else is known about the reasons for the variability observed. The literature provides little insight into the connection between perceptually salient aspects of voices and differences that predict subsequent recognition performance.

5.1.3 Studies Focusing on Stimuli

5.1.3.1 Sample Content and Duration

Hecker (1971) and Bricker and Pruzansky (1976) provide extensive reviews of studies examining how changes in the sample of speech a listener hears (e.g., vowels vs. phrases, phonemic content, duration) affect recognition and discrimination performance. These studies suggest that performance on recognition or discrimination tasks is much better predicted by the size of the sample of the speaker's phonetic repertoire than by the duration of the sample, with performance generally peaking with sample durations of about 1 s (Bricker & Pruzansky, 1966; Pollack, Pickett, & Sumby, 1954). A number of recent forensically oriented studies have further examined the contribution of voice sample duration to speaker recognizability. Clifford (1980) found no improvement in immediate recall for voices when stimuli increased in duration from one to four sentences; a subsequent experiment reported that percent correct recognition was greater when listeners heard two rather than one sentence. Legge, Grosmann, and Pieper (1984) reported that, after a retention interval of 15 min, the percentage of correct recognitions increased as sample duration increased from 6 to 60 s in a two-alternative forced-choice task; recognition of 6-s stimuli did not exceed chance levels. In a series of delayed recognition tasks, with delays ranging from a few minutes to 1 week, Yarmey (1991) and Yarmey and Matthys (1992) reported that both hit and false alarm rates increased at all delays as sample durations increased; stimuli ranged in duration from 18 s to 7.8 min. In contrast, Read and Craik (1995) found good recognition with sample durations of only 4 to 5 s after 17 days, provided identical voice samples were used at learning and recall. Emotionally laden samples did not produce better recall than did samples with neutral content. Finally, Deffenbacher et al. (1989) suggested that effects of stimulus duration on recognition accuracy may depend on the delay between learning and testing. They reported no effect of stimulus duration for an immediate recall task, but a significant effect as delay increased.

5.1.3.2 Source versus Vocal Tract Contributions to Individual Voice Quality

A number of studies have used whisper, artificial voicing sources, and analysis-by-synthesis techniques to estimate the relative contributions of source and vocal tract information to personal quality. Early studies suggested vocal tract information contributes more to personal quality than source information does; however, eliminating either source of information reduces performance, but not to chance levels (see Bricker & Pruzansky, 1976). Abberton and Fourcin (1978) asked listeners to identify familiar voices from the output of a laryngograph, thus eliminating vocal tract and source–tract interaction information from the signal. They concluded that the source alone provides enough information to identify a familiar speaker from a small set, although they reported large differences among listeners in their performance. Tartter (1991) found that listeners were able to match whispered to phonated vowels produced by the same speaker, suggesting that vocal tract information is also adequate to identify speakers (although listeners again varied widely in performance, from 39–96% correct). Kuwabara and Takagi (1991) used analysis-by-synthesis to manipulate formant frequencies, bandwidths, and fundamental frequency (F0). They concluded that vocal tract information is more important than source information for identifying known speakers: Changes in formant frequencies exceeding 5% destroyed personal quality, whereas changes in F0 and bandwidths had little impact.

5.1.3.3 Signal Distortion

Previous studies (reviewed in Bricker & Pruzansky, 1976) indicate that playing voice samples backward reduces performance on voice perception tasks. Van Lancker and colleagues (Van Lancker, Kreiman, & Emmorey, 1985; Van Lancker, Kreiman, & Wickens, 1985) evaluated the effects of rate-altering signals or playing them backwards on recognition of famous voices. Performance in all conditions depended on the voice: Some voices were identified equally well in distorted and normal conditions; some were unrecognizable when played backward, and others when rate-altered. These studies are discussed further below.

5.1.3.4 Disguise and Mimicry

Disguise significantly reduces both discrimination scores and recognition scores, for unfamiliar and familiar voices, and for voices listeners have been trained to identify (Clifford, 1980; Hirson & Duckworth, 1993; Hollien, Majewski, & Doherty, 1982; Reich, 1981; Reich & Duke, 1979). On the other hand, mimics are seldom mistaken for their targets (Hall & Tosi, 1975; Hollien et al., 1982; Rosenberg, 1973).

5.1.3.5 Effects of Stimulus Familiarity on Voice Perception

Listeners recognize familiar voices well, but not perfectly. Ladefoged and Ladefoged (1980) reported 31% of a set of familiar voices were successfully identified from the word *hello;* 66% were correctly recognized from a single sentence, with an overall false identification rate of 11%. Rose and Duncan (1995) reported that hello produced correct recognition rates ranging from 47–60% for a smaller set of voices. Listeners who knew the speakers well failed to identify 25% of samples and produced 18% false identifications. Schmidt-Nielsen and Stern (1985) reported that co-workers recognized each others' voices well (88% correct). The rate of correct identifications increased with rated familiarity; no relationship was found between the rated distinctiveness of a voice and the rate of correct identifications.

Other studies suggest listeners are not particularly good judges of whom they will recognize. Van Lancker, Kreiman, and Emmorey (1985) and Van Lancker, Kreiman, and Wickens (1985) asked listeners to identify 45 famous male speakers by name from 2-s voice samples. For voices that listeners claimed were familiar, naming averaged 27% correct in this unlimited response set task, and 70% correct in a six-alternative multiple-choice task. Read and Craik (1995) also found that a priori familiarity is not a good index of recognizability. Familiarity did not enhance performance on a delayed recognition task if the listener failed to identify the voice in a pretest, even if the listener claimed to know the voice very well.

5.1.3.6 Effects of Native Language, Accent, and Tone of Voice on Voice Perception

Perception of personality from accented speech is subject to the same kinds of stereotyping as other judgments of personality from speech (e.g., Gallois & Callan, 1981; Strongman & Woosley, 1967). A speaker's accent or tone of voice has produced variable effects on recognition scores. In an immediate recall task, Goldstein, Knight, Bailis, and Conover (1981) found effects of foreign accent on recognition scores for short stimuli, but not for longer utterances. Thompson (1987) reported that hit rates for native speakers of English were higher when stimuli were spoken in unaccented English than when they were in Spanish, but that hit rates for accented English did not differ from either English or Spanish speech. (False alarm rates did not differ for any of the conditions.) Hollien et al. (1982) found lower recognition scores when listeners did not know the language spoken than when they did. Spanish/English bilingual listeners recognized voices equally well when either language was spoken; bilingual speakers were better recognized when speaking the listener's native language (Goggin, Thompson, Strube, & Simental, 1991). Changing the emotional tone of utterances appears to have drastic effects on speaker recognizability. Saslove and Yarmey (1980) found that when listeners heard a hostile voice but were asked to recognize it from a neutral sample, recognition was at chance. Similarly, Read and Craik (1995) found that recognition was at chance when the emotional tone of a voice was different at learning and test.

5.1.4 Studies Focusing on Differences among Tasks

A number of studies have manipulated the conditions under which voices are learned and/or recognized.

5.1.4.1 Retention Set Size

Increasing the number of voices to be remembered decreases the likelihood that a target will be correctly identified after a delay (Carterette & Barnebey, 1975; Legge et al., 1984).

5.1.4.2 Effects of Increasing the Number of Exposures to the Target Voice

Goldstein and Chance (1985, cited in Deffenbacher et al., 1989) reported that recognition improved when a voice sample was divided into segments and presented over several days, as compared to presentation of the entire sample at one session. Yarmey and Matthys (1992) found variable effects of such distributed stimulus presentations. Hit rates improved when stimuli were presented in two pieces, but not three, and false-alarm rates were not affected by the distributed presentation. Playing a *distractor* (nontarget) voice in a mock one-voice lineup between learning and final test tripled the false-alarm rate (Thompson, 1985b).

5.1.4.3 Passive versus Active Learning

Hammersley and Read (1985) compared recognition of tape-recorded voices with recognition after participation in a conversation. After a 48-hr delay, recognition of the taped voices was at chance levels, but listeners were able to identify voices heard in active conversation with better than chance accuracy.

5.1.4.4 Does Seeing a Face Improve Voice Recognition?

Seeing a face when a target voice is initially presented may or may not help listeners identify that voice later. Legge et al. (1984) found that the percentage of correct identifications was higher when a face was presented at both learning and testing; seeing a face at learning, but not recall, provided no advantage. Yarmey (1993) also reported that seeing a face when learning a voice produced higher hit rates and lower false-alarm rates than when the voice was learned and recognized alone. In contrast, McAllister, Dale, Bregman, McCabe, and Cotton (1993) reported that hit rates were higher and false-alarm rates unchanged when a face was *not* present during learning.

5.1.4.5 Retention Interval

Studies comparing recognition accuracy for unfamiliar voices with short and long delays between learning and testing have produced highly variable results. Kreiman and Papcun (1991) found no differences between discrimination scores and recognition accuracy after 1 week, although patterns of confusions and perceptual strategies differed across delays. (This study is discussed further below). Saslove and Yarmey (1980) reported no difference in accuracy between immediate testing and a delay of 24 hr. Clifford (1980; Clifford et al., 1981) found better performance after a 10-min delay than after 1, 7, or 14 days; the longer delays did not differ, with performance near chance after 24 hr. In contrast, Legge et al. (1984) found no difference between delays of 15 min and 10 days in percent correct recognition; and Yarmey (1991) reported no difference between immediate recall and recognition after 2–3 days. Yarmey and Matthys (1992) compared immediate testing and delays of 24 hr and 1 week. They also found no differences in hit or false-alarm rates among conditions, but reported many confusing interactions between delay, stimulus duration, and frequency of exposure to the target voice.

Studies comparing long retention intervals have also produced conflicting results. Papcun et al. (1989) reported a linear decline in recognition accuracy as retention interval increased from 1 to 4 weeks, with scores above chance at all delays. Read and Craik (1995) found no differences among delays ranging from 6–37 days. Finally, Hollien, Bennett, and Gelfer (1983) reported no difference in performance for delays of 1 day, 1 week, and 2 weeks, with performance at chance for all delays.

5.1.5 Studies Focusing on Effects of Different Transmission Systems

Studies assessing the effects of acoustic filtering on voice recognizability or discriminability are reviewed in Bricker and Pruzansky (1976). Filtering generally reduces recognition and discrimination scores, but not to chance levels, suggesting that listener performance does not depend on any particular part of the speech-frequency spectrum. Linear predictive coding (LPC) also reduces voice recognizability, but not to chance levels: hit rates for familiar voices were lower for coded than for unprocessed recordings, but remained well above chance in both conditions (88 vs. 69%; Schmidt-Nielsen & Stern, 1985).

Several studies have examined voice recognizability over the telephone. McGonegal, Rabiner, and McDermott (1978) compared recognition of taped and live voices to recognition of voices heard over the telephone, and found no difference between systems as long as learning and testing took place over the same system. Rathborn, Bull, and Clifford (1981) reported that hit rates were significantly higher when voices were presented live than over the telephone, but confirmed that the best performance occurs when learning and testing use the same system.

5.1.6 Studies Focusing on Listeners

5.1.6.1 Voice Perception Abilities of Different Listener Populations

Although not a uniquely human ability (Cheney & Seyfarth, 1980; Goldman, Phillips, & Fentress, 1995; White, White, & Thorpe, 1970), the ability to recognize voices appears to be innate, and voice learning may begin in utero. Fetuses at 36-weeks gestation did not discriminate between the voice of their mother and other maternal voices when stimuli were played via a loudspeaker on the abdomen, but did discriminate between their mother's voice played over the loudspeaker and their mother speaking normally (Hepper, Scott, & Shahidullah, 1993). Two-day old infants preferred voices filtered to mimic the uterine environment to unfiltered voices (Fifer & Moon, 1989), and could discriminate among male voices (but not recognize their father's voice; DeCasper & Prescott, 1984). Three-day old infants can recognize the voice of their mother from a set of maternal voices (DeCasper & Fifer, 1980). Four-month-old infants can discriminate their parents' voices from those of same-sex strangers (Brown, 1979). By age 7–8 months, infants can learn to recognize unfamiliar voices (Jusczyk, Hohne, Jusczyk, & Redanz, 1993); and voice recognition abilities reach adult levels by age 10 (Mann, Diamond, & Carey, 1979).

Normal adult listeners differ widely in their abilities to recognize or discriminate among speakers (e.g., Hollien et al., 1982; Nygaard & Pisoni, 1996). Kreiman (1987) reported that discrimination performance declined significantly with a listener's age. Male and female listeners apparently do not differ in voice recognition accuracy (Thompson, 1985a).

Phoneticians are not more accurate than naive listeners in voice discrimination tasks (Shirt, 1983). Expert and naive listeners do differ significantly in the strategies they use when evaluating pathological voice quality (Kreiman, Gerratt, & Precoda, 1990). Naive listeners used relatively simple perceptual strategies and generally attended to a consistent set of voice "features," whereas experts differed considerably from one another and from the naive listeners in the strategies applied when judging quality (Kreiman, Gerratt, Precoda, & Berke, 1992).

The voice recognition abilities of blind listeners may exceed those of sighted controls (Ball, Rathborn, & Clifford, 1983) or may not (Winograd, Kerr, & Spence, 1984). Neurological disease may interfere with voice recognition or discrimination abilities. Studies by Van Lancker and colleagues (e.g., Van Lancker, Kreiman, & Cummings, 1989) showed that deficits in voice discrimination are associated with temporal lobe damage to either hemisphere, whereas deficits in recognizing familiar voices are associated with damage to the right parietal lobe. (These studies are reviewed further in the next sections.) A case study of a blind Capgras patient revealed a deficit in recognizing familiar voices (Reid, Young, & Hellawell, 1993), and Korsakoff amnesia also interferes with familiar-voice recognition (although memories from the remote past are relatively preserved; Meudell, Northen, Snowden, & Neary, 1980). Adults with dyslexia showed significant impairment compared to control subjects when judging if a presented voice was a new or old stimulus, but not on a similar facial recognition task (Brachacki, Fawcett, & Nicolson, 1994).

5.1.6.2 Confidence in Responses and Listener Accuracy

Many studies have reported that listeners' confidence in their responses is not a significant predictor of response accuracy (Bull & Clifford, 1984; Hollien et al., 1983; Yarmey, 1986, cited in Deffenbacher et al., 1989; Yarmey, 1991; Yarmey & Matthys, 1992; Yarmey, Yarmey, & Yarmey, 1994). Many others have reported significant but small associations between confidence and accuracy (Rathborn et al., 1981; Saslove & Yarmey, 1980; Thompson, 1985a, 1985b). Read and Craik (1995) argued that confidence predicts performance when the task is easy (for example, when the stimuli played at learning and test match in text and emotional tone), but not otherwise. Finally, Rose and Duncan (1995) reported large positive correlations (ρ = .90–.92) between confidence and accuracy when speakers are well known to listeners.

5.1.6.3 Studies Examining Listeners' Perceptual Strategies

A number of studies (Carterette & Barnebey, 1975; Fagel, van Herpt, & Boves, 1983; Gelfer, 1993; Kreiman & Papcun, 1991; Matsumoto, Hiki, Sone, & Nimura, 1973; Murry & Singh, 1980; Singh & Murry, 1978; Walden, Montgomery, Gibeily, Prosek, & Schwartz, 1978) have used multidimensional scaling (MDS) or factor analysis to examine the features that underlie perceived differences in the quality of normal voices. Results are summarized in Table I. Fundamental frequency or pitch characteristics, vowel formant frequencies, and stimulus duration have emerged as perceptually significant features of voice on a fairly regular basis, as has a "voice quality" dimension (whose appearance in studies attempting to derive the dimensions underlying judgments of voice quality is somewhat disappointing). However, many discrepancies exist between studies. Some may be attributable to the variety of subject and listener populations studied and to the variety of stimuli employed. Singh and Murry (1978) suggested that different perceptual features may be used in processing male and female voices, and argued that the cues used to judge voices depend on both the stimulus and the gender of the speaker (Murry & Singh, 1980). However, the dimensions reported by Gelfer (1993) for female voices have also emerged from studies of male voices, and she argued that gender differences probably do not contribute significantly to differences among studies.

Few studies have attempted to relate perceptual dimensions to characteristics of the stimuli or the listeners. Listeners' experience may contribute to differences in perceptual strategies. In a study of pathological voices, Kreiman et al. (1990) found that different dimensions underlie quality judgments by expert and naive listeners, and Gelfer (1993) reported similar findings for expert and naive judgments of normal female quality. Individual expert listeners also differ from one another in their perceptual strategies (Kreiman, Gerratt, & Berke, 1994; Kreiman et al., 1992). Listener agreement on ratings of pathological voice can be predicted

TABLE I Multidimensional Scaling and Factor Analysis Studies of Normal Voice Quality

Study	Dimensions/features[a]
Matsumoto et al. (1973)	F0; glottal source spectrum; jitter; formant frequencies
Carterette and Barnebey (1975)	F0; intensity; intonation pattern
Walden et al., (1978)	F0; stimulus duration; speaker's age; "superior" vs. "inferior" voice quality
Singh and Murry (1978)	Speaker gender; pitch (male speakers only); stimulus duration (female speakers only)
Murry and Singh (1980)	F0; formants; nasality; F2 (male voices, vowel)
	F0; hoarseness; formants (male voices, phrase)
	F0; breathiness; formants; breathiness (female voices, vowel)
	Effort/nasality; F0; stimulus duration (female voices, phrase)
Fagel et al. (1983)	Melodiousness; articulation quality; voice quality; pitch; tempo (factor analysis)
Kreiman and Papcun (1991)	Masculinity; creakiness; variability; mood (discrimination task)
	Masculinity; breathiness; liveliness (long-term memory task)
Gelfer (1993)	Pitch; loudness; age/stimulus duration; perceived variability; quality (expert listeners)
	Pitch/resonant quality; variability/age/rate (naive listeners)

[a] F0, Fundamental frequency; F2, formant 2.

from perceptual strategies (as estimated with MDS). Listeners with similar perceptual spaces agreed better on ratings of breathiness and roughness than did listeners whose perceptual spaces differed (Kreiman et al., 1994). To some extent, listeners' attention to particular stimulus dimensions can be predicted by the extent of stimulus variability on those dimensions. Variability above a certain threshold is a necessary, but not sufficient, condition for a dimension to emerge as perceptually salient (Kreiman et al., 1992). Listener preferences for different dimensions with equal variability are presumably related to differences in their perceptual habits and experience with the class of stimuli, but the origin and nature of these differences are not well understood. Studies relating characteristics of stimuli, listener perceptual strategies, and performance on voice perception tasks have not been undertaken for normal voices, and it is not presently possible to explain why listeners differ in accuracy, why they attend to a particular characteristic on one occasion and not on another, or how or why listeners differ from one another in perceptual strategy when judging normal voice quality.

5.1.7 Theoretical Perspectives

As this review indicates, a significant body of research on voice perception has produced many discrepant results. Such discrepancies have led authors to call for (and frequently to conduct) further research, but seldom to speculate about why a particular finding emerged, or why other studies have produced different results, and rather little theory exists to explain why results differ from study to study.

A few authors have attempted to investigate the perceptual and memory processes underlying recognition, discrimination, or evaluative tasks in voice perception. One group of studies (Kreiman, 1987; Kreiman & Papcun, 1991; Papcun et al., 1989) examined long- (LTM) and short-term memory (STM) for unfamiliar voices. Listeners in Papcun et al. (1989) heard a speaker making a telephone survey call, and attempted to identify that speaker from a set of 10 recordings after a delay of 1, 2, or 4 weeks. (Listeners also rated their confidence in their response and the similarity of the probe voice to the remembered target.) Signal-detection analyses showed that recognition accuracy declined significantly with delay. Target voices did not differ in how likely they were to be correctly identified. However, foils that were "average-sounding" were more likely to be falsely identified as a target than were more distinctive-sounding foils. These findings were interpreted in terms of a prototype model of memory for voices. The authors speculated that listeners encode vocal quality in terms of a central category member (a "prototype") and a set of deviations from that prototype. Over time, the deviations are forgotten, and recognition responses converge on the most average-sounding voice, whatever target was originally heard.

A second study (Kreiman & Papcun, 1991) compared the discriminability of the voices studied by Papcun et al. (1989) to their recognizability after 1 week, to determine how stored representations of voice quality change over time. The recognition task was identical to that used by Papcun et al.; in the discrimination task, listeners heard pairs of sentences excerpted from the telephone surveys. They were asked to determine whether the speakers were the same or different, to rate their confidence in their response, and to rate the similarity of the two voices. MDS analyses of similarity ratings from the two tasks indicated that rather different perceptual strategies were used. The perceptual space for the LTM task included fewer dimensions, but accounted for more variance, than did the space for the discrimination task. A single perceptual dimension (labeled "masculinity") was shared by the two scaling solutions, but no other significant correspondences between spaces emerged. However, the changes in stored representations over time did not correspond to a loss of ability to distinguish among voices: signal-detection analyses indicated that discrimination accuracy did not differ significantly from recognition accuracy. Patterns of confusions did vary across tasks, in a manner consistent with the prototype model proposed by Papcun et al. Identification responses converged on the least-distinctive voices in the LTM task, again suggesting that over time the "distinctive characteristics" of a voice are forgotten and a "typical" pattern is retained in memory.

A group of studies by Van Lancker and colleagues examined perception of and memory for familiar voices. Several studies of normal listeners (Van Lancker, Kreiman, & Emmorey, 1985; Van Lancker, Kreiman, & Wickens, 1985) used naming and multiple-choice tasks to examine recognition of famous voices under various conditions of signal distortion. These studies suggested that the cues to personal identity vary from voice to voice (see also Van Dommelen, 1990). Furthermore, the perceptual context in which a cue occurred was important in evaluating its usefulness. For example, a distinctive accent was not critical to recognizing a voice if that voice was also very distinctive on some other dimension(s). These data suggested that no single set of voice features exists that characterizes all voices. Instead, the authors proposed, only the salient features are stored for any familiar voice, and each voice constitutes a unique pattern of features. In the framework of Papcun et al. (1989), familiar voices are no longer remembered in terms of a prototype and deviations from that prototype. Rather, only the deviations (the distinctive aspects) are retained in LTM. (Note, however, that Walden et al. (1978) found no obvious effects of familiarity on perceptual strategy in an MDS study.)

Direct evidence for differences in the processing of familiar and unfamiliar voices comes from studies of subjects with focal brain damage (e.g., Van Lancker, Cummings, Kreiman, & Dobkin, 1988; Van Lancker & Kreiman, 1987; Van Lancker et al., 1989). In these studies, performance on a voice discrimination task [using a subset of the unfamiliar voice stimuli studied by Kreiman and Papcun (1991)] and on a familiar voice recognition task was correlated with the site of lesion. Subjects were observed who could recognize familiar voices but not discriminate among unfamiliar voices, and vice versa, indicating that voice recognition and discrimination are dissociated neurological functions. As a group, left-brain-damaged subjects did not differ from normal controls on the voice recognition task, but right-brain-damaged patients were significantly impaired in recognizing familiar voices. Both brain-damaged groups differed overall from controls on the voice discrimination task. Impaired familiar voice recognition was associated with damage to the right parietal lobe, whereas deficits in voice discrimination were associated with temporal lobe damage to either hemisphere.

Finally, recent studies of pathological voice quality (Kreiman & Gerratt, 1996; Kreiman et al., 1990, 1992, 1994) suggest that listeners may contribute nearly as much variance to ratings of quality as do differences between voices. In these studies, listeners judged the dissimilarity of pairs of pathological voices, and the resultant ratings were analyzed with MDS to determine the perceptually important voice "features" that underlie similarity judgments. Results of these studies indicated that quality judgments depend critically on the particular listener and act of listening. Although individual listeners were quite reliable in their judgments, perceived similarity was not constant across listeners, and the scaling analyses revealed only a single perceptual dimension (severity of pathology) that was common to all the listeners. These studies used pathological voices and evaluation tasks, which limits their generalizability to recognition and discrimination of normal voices, but they suggest that voice perception cannot be modeled solely as a function of differences between voices, and that listeners' contributions to voice perception cannot be neglected. If listeners did not differ in their perceptual strategies, vocal quality could be modeled solely as an attribute of voices. That is, when listeners are interchangeable, observed differences in the ratings different voices receive must be due to differences among voices. However, differences among listeners in perceptual strategies are large enough to suggest that it is imprudent to continue the traditional practice of treating differences among listeners as "noise" to be ignored or controlled.

Many limitations to these studies (and to the models they propose) are evident. Although large sets of listeners have been employed, the voice sets studied were rather small (only 10 unfamiliar voices in the Papcun et al. studies, and 26 pairs of unfamiliar voices and 25 familiar voices in the Van Lancker et al. studies). Results have not been replicated in different laboratories or with different samples of speakers and listeners. Finally, the models proposed are mere outlines, and competing explanations are possible for the data presented. Unfortunately, efforts to refine these proposals have not been undertaken.

Although previous studies point to prototype models of voice perception, there is not enough evidence at present to determine whether such models will ultimately serve to describe the processes by which listeners evaluate and recognize voices. However, existing data do suggest that other classes of model are probably inappropriate. For example, linguistic-style distinctive feature models of vocal quality (e.g., Gelfer, 1988; Hammarberg & Gauffin, 1995; Laver, 1980) are unlikely to predict listener performance in voice perception tasks. However elegant or detailed the manner in which such models specify the ways in which voices may differ, they do not model listeners' contributions to the perceptual process (nor are they intended to model listeners' behavior). Thus they cannot explain the relative perceptual importance of different quality "settings," or predict which cues listeners will attend to; and they cannot account for variability in the cues used for different voices or in perceptual strategy across listeners.

5.2 DISCUSSION

As this review indicates, very little is actually known about voice perception (despite common belief; cf. Hollien's statement that "we now know a great deal about people's ability to make aural perceptual speaker identifications" [1990, p. 205]). Experimenters have varied the speaker, stimulus, task, transmission system, and listener population, but conflicting results have emerged in nearly every area of study.[2] No basis exists for linking variability in listener performance to manipulations in other domains, in part because performance is generally measured in terms of response accuracy. Other data that might shed light on how perceptual strategies vary with experimental manipulations (for example, changes

[2] A similar state of affairs exists in the study of pathologic vocal quality, where the literature contains many papers with titles like, "Have the major issues in voice disorders been answered by research in speech science? A 50-year retrospective" (Moore, 1977) and "Voice therapy: A need for research" (Reed, 1980).

in patterns of confusions or similarity ratings) generally are not examined. Thus it is unlikely such studies will ever explain why results differ from paper to paper.

Response accuracy is not without interest, and a reasonable amount of description is necessary before theory can be generated. However, the majority of voice perception studies are not designed to investigate the perceptual processes by which listeners recognize, discriminate among, or evaluate voice signals, and thus do not contribute to developing an understanding of perceptual processes. Instead, studies often seem to "fill in the cells" in a paradigm. (A particularly egregious example of this is a series of papers using direct estimations and paired comparison tasks to examine the effects of disguise, filtering, temporal alterations, phonetic complexity, and voicing on listeners' evaluations of height, weight, gender, and race.) Other papers repeatedly replicate previous findings, without obvious motivation for the replication (for example, the many investigations of the relationship between listeners' confidence and accuracy, or of the effects of response interval on recognition accuracy). In this system, discrepant results are defined with reference to previous findings, not in terms of the predictions of a model. Consequently, they do not lead to modifications of a model and new predictions, but instead generate more studies with more discrepant results. Thus, research questions are never resolved, but are investigated over and over again, as the review above demonstrates. Combined with a general lack of new research foci, this pattern suggests that the descriptive level of study is saturated. Only the development of a theoretical basis for research into voice quality can stem the proliferation of repetitive, inconclusive studies.

Lack of a viable model has also begun to limit progress in other disciplines. For example, broader questions of the acoustic correlates and physiological underpinnings of vocal quality cannot be answered in the absence of an understanding of voice perception. Furthermore, voice research provides no guidance for investigators studying spoken-word recognition, who as a result must select the particular manipulations of voice they use in a somewhat arbitrary fashion. For example, recent work in speech perception has examined how differences in a speaker's gender, speaking rate, and dialect affect spoken-word recognition, but it is unclear why these particular factors were examined, and not others (see Pisoni, 1993, for review). Better models of voice perception would provide a principled basis for developing hypotheses about the acoustic and physiological correlates of perceived quality, and about how voice quality interacts with lexical information in speech recognition.

Finally, systematic investigation of the role of listeners in voice perception has not taken place. Quality is *perceptual* in nature: It is a function of both listeners and stimuli, not just of stimuli. However, the great majority of voice perception studies focus on how a manipulation affects response accuracy, the goal being to determine how well voices are recognized, not to learn what listeners are doing. This approach is essentially "stimulus-driven": stimuli or test conditions are manipulated, and responses tabulated in terms of the effects of these manipulations, but changes in listeners' perceptual processes across conditions and differences among listeners within conditions are generally ignored. In other words, these studies examine main effects of stimulus or task conditions, but neglect the main effect of listeners and interactions between stimuli, tasks, and listeners.

The importance of modeling both listener and interaction effects in voice perception has long been known. For example, a factor analysis study by Voiers (1964) produced both listener-specific terms and interactions between specific listeners and voices, which he termed *extrastimulus factors* in speaker recognition. Recent studies of pathological voice quality also suggest that differences among listeners may explain as much variance in ratings of quality as differences among voices do (Kreiman & Gerratt, 1996), as described above. Note that the traditional view that voice recognition and discrimination depend on the extent to which interspeaker variability in quality exceeds intraspeaker variability also assumes that voice perception can be modeled as a function of differences among signals, and consequently may require modification.

One possible cause of the lack of theoretical development, relative neglect of listener factors, and reliance on measures of response accuracy that characterize voice perception research, is the persistent focus of most voice research on specific, practical questions. Bricker and Pruzansky's statement remains true today: "While some studies have been undertaken solely to increase our basic knowledge of the process, by far the greater number have been motivated by some practical considerations" (1976, p. 296). Researchers in different disciplines ask different questions: Forensic scientists are interested in earwitness accuracy under different conditions, neurologists are interested in the effects of disorders on perception, otolaryngologists are interested in the effects of disease or treatment on voice quality, and so on. The variety of practical questions motivating voice perception studies has resulted in a literature that is fragmented across disciplines. A reference database maintained in the University of California, Los Angeles (UCLA) Voice Laboratory lists studies in more than 200 journals, spanning a huge range of disciplines (Table II). Lack of a body of theory promotes this fragmentation, and fragmentation also inhibits the development of theory, perpetuating the problem. Thus the pursuit of answers to specific questions has limited the development of voice perception research as a coherent discipline, and has paradoxically contributed to the development of a research climate in which these very questions cannot be answered.

The fragmentation of voice research across disciplines may also have acted to limit the number of researchers investigating voice perception. The UCLA reference database, which covers 63 years of research, lists 1740 authors who have published on some aspect of voice perception or production, 84% of whom have produced only one or two papers on voice-related topics. Less than 6% of the authors indexed have authored more than five papers on voice. Many factors serve to perpetuate this situation. Students at the beginning of their studies may find it difficult to acquire the necessary interdisciplinary expertise within the constraints of doctoral program requirements, to assemble a suitable dissertation

TABLE II Academic Disciplines that Include Studies of Voice

Acoustics
Animal behavior
Electrical engineering/computer science/signal processing
Forensic/police science
Linguistics
Medicine
Developmental biology
Gerontology
Neurology
Obstetrics/Gynecology
Otolaryngology
Pediatrics
Respiration
Surgery
Music
Phonetics
Psychology
Cognitive
Clinical
Social
Neuropsychology
Psychophysics
Psycholinguistics
Sociology
Speech pathology
Speech science

committee, and to convince that committee that voice studies are an appropriate dissertation topic. Students who pursue the study of voice perception may find it difficult to affiliate with a particular department when their graduate work is completed. Given its interdisciplinary nature, the study of vocal quality has no clear academic home. Maintaining the necessary expertise on voice is difficult: Even the most diligent researcher may find it difficult to consistently monitor the contents of 200 or more journals. Finally, it can be difficult to assemble and maintain an interdisciplinary laboratory group, even at a large university.

A number of changes in research practices are required to remedy this situation. First, scientific method must be consistently applied in studies of voice perception. Authors, reviewers, and editors must insist that the questions addressed are motivated by theoretical concerns, and that the manipulations introduced will resolve these questions, not simply add one more study to the weight of evidence on one side or the other of a question. Studies must address the issues of *why* a particular result occurred, and not merely tally the number of voices correctly recognized under particular circumstances. More researchers must work systematically on voice perception, and funding for basic, rather than applied, studies of voice must be secured. (Development of a theoretical base for such studies should facilitate this process.) Researchers must resist the temptation to reduce the study of voice perception to the study of stimuli, unless they provide a clear explanation of how the particular manipulation will elucidate the larger issues at hand. Finally, much more effort must be devoted to understanding listeners' contribution to voice perception. The problem of how speakers perceive and identify voices is a difficult one, but it will not be solved if the current practice of neglecting theory in favor of simplification of the questions continues.

ACKNOWLEDGMENTS

Preparation of this chapter was supported by grant DC01797 from the National Institute on Deafness and Other Communication Disorders. Thanks to Abeer Alwan, Bruce Gerratt, Peter Ladefoged, and the UCLA voice community for many helpful comments on earlier versions.

REFERENCES

Abberton, E., & Fourcin, A. J. (1978). Intonation and speaker identification. *Language and Speech, 21,* 305–318.

Apple, W., Streeter, L. A., & Krauss, R. M. (1979). The effects of pitch and speech rate on personal attributions. *Journal of Personality and Social Psychology, 37,* 715–727.

Aronovitch, C. D. (1976). The voice of personality: Stereotyped judgments and their relation to voice quality and sex of speaker. *Journal of Social Psychology, 99,* 207–220.

Berke, G. S., & Gerratt, B. R. (1993). Laryngeal biomechanics: An overview of mucosal wave mechanics. *Journal of Voice, 7,* 123–128.

Brachacki, G. W., Fawcett, A. J., & Nicolson, R. I. (1994). Adults with dyslexia have a deficit in voice recognition. *Perceptual and Motor Skills, 78,* 304–306.

Bricker, P. D., & Pruzansky, S. (1966). Effects of stimulus content and duration on talker identification. *Journal of the Acoustical Society of America, 40,* 1441–1449.

Bricker, P. D., & Pruzansky, S. (1976). Speaker recognition. In N. J. Lass (Ed.), *Contemporary issues in experimental phonetics* (pp. 295–326). New York: Academic Press.

Brown, C. J. (1979). Reactions of infants to their parents' voices. *Infant Behavior and Development, 2,* 295–300.

Bull, R., & Clifford, B. R. (1984). Earwitness voice recognition accuracy. In G. L. Wells & E. F. Loftus (Eds.), *Eyewitness testimony* (pp. 92–123). New York: Cambridge University Press.

Bull, R., Rathborn, H., & Clifford, B. R. (1983). The voice-recognition accuracy of blind listeners. *Perception, 12,* 223–226.

Carterette, E. C., & Barnebey, A. (1975). Recognition memory for voices. In A. Cohen & S. G. Nooteboom (Eds.), *Structure and process in speech perception* (pp. 246–265). New York: Springer.

Cheney, D. L., & Seyfarth, R. (1980). Vocal recognition in free-ranging vervet monkeys. *Animal Behaviour, 28,* 362–367.

Childers, D. G., & Lee, C. K. (1991). Vocal quality factors: Analysis, synthesis, and perception. *Journal of the Acoustical Society of America, 90,* 2394–2410.

Clifford, B. R. (1980). Voice identification by human listeners: On earwitness reliability. *Law and Human Behavior, 4,* 373–394.

Clifford, B. R., Rathborn, H., & Bull, R. (1981). The effects of delay on voice recognition accuracy. *Law and Human Behavior, 5,* 201–208.
DeCasper, A. J., & Fifer, W. P. (1980). Of human bonding: Newborns prefer their mothers' voice. *Science, 208,* 1174–1176.
DeCasper, A. J., & Prescott, P. A. (1984). Human newborns' perception of male voices: Preference, discrimination, and reinforcing value. *Developmental Psychobiology, 17,* 481–491.
Deffenbacher, K. A., Cross, J. F., Handkins, R. E., Chance, J. E., Goldstein, A. G., Hammersley, R., & Read, J. D. (1989). Relevance of voice identification research to criteria for evaluating reliability of an identification. *Journal of Psychology, 123,* 109–119.
Denes, P. B., & Pinson, E. N. (1993). *The speech chain: The physics and biology of spoken language* (2nd ed.). New York: Freeman.
Disner, S. F. (1982). Stress evaluation and voice lie detection: A review. *UCLA Working Papers in Phonetics, 54,* 78–92.
Fagel, W. P. F., van Herpt, L. W. A., & Boves, L. (1983). Analysis of the perceptual qualities of Dutch speakers' voice and pronunciation. *Speech Communication, 2,* 315–326.
Fifer, W. P., & Moon, C. (1989). Psychobiology of newborn auditory preferences. *Seminars in Perinatology, 13,* 430–433.
Gallois, C., & Callan, V. J. (1981). Personality impressions elicited by accented English speech. *Journal of Cross-Cultural Psychology, 12,* 347–359.
Garvin, P. L., & Ladefoged, P. (1963). Speaker identification and message identification in speech recognition. *Phonetica, 9,* 193–199.
Gelfer, M. P. (1988). Perceptual attributes of voice: Development and use of rating scales. *Journal of Voice, 2,* 320–326.
Gelfer, M. P. (1993). A multidimensional scaling study of voice quality in females. *Phonetica, 50,* 15–27.
Goggin, J. P., Thompson, C. P., Strube, G., & Simental, L. R. (1991). The role of language familiarity in voice identification. *Memory & Cognition, 19,* 448–458.
Goldman, J. A., Phillips, D. P., & Fentress, J. C. (1995). An acoustic basis for maternal recognition in timber wolves (*Canis lupus*)? *Journal of the Acoustical Society of America, 97,* 1970–1973.
Goldstein, A. G., & Chance, J. E. (1985). *Voice recognition: The effects of faces, temporal distribution of "practice," and social distance.* Paper presented at the meeting of the Midwestern Psychological Association, Chicago.
Goldstein, A. G., Knight, P., Bailis, K., & Conover, J. (1981). Recognition memory for accented and unaccented voices. *Bulletin of the Psychonomic Society, 17,* 217–220.
Granström, B. (1992). The use of speech synthesis in exploring different speaking styles. *Speech Communication, 11,* 347–355.
Gunter, C. D., & Manning, W. H. (1982). Listener estimations of speaker height and weight in unfiltered and filtered conditions. *Journal of Phonetics, 10,* 251–257.
Hall, M., & Tosi, O. I. (1975). Spectrographic and aural examination of professionally mimicked voices [Abstract]. *Journal of the Acoustical Society of America, 58,* S107.
Hammarberg, B., & Gauffin, J. (1995). Perceptual and acoustic characteristics of quality differences in pathological voices as related to physiological aspects. In O. Fujimura & M. Hirano (Eds.), *Vocal fold physiology: Voice quality control* (pp. 283–303). San Diego, CA: Singular.
Hammersley, R., & Read, J. D. (1985). The effect of participation in conversation on recognition and identification of the speakers' voices. *Law and Human Behavior, 9,* 71–81.
Hartman, D. E., & Danauer, J. L. (1976). Perceptual features of speech for males in four perceived age decades. *Journal of the Acoustical Society of America, 59,* 713–715.
Hecker, M. H. L. (1971). Speaker recognition: An interpretive survey of the literature. *ASHA Monographs, 16.*
Helfrich, H. (1979). Age markers in speech. In K. R. Scherer & H. Giles (Eds.), *Social markers in speech* (pp. 63–108). Cambridge, England: Cambridge University Press.

Hepper, P. G., Scott, D., & Shahidullah, S. (1993). Newborn and fetal response to maternal voice. *Journal of Reproductive and Infant Psychology, 11,* 147–153.

Hirson, A., & Duckworth, M. (1993). Glottal fry and voice disguise: A case study in forensic phonetics. *Journal of Biomedical Engineering, 15,* 193–200.

Hollien, H. (1990). *The acoustics of crime: The new science of forensic phonetics.* New York: Plenum.

Hollien, H., Bennett, G. T., & Gelfer, M. P. (1983). Criminal identification comparison: Aural vs. visual identifications resulting from a simulated crime. *Journal of Forensic Sciences, 28,* 208–221.

Hollien, H., Majewski, W., & Doherty, E. T. (1982). Perceptual identification of voices under normal, stress, and disguise speaking conditions. *Journal of Phonetics, 10,* 139–148.

Hunt, R. G., & Lin, T. K. (1967). Accuracy of judgments of personal attributes from speech. *Journal of Personality and Social Psychology, 6,* 450–453.

Jacques, R., & Rastatter, M. (1990). Recognition of speaker age from selected acoustic features as perceived by normal young and older listeners. *Folia Phoniatrica, 42,* 118–124.

Jusczyk, P., Hohne, E., Jusczyk, A. M., & Redanz, N. J. (1993) Do infants remember voices? [Abstract]. *Journal of the Acoustical Society of America, 93,* 2373.

Karlsson, I. (1992). *Analysis and synthesis of different voices with emphasis on female speech.* Stockholm: Royal Institute of Technology (KTH), Department of Speech Communication and Musical Acoustics.

Klatt, D. H., & Klatt, L. C. (1990). Analysis, synthesis, and perception of voice quality variations among female and male talkers. *Journal of the Acoustical Society of America, 87,* 820–857.

Kramer, E. (1963). Judgment of personal characteristics and emotions from nonverbal properties of speech. *Psychological Bulletin, 60,* 408–420.

Kreiman, J. (1987). *Human memory for unfamiliar voices.* Unpublished doctoral dissertation, University of Chicago, Chicago.

Kreiman, J., & Gerratt, B. R. (1996). The perceptual structure of pathologic voice quality. *Journal of the Acoustical Society of America, 100,* 1787–1795.

Kreiman, J., Gerratt, B. R., & Berke, G. S. (1994). The multidimensional nature of pathologic vocal quality. *Journal of the Acoustical Society of America, 96,* 1291–1302.

Kreiman, J., Gerratt, B. R., Kempster, G. B., Erman, A., & Berke, G. S. (1993). Perceptual evaluation of voice quality: Review, tutorial, and a framework for future research. *Journal of Speech and Hearing Research, 36,* 21–40.

Kreiman, J., Gerratt, B. R., & Precoda, K. (1990). Listener experience and perception of voice quality. *Journal of Speech and Hearing Research, 33,* 103–115.

Kreiman, J., Gerratt, B. R., Precoda, K., & Berke, G. S. (1992). Individual differences in voice quality perception. *Journal of Speech and Hearing Research, 35,* 512–520.

Kreiman, J., & Papcun, G. (1991). Comparing discrimination and recognition of unfamiliar voices. *Speech Communication, 10,* 265–275.

Kunzel, H. J. (1989). How well does average fundamental frequency correlate with speaker height and weight? *Phonetica, 46,* 117–125.

Kuwabara, H., & Takagi, T. (1991). Acoustic parameters of voice individuality and voice-quality control by analysis-synthesis method. *Speech Communication, 10,* 491–495.

Ladefoged, P. (1956). The classification of vowels. *Lingua, 5,* 113–128.

Ladefoged, P., & Ladefoged, J. (1980). The ability of listeners to identify voices. *UCLA Working Papers in Phonetics, 49,* 43–51.

Lass, N. J., Almerino, C. A., Jordan, L. F., & Walsh, J. M. (1980). The effect of filtered speech on speaker race and sex identifications. *Journal of Phonetics, 8,* 101–112.

Lass, N. J., Barry, P. J., Reed, R. A., Walsh, J. M., & Amuso, T. A. (1979). The effect of temporal speech alterations on speaker height and weight identification. *Language and Speech, 22,* 163–171.

Lass, N. J., Beverly, A. S., Nicosia, D. K., & Simpson, L. A. (1978). An investigation of speaker height and weight identification by means of direct estimations. *Journal of Phonetics, 6,* 69–76.

Lass, N. J., & Davis, M. (1976). An investigation of speaker height and weight identification. *Journal of the Acoustical Society of America, 60,* 700–703.

Lass, N. J., Hughes, K. R., Bowyer, M. D., Waters, L. T., & Bourne, V. T. (1976). Speaker sex identification from voiced, whispered and filtered isolated vowels. *Journal of the Acoustical Society of America, 59,* 675–678.

Lass, N. J., Mertz, P. J., & Kimmel, K. L. (1978). The effect of temporal speech alterations on speaker race and sex identifications. *Language and Speech, 21,* 279–290.

Lass, N. J., Phillips, J. K., & Bruchey, C. A. (1980). The effect of filtered speech on speaker height and weight identification. *Journal of Phonetics, 8,* 91–100.

Laver, J. (1980). *The phonetic description of voice quality.* Cambridge, England: Cambridge University Press.

Laver, J. (1981). The analysis of vocal quality: From the classical period to the 20th century. In R. Asher & E. Henderson (Eds.), *Toward a history of phonetics* (pp. 79–99). Edinburgh: Edinburgh University Press.

Legge, G. E., Grosmann, C., & Pieper, C. M. (1984). Learning unfamiliar voices. *Journal of Experimental Psychology: Learning, Memory, and Cognition, 10,* 298–303.

Linville, S. E., & Fisher, H. B. (1985). Acoustic characteristics of perceived versus actual vocal age in controlled phonation by adult females. *Journal of the Acoustical Society of America, 78,* 40–48.

Mann, V. A., Diamond, R., & Carey, S. (1979). Development of voice recognition: Parallels with face recognition. *Journal of Experimental Child Psychology, 27,* 153–165.

Matsumoto, H., Hiki, S., Sone, T., & Nimura, T. (1973). Multidimensional representation of personal quality of vowels and its acoustical correlates. *IEEE Transactions on Audio and Electroacoustics, AU-21,* 428–436.

McAllister, H. A., Dale, R. H. I., Bregman, N. J., McCabe, A., & Cotton, C. R. (1993). When eyewitnesses are also earwitnesses: Effects on visual and voice identifications. *Basic and Applied Social Psychology, 14,* 161–170.

McGonegal, C., Rabiner, L., & McDermott, B. (1978). Speaker verification by human listeners over several speech transmission systems. *Bell System Technical Journal, 57,* 2887–2900.

Meudell, P. R., Northen, B., Snowden, J. S., & Neary, D. (1980). Long term memory for famous voices in amnesic and normal subjects. *Neuropsychologia, 18,* 133–139.

Moore, P. (1977). Have the major issues in voice disorders been answered by research in speech science? A 50-year retrospective. *Journal of Speech and Hearing Disorders, 42,* 152–160.

Mullennix, J. W., Johnson, K. A., Topcu-Durgun, M., & Farnsworth, L. M. (1995). The perceptual representation of voice gender. *Journal of the Acoustical Society of America, 98,* 3080–3095.

Murry, T., & Singh, S. (1980). Multidimensional analysis of male and female voices. *Journal of the Acoustical Society of America, 68,* 1294–1300.

Nygaard, L. C., and Pisoni, D. B. (1996). *Learning voices.* Paper presented at the 131st meeting of the Acoustical Society of America, Indianapolis, IN.

Nygaard, L. C., Sommers, M. S., & Pisoni, D. B. (1994). Speech perception as a talker-contingent process. *Psychological Science, 5,* 42–46.

Papcun, G., Kreiman, J., & Davis, A. (1989). Long-term memory for unfamiliar voices. *Journal of the Acoustical Society of America, 85,* 913–925.

Peters, R. W. (1954). *Studies in extra messages: Listener identification of speakers' voices under conditions of certain restrictions imposed upon the voice signal* (Joint Project Report No. 30, Project No. NM 001-064-01). Pensacola, FL: Naval School of Aviation Medicine, Naval Air Station.

Pisoni, D. B. (1993). Long-term memory in speech perception: Some new findings on talker variability, speaking rate and perceptual learning. *Speech Communication, 13,* 109–125.

Pisoni, D. B., & Martin, C. S. (1989). Effects of alcohol on the acoustic-phonetic properties of speech: Perceptual and acoustic analyses. *Alcoholism: Clinical and Experimental Research, 13,* 577–587.

Pittam, J., & Scherer, K. R. (1993). Vocal expression and communication of emotion. In M. Lewis & J. M. Haviland (Eds.), *Handbook of emotions* (pp. 185–197). New York: Guilford Press.

Pollack, I., Pickett, J., & Sumby, W. H. (1954). On the identification of speakers by voice. *Journal of the Acoustical Society of America, 26,* 403–406.

Ptacek, P. H., & Sander, E. K. (1966). Age recognition from voice. *Journal of Speech and Hearing Research, 9,* 273–277.

Rathborn, H., Bull, R., & Clifford, B. R. (1981). Voice recognition over the telephone. *Journal of Police Science and Administration, 9,* 280–284.

Read, J. D., & Craik, F. I. M. (1995). Earwitness identification: Some influences on voice recognition. *Journal of Experimental Psychology: Applied, 1,* 6–18.

Reed, C. (1980). Voice therapy: A need for research. *Journal of Speech and Hearing Disorders, 45,* 157–189.

Reich, A. R. (1981). Detecting the presence of vocal disguise in the male voice. *Journal of the Acoustical Society of America, 69,* 1458–1461.

Reich, A. R., & Duke, J. E. (1979). Effects of selected vocal disguise upon speaker identification by listening. *Journal of the Acoustical Society of America, 66,* 1023–1028.

Reid, I., Young, A. W., & Hellawell, D. J. (1993). Voice recognition impairment in a blind Capgras patient. *Behavioral Neurology, 6,* 225–228.

Rose, P., & Duncan, S. (1995). Naive auditory identification and discrimination of similar voices by familiar listeners. *Forensic Linguistics, 2,* 1–17.

Rosenberg, A. E. (1973). Listener performance in speaker verification tasks. *IEEE Transactions on Audio and Electroacoustics, AU-21,* 221–225.

Saslove, H., & Yarmey, A. D. (1980). Long-term auditory memory: Speaker identification. *Journal of Applied Psychology, 65,* 111–116.

Scherer, K. R. (1979). Personality markers in speech. In K. R. Scherer & H. Giles (Eds.), *Social markers in speech* (pp. 147–210). Cambridge, England: Cambridge University Press.

Scherer, K. R. (1986). Vocal affect expression: A review and a model for future research. *Psychological Bulletin, 99,* 143–165.

Schmidt-Nielsen, A., & Stern, K. R. (1985). Identification of known voices as a function of familiarity and narrow-band coding. *Journal of the Acoustical Society of America, 77,* 658–663.

Shipp, T., Qi, Y., Huntley, R., & Hollien, H. (1992). Acoustic and temporal correlates of perceived age. *Journal of Voice, 6,* 211–216.

Shirt, M. (1983). An auditory speaker-recognition experiment comparing the performance of trained phoneticians and phonetically naive listeners. *Papers in Linguistics and Phonetics, 1,* 115–117.

Siegman, A. W. (1987). The telltale voice: Nonverbal messages of verbal communication. In A. W. Siegman & S. Feldstein (Eds.), *Nonverbal behavior and communication* (pp. 351–434). Hillsdale, NJ: Erlbaum.

Singh, S., & Murry, T. (1978). Multidimensional classification of normal voice qualities. *Journal of the Acoustical Society of America, 64,* 81–87.

Strongman, K., & Woosley, J. (1967). Stereotyped reactions to regional accents. *British Journal of Social and Clinical Psychology, 6,* 164–167.

Tartter, V. C. (1991). Identifiability of vowels and speakers from whispered syllables. *Perception & Psychophysics, 49,* 365–372.

Taylor, H. C. (1934). Social agreement on personality traits as judged from speech. *Journal of Social Psychology, 5,* 244–248.

Thompson, C. P. (1985a). Voice identification: Speaker identifiability and a correction of the record regarding sex effects. *Human Learning, 4,* 19–27.

Thompson, C. P. (1985b). Voice identification: Attempted recovery from a biased procedure. *Human Learning, 4,* 213–224.

Thompson, C. P. (1987). A language effect in voice identification. *Applied Cognitive Psychology, 1,* 121–131.

Titze, I. R. (1994). *Principles of voice production.* Englewood Cliffs, NJ: Prentice-Hall.

Van Dommelen, W. A. (1990). Acoustic parameters in human speaker recognition. *Language and Speech, 33,* 259–272.

Van Dommelen, W. A. (1993). Speaker height and weight identification: A re-evaluation of some old data. *Journal of Phonetics, 21,* 337–341.

Van Lancker, D., Cummings, J., Kreiman, J., & Dobkin, B. H. (1988). Phonagnosia: A dissociation between familiar and unfamiliar voices. *Cortex, 24,* 195–209.

Van Lancker, D., & Kreiman, J. (1987). Voice discrimination and recognition are separate abilities. *Neuropsychologia, 25,* 829–834.

Van Lancker, D., Kreiman, J., & Cummings, J. (1989). Voice perception deficits: Neuroanatomical correlates of phonagnosia. *Journal of Clinical and Experimental Neuropsychology, 11,* 665–674.

Van Lancker, D., Kreiman, J., & Emmorey, K. (1985). Familiar voice recognition: Patterns and parameters. Part I: Recognition of backward voices. *Journal of Phonetics, 13,* 19–38.

Van Lancker, D., Kreiman, J., & Wickens, T. D. (1985). Familiar voice recognition: Patterns and parameters. Part II: Recognition of rate-altered voices. *Journal of Phonetics, 13,* 39–52.

Voiers, W. D. (1964). Perceptual bases of speaker identity. *Journal of the Acoustical Society of America, 36,* 1065–1073.

Walden, B. E., Montgomery, A. A., Gibeily, G. J., Prosek, R. A., & Schwartz, D. M. (1978). Correlates of psychological dimensions in talker similarity. *Journal of Speech and Hearing Research, 21,* 265–275.

Walton, J. H., & Orlikoff, R. F. (1994). Speaker race identification from acoustic cues in the vocal signal. *Journal of Speech and Hearing Research, 37,* 738–745.

White, S., White, R., & Thorpe, W. (1970). Acoustic basis for individual recognition by voice in the gannet. *Nature (London), 225,* 1156–1158.

Williams, C. E. (1964). *The effects of selected factors on the aural identification of speakers* (Section III of Report ESD-TDR-65-153). Hanscom Field, MA: Air Force Systems Command, Electronics Systems Division, Hanscom AFB.

Winograd, E., Kerr, N., & Spence, M. (1984). Voice recognition: Effect of orienting task, and a test of blind versus sighted listeners. *American Journal of Psychology, 97,* 57–70.

Yarmey, A. D. (1986). Verbal, visual, and voice identification of rape suspect under different levels of illumination. *Journal of Applied Psychology, 71,* 363–370.

Yarmey, A. D. (1991). Voice identification over the telephone. *Journal of Applied Social Psychology, 21,* 1868–1876.

Yarmey, A. D. (1993). Stereotypes and recognition memory for faces and voices of good guys and bad guys. *Applied Cognitive Psychology, 7,* 419–431.

Yarmey, A. D. (1995). Earwitness speaker identification. *Psychology, Public Policy, and Law, 1,* 792–816.

Yarmey, A. D., & Matthys, E. (1992). Voice identification of an abductor. *Applied Cognitive Psychology, 6,* 367–377.

Yarmey, A. D., Yarmey, A. L., & Yarmey, M. J. (1994). Face and voice identifications in showups and lineups. *Applied Cognitive Psychology, 8,* 453–464.

6

Talker Normalization

Phonetic Constancy as a Cognitive Process

HOWARD NUSBAUM
JAMES MAGNUSON

6.1 LACK OF INVARIANCE AND THE PROBLEM OF PHONETIC CONSTANCY

Human listeners recognize and understand spoken language quite effectively regardless of the vocal characteristics of the talker, or how quickly the speech is produced, or what the talker has said previously. Even at the most basic level of recognizing spoken consonants and vowels, most humans have little difficulty maintaining phonetic constancy—stable recognition of the phonetic structure of utterances (Shankweiler, Strange, & Verbrugge, 1977) in spite of variation in the relationship between the acoustic patterns of speech and phonetic categories that results from these sources of variability (e.g., Liberman, Cooper, Shankweiler, & Studdert-Kennedy, 1967). Indeed, the perceptual ability of human listeners has still not been matched in engineering efforts to develop computer speech-recognition systems.

Furthermore, even after more than 30 years of scientific endeavor, there are no theories of speech perception that can adequately explain how humans recognize spoken consonants and vowels (see Nusbaum & Henly, in press). Although the theoretical problem posed by the lack of invariance in the relationship between linguistic categories and their acoustic manifestations in the speech signal has been attacked from a number of different perspectives, such as the use of articu-

Talker Variability in Speech Processing

latory knowledge (see Liberman, Cooper, Harris, & MacNeilage, 1962; Liberman & Mattingly, 1985; Stevens & Halle, 1967) or linguistic knowledge (G.A. Miller, 1962; Newell, 1975) or biologically plausible mechanisms such as feature detectors (Abbs & Sussman, 1971; McClelland & Elman, 1986), none of these approaches has credibly accounted for phonetic constancy. In theoretical terms, perhaps the most critical feature of the lack of invariance problem is that it makes speech recognition an inherently nondeterministic process.

In order to understand the significance of this, we need to consider briefly the definition of a finite state automaton (Gross, 1972; Hopcroft & Ullman, 1969). A finite state automaton is an abstract computational mechanism that can represent (in terms of computational theory) a broad class of different "real" computational processes. A finite state automaton (FSA) consists of a set of states (that differ from each other), a vocabulary of symbols representing inputs, a mapping process that denotes how to change to a new state given an old state and an input symbol, a starting state, and a set of ending states. Finite state automata have been used to represent and analyze grammars (e.g., Gross, 1972) and other formal computational problems (Hopcroft & Ullman, 1969). For our purposes, the states in an FSA representing speech perception can be regarded as denoting internal linguistic states, such as phonetic features or categories, and the input symbols can be thought of as acoustic properties present in an utterance. The possible orderings of sequences of permissible states in the processing carried out by the automaton can be thought of as the phonotactic constraints inherent in language. The transition from one state to another, which determines those orderings, is based on acoustic input with acoustic cues serving as the input symbols to the system. This is a relatively uncontroversial conceptualization of speech recognition (e.g., Klatt, 1979; Levinson, Rabiner, & Sondhi, 1983; Lowerre & Reddy, 1980) and is similar to the use of finite state automata in other areas of language processing, such as syntactic analysis (e.g., Charniak, 1993; Woods, 1973).

A deterministic finite state automaton changes from one state to another such that the new state is *uniquely* determined by the information (i.e., next symbol) that is processed. In speech this means that if there were a one-to-one relationship between acoustic information and the phonetic classification of that information (i.e., each acoustic cue denotes one and only one phonetic category or feature), a wide variety of relatively simple deterministic computational mechanisms (e.g., some simple context-free grammars, Chomsky, 1957; feature detectors, Abbs & Sussman, 1971) could be invoked to explain the apparent ease with which we recognize speech. Unfortunately, as researchers know all too well by now, this relationship is much more complex. Instead, there is a many-to-many mapping between acoustic patterns and phonetic categories, which is referred to as the lack of invariance problem.

Any particular phonetic category (or feature) may be instantiated acoustically by a variety of different acoustic patterns. Conversely, any particular acoustic pattern may be interpreted as a variety of different phonetic categories (or features). Although a many-to-one mapping can still be processed by a deterministic finite state automaton, because each new category or state is still uniquely determined, albeit by different symbols or information (e.g., the set of different cues any one of which could denote a particular feature), the one-to-many mapping represents a nondeterministic computational problem. Given the current state of an FSA and the input acoustic information, there are often multiple possible states to which the system could change. There is nothing inherent in the input symbol or acoustic information, or in the system itself, that uniquely determines the classification of that information (i.e., the next state of the system). In other words, there is a computational ambiguity that is unresolvable given just the information that describes the system.

The classic empirical demonstrations of the lack of invariance problem come from early research on perception of synthetic speech (Liberman, Cooper, Harris, MacNeilage, & Studdert-Kennedy, 1967). Two different second formant (F2) transitions are heard as /d/ in the context of different vowels (Delattre, Liberman, & Cooper, 1955) demonstrating that very different acoustic patterns may be interpreted as signaling a single phonetic category. As already noted, this kind of many-to-one mapping between acoustic patterns and phonetic categories can be processed easily by a deterministic FSA mechanism, whereas the converse case of a one-to-many mapping has different computational-theoretic implications inherent in a nondeterministic mechanism. It is the demonstration that a single consonant release burst cue may be interpreted as either of two different phonetic categories /p/ or /k/ depending on the vowel context (Liberman, Delattre, & Cooper, 1952) which indicates that recognition of phonetic structure is inherently nondeterministic.

The problem for theories of speech perception is to explain how a listener can recover the phonetic structure of an utterance given the acoustic properties present in the speech signal. The real computational problem underlying this, which must be addressed by theories, is presented by those cases in which one acoustic cue can be interpreted as more than one phonetic feature or category. Because this is inherently a nondeterministic problem, it may require a different kind of computational solution than would be required by a deterministic problem.

6.2 COMPUTATIONAL CONSTRAINTS ON THEORIES OF SPEECH PERCEPTION

If the one-to-many mapping in speech specifically determines the class of computational mechanisms that can produce phonetic constancy, this should constrain the form of theories that are appropriate to explaining speech perception. Thus it is important to consider whether or not we need to be concerned about this kind of computational constraint. If this computational constraint is important (i.e., it cannot be dismissed or resolved by some trivial solution), it follows that it is important to consider how well extant theories of speech perception conform to this constraint.

Let us start by considering for a moment how we might distinguish between classes of computational mechanisms (Nusbaum & Schwab, 1986) and how this distinction relates to the issue of deterministic versus nondeterministic computational problems. Computational mechanisms can be thought of generally as consisting of three classes of elements: representations of information, transformations of the representations, and control structures. Control structures determine the sequencing of transformations that are applied to representations. When defined this way, computational mechanisms can be sorted into two types based on the nature of the control structure. In passive systems the sequence of transformations is carried out according to an open-loop control structure (MacKay, 1951, 1956). This means that given the same input at two different points in time, the same sequence of transformations will be carried out so that there is an invariant mapping from source to domain (in functional terms). For example, in motor control, a ballistic movement is considered to be controlled as an open-loop system. Also, feature detectors can be thought of as operating as passive mechanisms at least in the overly simplified form that is generally used in psychological models (Barlow, 1972). Passive systems constitute relatively simple and generally easily understood computational mechanisms. If speech perception could be carried out by a passive system, such as represented in a deterministic finite-state automaton, theories of speech perception would be relatively easy to specify and analyze.

By contrast, in an active system the sequence of transformations is adaptively controlled by a closed-loop control structure (Nusbaum & Schwab, 1986). This means that the flow of computation is contingent on the outcome of certain comparisons or tests in a feedback loop. This kind of system is generally used when there is a need for an error-correcting mechanism that allows systematic adjustment of processing based on the outcome of the transformations and can be used to address nondeterministic computational problems. Nusbaum and Schwab (1986) described two different types of active systems. These types of systems can be thought of as hypothesize-test-adjust or approximate-test-adjust systems. In the former, higher level knowledge-based processes propose hypotheses that are tested against bottom-up transformations of input. In the latter, an approximate classification or target is proposed from the bottom-up, and derived implications of this approximation are compared with other analyses from either top-down or bottom-up processing. Both types of active systems have been proposed as important in various cognitive processes (e.g., Grossberg, 1986; Minsky, 1975; Neisser, 1967). In an active system, the sequence of transformations may differ given the same input in different contexts.

Because the relation between input and output is formally a mathematical function or computationally deterministic in passive systems, this class of systems cannot generally address nondeterministic computational problems, where one input may lead to either of two different states. (This is similar to the constraint that a mathematical function must produce one and only one value for each input.) Typically, an active system would be required to address these nondeterministic problems. Of course there are some exceptions, such as Hidden Markov Models (HMM) (Charniak, 1993; Levinson et al., 1983, for reviews and discussion). HMMs are nondeterministic finite state automata that handle nondeterministic computational problems without a closed-loop control structure. Instead they select one of the alternative states based on statistics estimated from a set of "observations" made during a "training" process. An HMM resolves nondeterministic choices by estimating the distributional statistics for those choices and basing the decision on those statistics.

In general, HMMs have provided the most successful engineering solutions to the development of speech recognition systems because they explicitly recognize the inherent nondeterministic nature of the recognition problem. The most accurate and robust commercially available recognition systems are based on HMMs (e.g., Nusbaum & Pisoni, 1987). However, even though HMM-based systems are the most successful recognition systems, they do not perform as well as human listeners (e.g., Klatt, 1977; Nusbaum & Pisoni, 1987). These systems cannot recognize words in fluent, continuous speech as well as human listeners can, nor do they handle the effects of background noise or changes in speaking rate as well as human listeners do. In part, this may reflect the fact that the states and units of acoustic analysis are more rigid than are employed by human listeners (e.g., Nusbaum & Henly, 1992). This may also be partly due to the use of statistics to resolve the nondeterministic nature of the recognition problem; this kind of statistical approach may really only be a statistical approximation of the kind of mechanism used in human speech perception.

Rather than approximate a nondeterministic solution statistically, an alternative is to find a way of restructuring a nondeterministic problem (such as the lack of invariance problem) that eliminates the nondeterminism. This would make it possible to use a deterministic mechanism as the basis for phonetic constancy in speech perception. In computational theory of formal languages, there is a theorem that states that for any nondeterministic system there exists an equivalent deterministic system (Hopcroft & Ullman, 1969). Another way to say this is if there is a nondeterministic system such as the relationship between acoustic cues and phonetic categories, there exists a deterministic system that can account for this relationship. On the face of it, this suggests that although there are aspects of spoken language that might be characterized as requiring nondeterministic processing, it is possible to construct a deterministic mechanism to account for processing this information. Some deterministic automaton can be constructed that can provide a complete description of the nondeterministic problem represented by the mapping of acoustic cues onto phonetic structure. If such a deterministic description is possible, then this may describe the processing mechanism used in human speech perception and would allow the use of simpler computational devices such as passive mechanisms.

However, the proof of the theorem regarding the equivalence of a deterministic and nondeterministic system places certain constraints on the form of the deterministic system (Hopcroft & Ullman, 1969). The proof requires the construction of a deterministic system that contains states that are different from the nondeterministic system. Specifically, the new deterministic version of a nondeterministic system requires states that represent the *disjunction* of the set of states that would have been alternatives in the nondeterministic system. Thus these new states in the deterministic machine are actually compounds of the old states in the nondeterministic system. In other words, this does not deterministically resolve the ambiguity as to which of the states the machine should be in given an input. Rather it represents and recognizes the ambiguity explicitly as ambiguous states. So in the /pi/-/ka/-/pu/ example, when given the burst information, a nondeterministic machine could go to either the /p/ state or the /k/ state. A deterministic machine would have a single state called /p/-or-/k/. Clearly this does not resolve the lack of invariance problem in a satisfactory way because moving to the /p/-or-/k/ state would leave ambiguous the phonetic interpretation of the burst cue. Moreover, because phonetic segments are categorically perceived (Studdert-Kennedy, Liberman, Harris, & Cooper, 1970), this kind of phonetic perceptual ambiguity is never found in human listeners.

Another possible way of addressing the problem of a nondeterministic computational problem (or the lack of invariance) may be to change the definition of the states and the assumed form of the input. In a nondeterministic machine, there must be at least one state from which there are several alternative states that may be entered given exactly the same input information. By restructuring either the states or the input patterns, it might be possible to change a nondeterministic problem into a deterministic one, without retaining the ambiguity noted above. (However, I am unaware of any proof of this conjecture.)

For example, take the basic case in which one acoustic cue could lead to either of two states. If we consider the sequence of states that follow from each of those two possibilities given subsequent inputs, and the different sequences of inputs that would give rise to those sequences of states, it may be possible to convert the nondeterministic system into a deterministic system. Thus, rather than create compound states from the alternative states as described above, it is possible to create compound states that represent the alternative sequences of states that would be entered given a particular sequence of input symbols. This might require changing the definition of the states to be sequentially constituted and the definition of the next input to allow different lengths of sequences of acoustic cues depending on the current state. By the example from the /pi/-/ka/-/pu/ experiment, this would mean that to construct a deterministic system, we would need states /pi/, /ka/, and /pu/ (i.e., combining the consonant state with the subsequent vowel state to form a single sequentially defined state). To distinguish among these states, the input would then need to include information about the vowel in addition to the burst. In other words, we would be converting a system that is nondeterministic in phonetic terms to one that is deterministic in syllabic terms.

Of course, some speech researchers have proposed just this kind of approach by redefining the basic units of speech perception (see Pisoni, 1978, for a discussion) from phonemes to syllables (e.g., Massaro, 1972), or other context-sensitive units (e.g., Wickelgren, 1969) or to entire linguistic phrases (G. A. Miller, 1962). Unfortunately, this does not actually solve the problem because the coarticulatory processes that encode linguistic structure into sound do not respect any particular unit boundaries (e.g., for syllables, Ohman, 1966) so that the same problem of lack of invariance arises regardless of the size of the unit of analysis. Furthermore, empirical evidence suggests that listeners do not have a fixed size unit of analysis for recognizing speech (Nusbaum & Henly, 1992). The listener does not process a fixed amount of speech signal in order to recognize a particular unit. Nusbaum and Henly (1992) have argued that listeners dynamically adapt the analysis of the acoustic structure of speech as a result of available linguistic and informational constraints and the immediate linguistic-perceptual goals.

An alternative approach to restructuring the states and analysis of input is to change the definition of what is being recognized. For example, the ecological perspective on speech perception asserts that the states that are being recognized are phonetic gestures (because these are the distal objects of perception) and the input is considered to be gestural rather than acoustic (see Best, 1994; Fowler, 1989). Indeed, if we consider theories of speech perception generally, there has been a tendency to approach the problem of phonetic constancy by redefining the type of knowledge that is used in perception, often without considering the role or nature of the computational mechanism that is required. For example, articulatory theories (e.g., different forms of motor theory, Liberman et al., 1962; Liberman & Mattingly, 1985; and analysis-by-synthesis, Stevens & Halle, 1967) argue that knowledge of the process of speech production by which linguistic units are encoded into sound would resolve the lack of invariance problem. By contrast, Newell (1975) claimed that the acoustic signal underdetermines the linguistic structure that must be recovered, and so broader linguistic knowledge about lexical structure, syntax, and semantics must be used to constrain the recognition process (also see Klatt, 1977; G. A. Miller, 1962). From yet another perspective Stevens and Blumstein (1978, 1981) have argued, in essence, that the lack of invariance problem is a result of selecting the wrong acoustic properties for mapping onto phonetic features. Thus, their claim is that it is important to carefully define which acoustic properties are selected as the input tokens. In the Lexical Access From Spectra (LAFS) model, Klatt (1979) essentially combined this claim with a redefinition of which linguistic categories were actually being recognized.

However, none of these approaches has been entirely successful or convincing in explaining phonetic constancy. All depend on the assumption that the appropriate kind of knowledge or representation will be sufficient to restructure the nondeterministic relationship between the acoustic patterns of speech and the linguistic interpretation into a deterministic relationship, but empirical studies are not encouraging. Measures of speech production show as much lack of invariance in the motor system as there is in the relationship between acoustics and phonetics (e.g., MacNeilage, 1970). Similarly, there is as much lack of invariance between sound patterns and larger linguistic units (e.g., syllables, words, etc.) as there is with phonemes or phonetic features. And the perspective that better acoustic knowledge or the right acoustic analysis would provide an invariant mapping has failed as well. For the paradigm case of place of articulation perception, it turns out that listeners do not make use of the information that Stevens and Blumstein (1978, 1981) claimed was the invariant cue. Walley and Carrell (1983) demonstrated that listeners carry out phonetic classification by using the noninvariant portions of the signal rather than the invariant portions.

Perhaps theories of speech perception have largely failed to explain phonetic constancy given the problem of lack of invariance because they have taken the wrong tack on analyzing the problem. By focusing on a content analysis of the lack of invariance problem, these theories have tried to specify the type of information or knowledge that would permit accurate recovery of phonetic structure from acoustic patterns. As we have argued, this is an attempt to change the computational structure of the lack of invariance problem from a nondeterministic problem to a deterministic problem. Perhaps the failure of these theories to yield convincing and completely explanatory accounts of phonetic constancy is a consequence of focusing on trying to find a kind of knowledge, information, or representation that resolves the lack of invariance problem. Instead, a more successful approach may depend on acknowledging and analyzing the computational considerations inherent in a nondeterministic system. The point of this section has been to argue that it is important to shift the focus of theories from a consideration of the problem of lack of invariance as a matter of determining the correct representation of the information in speech to a definition of the problem in computational terms. We claim speech perception is a nondeterministic computational problem. Furthermore, we claim that deterministic mechanisms and passive systems are incapable of accounting for phonetic constancy. Human speech perception requires an active control system in order to carry out processing. By focusing on an analysis of the specific nature of the active system used in speech perception it will be possible to develop theories that provide better explanations of phonetic constancy.

Active systems have been proposed as explanations of speech perception in the past (see Nusbaum & Schwab, 1986), including analysis-by-synthesis (Stevens & Halle, 1967) and Trace (McClelland & Elman, 1986). These theories have indeed acknowledged the importance of complex control systems in accounting for phonetic constancy. However, even in these theories, the focus has been on the nature of the information (e.g., articulatory in analysis-by-synthesis and acoustic-phonetic, phonological, and lexical in Trace); the active control system has subserved the role of delivering the specific information at the appropriate time or in the appropriate manner. Unfortunately, from our perspective, these earlier theories took relatively restricted views of the problem of lack of invariance (see Nusbaum & Henly, in press, for a discussion). Although all theories of speech perception have generally acknowledged that lack of invariance arises from variation in phonetic context, speaking rate, and the vocal characteristics of talkers, most theories have focused on the problem of variation in phonetic context alone. By focusing on the specific knowledge or representations needed to maintain phonetic constancy over variability in context, these theories developed highly specific approaches that do not generalize to problems of talker variability or variability in speaking rate (e.g., see Klatt, 1986, for a discussion of this problem in Trace; Nusbaum & Henly, in press). For these theories, there is no clear set of principles for dealing with nondeterminism in speech that would indicate how to generalize these theories to other sources of variability, such as talker variability.

Our goal is to specify a general set of computational principles that can address the nondeterministic problem posed to the listener by the lack of invariance between acoustic patterns and linguistic categories (see Nusbaum & Henly, in press). If these principles are sufficiently general, they may constitute the basic framework for a theory of speech perception that can account for phonetic constancy regardless of the source of acoustic-phonetic variability.

6.3 TALKER VARIABILITY AND TALKER NORMALIZATION

Two talkers can produce the same phonetic segment with different acoustic patterns and different segments with the same acoustic pattern (Peterson & Barney, 1952). As a result, there is the same many-to-many relationship between acoustic patterns and linguistic categories as a result of differences in the vocal characteristics of talkers. Nonetheless, human listeners are usually quite accurate in recognizing speech regardless of who produces it.

Engineers would love to build a speech recognition system that would accurately recognize speech regardless of who produced it, but this has yet to be done. Most speech recognition systems require some amount of training on the voice of the person who will be using the system in order to achieve accurate levels of performance (Nusbaum, DeGroot, & Lee, 1995; Nusbaum & Pisoni, 1987). Speech recognition systems would be much more useful if they did not require this kind of training on a talker's voice. Nonetheless, in spite of two decades of intense engineering effort directed at building speaker-independent speech recognition systems, this goal has been realized in only the most restricted sense: There are recognition systems that are relatively accurate for a very small vocabulary and there are systems that are relatively inaccurate (compared to humans) for larger vocabularies. In all cases, there are limitations to the set of talkers whose speech can be recognized. For example, one system that used statistical modeling techniques achieved a relatively high level of accuracy for speech produced by talkers from New Jersey, but performance was terrible when the same system was tested on speech produced by talkers from another dialect of American English (Wilpon, 1985). Thus from the engineering perspective, it is clear that speaker-independent speech recognition is an extremely difficult computational task, albeit one that we, as human listeners, solve all the time, such as whenever we answer the phone. The correct solution to this problem is probably not based solely on the perceptual experience listeners have with a wide range of talkers' vocal characteristics because unlike computer speech recognition systems, we can quickly generalize to an accent we have never heard before.

There is no deep mystery about why speaker-independent speech recognition is computationally challenging. Talkers differ in the structure of their vocal tracts and in the way they produce speech (e.g., Fant, 1973). This results in a nondeterministic relationship between acoustic properties and phonetic categories, which means that if given a particular acoustic pattern, there is uncertainty about how to classify it. In order to classify a pattern correctly (i.e., as the talker intended it), it is necessary to know something about the vocal characteristics of the talker who produced the speech. This is the crux of the purported solution to phonetic constancy given talker variability, and this is what distinguishes the problem of talker variability from the problem of variability in phonetic context.

When we consider the problem of talker variability and the theoretical approaches to speech recognition across talkers, we see very different kinds of theories than the more general theories described above such as motor theory or Trace (see Nusbaum & Henly, in press, for a discussion). First, whereas general theories of speech perception focus on the problem of consonant recognition, models of talker normalization address the problem of vowel perception. Thus, different classes of segments are generally targeted by these theories. This is probably because consonants are most greatly affected by changes in phonetic context (e.g., Liberman, Cooper, Shankweiler et al., 1967), whereas the effects of talker differences on vowel spaces are much better understood (e.g., Fant, 1973; Peterson & Barney, 1952) than differences in the way talkers produce consonants. Second, theories of talker normalization fall into two categories depending on the kind of information used in normalizing talker differences (Ainsworth, 1975; Nearey, 1989). Some theories use extrinsic information (information from preceding context) to estimate or calibrate the talker's vowel space (e.g., Gerstman, 1968); other theories use intrinsic information, meaning that information within the acoustic pattern of the segment being recognized is used to achieve phonetic constancy (e.g., Shankweiler et al., 1977; Syrdal & Gopal, 1986).

Talker normalization is the purported process by which listeners compensate for differences among talkers in order to maintain phonetic constancy regardless of the vocal characteristics of the talker. Is this truly a different process from the process that characterizes the recognition of phonemes in spite of the variability in acoustic patterns produced by different phonetic contexts? From the term *normalization,* one might think so. For example, the term normalization has been used in computational vision to describe a set of passive and simple transformations that render an input pattern into a canonical form for pattern matching. In Roberts' (1965) early object recognition system, a set of prototypes or object templates were used as the basis for determining the identity of an input pattern. However, it was important to modify the input pattern by appropriate rotation, size expansion or compaction, and translation across spatial position, to optimally register the input pattern against the set of templates. If the size of the input and templates were different, or their major axes were not in registration, the contours or other visual features of the input and template set would mismatch for reasons unrelated to the basic level differences among the pattern properties of the objects to be recognized. Simple pattern differences due to orientation, distance, or location of an object should not affect the recognition of the object, so normalization processes were proposed, based on relatively simple criteria, that would eliminate these effects prior to pattern matching.

From this kind of work on computational vision and pattern matching, pattern normalization has been viewed as a distinct process from the process of recognition (e.g., see Uhr, 1973). First, normalization processes are typically viewed as preceding pattern recognition for the purpose of eliminating variation that is not intrinsic to the definition of a pattern. Second, normalization processes have been viewed as linear (simple) transformations of the input such as rotation, translation, and magnification. Finally, these processes have been viewed as passive filtering mechanisms.

In speech perception, some researchers have assumed that talker normalization operates in much the same way, although it is not clear why this should necessarily be the case. For example, Palmeri, Goldinger, and Pisoni (1993) have argued from recent data that talker information is retained within the episodic trace that is encoded during the perception of spoken words. They suggest that if normalization transforms an input pattern into some canonical form, thereby stripping out talker vocal characteristics, this kind of normalization cannot be carried out (see also Nygaard, Sommers, & Pisoni, 1994). (We can ignore for present purposes the fact that there exist parallel multiple representations of any stimulus pattern in the auditory system such that some may represent transforms of one kind and others may be relatively untransformed, rendering this logic questionable.) This assumption is largely based on the structure of many models of talker normalization: As in computational vision, these may take the form of a passive filtering process that transforms an input stimulus into some canonical or talker-independent form for subsequent matching to phonetic categories. The model proposed by Syrdal and Gopal (1986) is just this kind of system. Bark scaling by F0 and F3 is used to modify the pattern of F1 and F2 of vowels in order to be compared to a set of prototype vowels. In this regard then, talker normalization is simply a passive filtering process that precedes the "real" computational work of recognizing phonetic structure.

Furthermore, the kind of knowledge and information that is used during talker normalization is thought to be different from the knowledge used to account for phoneme recognition. In order to carry out talker normalization, it is necessary to derive information about the talker's vocal characteristics. For example, in Gerstman's (1968) model, the point vowels are used to scale the location of the F1–F2 space of all the other vowels produced by a given talker. Because the point vowels represent the extremes of a talker's vowel space, they can be used to characterize the talker's vocal tract extremes and therefore bound the recognition space. Similarly, Syrdal and Gopal's model scales F1 and F2 using the talker's fundamental frequency and F3 because these are considered to be more characteristic of the talker's vocal characteristics rather than of vowel quality (e.g., Fant, 1973; Peterson & Barney, 1952). Thus, talker normalization models use information about the talker's vocal characteristics rather than information about the specific message or phonetic context, as in models of phoneme perception such as Trace (McClelland & Elman, 1986) or Motor Theory (Liberman, Cooper, Harris, & MacNeilage, 1962) or analysis-by-synthesis (Stevens & Halle, 1967) or the Fuzzy Logical Model of Perception (Massaro, 1987; Massaro & Oden, 1980).

From all these considerations it appears that there is a belief among speech researchers that coping with talker variability is a different kind of process from coping with variability due to phonetic context. Thus in spite of the traditional acknowledgment that the lack of invariance problem in speech is manifest due to variability in context, speaking rate, and talker, this really means that there are different variability problems that require different theoretical solutions. Even in more recent models such as Trace, Elman and McClelland (1986) made the argument that speech perception requires a general approach to coping with "sources of lawful variability" in speech. However, Trace itself is highly specialized to address the specific problem of coping with variability due to phonetic context, and there is no set of general principles presented that would permit extension of this model to address talker variability or speaking rate variability (see Klatt, 1986, for a discussion). In spite of the general claims, and although seldom explicitly presented this way, the modal theoretical view of speech perception is that there are a set of specialized normalizing processes that act as passive filters (e.g., one for speaking rate, cf. J. L. Miller & Dexter, 1988; one for talker vocal characteristics, Syrdal & Gopal, 1986) that transform the input signal into some canonical form for comparison to a set of linguistic category prototypes. This final prototype-matching operation is the focus and concern of most theories of speech perception (e.g., Liberman et al., 1962; Massaro, 1987; McClelland & Elman, 1986).

Although this is the modal view, we claim that this balkanization of speech perception is part of the reason that adequate theories of speech perception have not emerged (see Nusbaum & Henly, in press). This kind of dissociation of spoken language understanding into separate perceptual problems may be a result of the fundamental approach that most theories have taken to speech perception. As we noted in the previous discussion of the general problem of lack of invariance, most theories have focused on an analysis of the kinds of knowledge or information representations needed by a perceiver to achieve phonetic constancy, even though this kind of content analysis or informational analysis cannot be expected to yield an effective account of phonetic constancy over variability in phonetic context without a consideration of the required computational control mechanisms. If a theory focuses only on the information that is relevant to determining a talker's vocal characteristics or relative speaking rate or identifying phonetic context, this will definitely make the effects of talker variability, context variability, and rate variability look like different kinds of perceptual problems. But a consideration of the computational structure of the problem leads to a different conclusion.

Because talker variability results in a one-to-many mapping between acoustic cues and phonetic categories, talker variability presents the same kind of nondeterministic computational problem that arises because of variation in phonetic context. This has two immediate implications. First, it is possible that a common computational architecture may mediate phonetic constancy resulting from either of these sources of variability. Indeed, it seems plausible to look for a general computational mechanism that could account for phonetic constancy as a general approach to coping with all forms of lawful variability (Elman & McClelland, 1986). Second, if talker variability results in a nondeterministic computational problem, as noted earlier, normalization cannot be accounted for by passive transformations, even if it may appear that way from some of the simple computational models and restricted analyses carried out (e.g., Gerstman, 1968; Syrdal & Gopal, 1986). These models take the simplest case possible and, because they are restricted to steady state vowels, may not be reflective of the entire scope of the talker normalization problem. Steady state vowels are seldom found in fluent speech where vowels are coarticulated into consonant contexts. However, even when constraining the problem of talker normalization to vowel space differences, these models are still not as accurate as human listeners (e.g., Syrdal & Gopal, 1986). By addressing only the problem of vocal tract scaling (Fant, 1973), these models cannot really address the problem of consonant perception. Vocal tract size differences will definitely affect the acoustic patterns of consonants but probably not in the simple way it does for steady state vowels. However, the speech of talkers differs in more than just the effects of differences in vocal tract size. Two talkers may use different cues, cue combinations, and coarticulation functions to express consonants (e.g., Dorman, Studdert-Kennedy, & Raphael, 1977). These kinds of effects are compensated for by the listener (e.g., Johnson, 1991; Nusbaum & Morin, 1992; but see Rand, 1971), and the vocal tract scaling models give no indication about how this is accomplished.

At this point, the concept of "lawful variability," introduced by Elman and McClelland (1986) becomes germane. They argued that speech is restructured in speech production to present a lack of invariance (cf. Liberman, Cooper, Shankweiler et al., 1967) not through capricious or random processes, but through structurally regular processes that impose this variability in systematic ways. To recognize speech, it is important to deconvolve these sources of lawful variability. At this level of description, this is also similar to claims made by Fowler and Smith (1986) regarding a "vector analysis" of speech. The moment-by-moment output acoustic signal is the instantaneous result of the convolution (or by their terminology, vector sum) of a set of sources of variability, including the phonetic context, the talker's vocal characteristics, and the speaking rate. In order to recover the phonetic structure, it is necessary to undo all these effects, although there is no explicit statement of how to accomplish that.

Both of these descriptions of speech perception share something in common, although neither provides a clear description of this commonality nor a clear theoretical solution. Both seem to acknowledge that there is a basic structural similarity to the recognition problem posed by variability in phonetic context and vocal characteristics but do not articulate its nature. Our claim is that this structural similarity is a consequence of the basic nondeterministic nature of the relationship between acoustic cues and linguistic categories that is imposed by these sources of variability. Furthermore, if it is the case that these sources of variability impose a nondeterministic computational structure on the problem of perception, then it must follow that we can reject all theories that have an inherently passive control structure. In other words, it is our contention that phonetic constancy must be achieved by an active computational system (e.g., Nusbaum & Henly, in press; Nusbaum & Morin, 1992; Nusbaum & Schwab, 1986).

6.4 EMPIRICAL EVIDENCE FOR ACTIVE PROCESSING IN TALKER NORMALIZATION

Active control systems employ a feedback loop structure to systematically modify computation in order to converge on a single, stable interpretation (MacKay, 1951, 1956). By comparison, passive control structures represent invariant computational mappings between inputs and outputs. In consideration of this distinction, there are two general patterns of behavioral performance that can be taken as empirical evidence for the operation of an active control system (see Nusbaum & Henly, in press; Nusbaum & Schwab, 1986, for a discussion). First, evidence of load sensitivity in processing should provide an argument for active processing. There are several ways to justify this claim. For example, automatized processing in perception occurs when there is an invariant mapping between targets and responses, whereas controlled—load-sensitive—processing occurs when there is uncertainty regarding the identity of targets and distractors over trials or when there is no simple single feature difference to distinguish targets and distractors (e.g., Shiffrin & Schneider, 1977; Treisman & Gelade, 1980). In other words, when there are multiple possible interpretations of a stimulus pattern, processing shows load sensitivity, which may be manifest as an increase in processing time, a decrease in recognition accuracy, or an interaction with an independent manipulation of cognitive load (Navon & Gopher, 1979) such as a digit preload task (e.g., Baddeley, 1986; Logan, 1979). Logically, if there are multiple interpretations for a particular pattern, these alternatives must be stored and processed simultaneously increasing possible memory load or processed in some serial fashion leading to an average increase in response time compared to conditions without this uncertainty.

Second, active processing is indicated by the appearance of processing flexibility as demonstrated by the effects of listener expectations, context effects, learning, or other forms of on-line strategic processing. Although an active process need not demonstrate this kind of flexibility, a passive process by virtue of its invariant computational mapping certainly cannot. This means, for example, that evidence for the effects of higher order linguistic knowledge on a lower level perceptual task, such as lexical influence on phonetic recognition (e.g., Ganong, 1980; Nusbaum & Henly, in press; Samuel, 1986), should implicate an active control system in processing.

There is definitely a great deal of evidence arguing that speech perception is load sensitive under conditions of talker variability. For example, the accuracy of word recognition in noise and word recall is reduced when there is talker variability (speech produced by several talkers) compared to a condition in which a single talker produced the speech (Creelman, 1957; Martin, Mullennix, Pisoni, & Summers, 1989; Mullennix, Pisoni, & Martin, 1989). Talker variability also slows recognition time for vowels, consonants, and spoken words in a number of different experiments using a range of different paradigms (Mullennix & Pisoni, 1990; Nusbaum & Morin, 1992; Summerfield & Haggard, 1975). This provides some basic evidence that perception of speech is sensitive to talker variability, but does not really indicate why this occurs.

One possibility is that the increase in recognition time could reflect the addition of a separate talker normalization process to the recognition process (e.g., Nusbaum & Morin, 1992; Summerfield & Haggard, 1975). This hypothesis of inserting a passive normalizing mechanism is consistent with the general perspective of this research area as we outlined earlier. However, Nusbaum and Morin (1992) demonstrated that an independent manipulation of load, using the digit preload method (Baddeley, 1986; Logan, 1979) produces an interaction with talker variability. When listeners hear speech produced by a single talker, recognition time is unaffected by increases in the size of this visually presented digit memory load. Talker variability by itself does slow recognition time (Nusbaum & Morin, 1992). However, when there is uncertainty about which talker could have produced the speech, increasing the memory load slows recognition time even more. There is no reason why adding a passive normalization stage would interact with the memory load. But if increasing talker variability increases the number of alternative interpretations that must be tested in order to recognize an utterance, we would expect this to interact with memory load (see Nusbaum & Morin, 1992).

These studies all indicate that talker variability increases the cognitive load of the listener and increases the difficulty of recognizing speech. On the one hand, as we argue above, this provides one kind of evidence supporting the idea that listeners recognize speech using an active computational mechanism to resolve the inherent nondeterminism presented by talker variability. On the other hand, there has been some research that implies that listeners may not engage in talker normalization during speech perception (Nygaard et al., 1994; Palmeri et al., 1993) based on two kinds of evidence: the first claim is that increasing the amount of talker variability (in terms of number of talkers) beyond simply having two talkers does not affect performance in a memory task (Palmeri et al., 1993). The second claim is that information about the talker is encoded into the episodic trace representing a spoken item in memory. This is considered critical because Nygaard et al. (1994) and Palmeri et al. (1993) assume that talker normalization must strip talker-specific information out of an utterance prior to—indeed as a precondition to—its recognition. Therefore, this information could not be present in an episodic trace of the item in a memory study.

Neither of these arguments presents a strong challenge to the claim that listeners engage in talker normalization, as Palmeri et al. acknowledge. The first issue is only significant if somehow the normalization process keeps track of how many talkers there are or somehow depends on variability defined over a very broad span of speech (i.e., many utterances). If talker normalization just uses information from the preceding talker to set a context of interpretation for a subsequent utterance or simply uses the presence of any talker variability to change the strategies used in recognition, the first part of this argument will not hold. Furthermore, the second argument depends on an overly simplistic view of normalization and of the human auditory system. If talker normalization is needed to address a nondeterministic mapping between acoustic properties and linguistic categories, it cannot operate as a passive filtering mechanism, as implied by Palmeri et al. and Nygaard et al. Instead, it must actively test hypotheses about the identity of an utterance using various sources of information about the talker's vocal characteristics. These could be derived from context or from the utterance itself (Ainsworth, 1975). But this information does not need to modify the auditory representation of an utterance as a precursor to recognition of that information. Furthermore, there is sufficient neurophysiological evidence about parallel representations in the human auditory system (Pickles, 1982) that there is no reason to assume that there is only one representation available to the listener. But of even greater theoretical concern is the fact that if, as suggested by this view, there is no talker normalization, how does the listener recognize speech given talker variability? Although there is a claim about storing auditory traces of spoken words, if recognition is conceived of as only based on a comparison of a stimulus utterance to these traces (as implied by Nygaard et al., 1994), this is exactly the approach that is used by many computer speech recognition systems and is quite possibly the reason that they fail to provide human levels of recognition performance.

Our view is that the evidence regarding the load sensitivity of the human listener when there is talker variability provides strong evidence that speech perception is carried out by an active process. Furthermore, evidence of the flexibility of human listeners in processing speech given talker variability provides additional support. For example, we have found that listeners shift attention to different acoustic cues when there is a single talker and when there is talker variability (Nusbaum & Morin, 1992). In one condition, subjects monitored a sequence of spoken vowels for a specified target vowel and all the vowels were produced by one talker. In a second condition, a mix of different talkers produced the vowels. Both of these conditions were given with four different sets of vowels that were produced by linear predictive coding (LPC) resynthesis of natural vowels used in our other experiments (Nusbaum & Morin, 1992). One set consisted of intact, four-formant voiced vowels. A second set consisted of the same vowels with voicing turned off to produce whispered counterparts. A third set was produced by filtering all information above F2 using hand-tuned digital filters. The final set combined whispering with filtering to eliminate F0 and formant information above F2.

If listeners recognize vowels using a mechanism similar to the one described by Syrdal and Gopal (1986), fundamental frequency and F3 information (although see Johnson, 1989, 1990a) should be necessary for recognition under all circumstances, because in their view this information provides a talker-independent specification of vowel identity. This predicts that in both the single-talker and mixed-talker conditions, the intact voiced vowels should be recognized most accurately, with whispering or filtering reducing performance somewhat, and the combination reducing performance the most, because these modifications eliminate critical information for vowel recognition. Our results showed that in the single-talker condition, recognition performance was uniformly high across all four sets of stimuli. In the mixed-talker condition, however, accuracy dropped systematically as a function of the modifications of the stimuli, with the voiced, intact vowels recognized most accurately and the whispered, filtered vowels recognized least accurately (Nusbaum & Morin, 1992). If vowel recognition were carried out by a passive, talker-independent mechanism (e.g., Syrdal & Gopal, 1986), the same pattern of results should have been obtained in both the single-talker and mixed-talker conditions. The results we obtained suggest that listeners only direct attention to F0 and F3 when there is talker variability (cf. Johnson, 1989, 1990b). This kind of strategic flexibility in recognition is strong evidence of an active mechanism. Furthermore, it suggests that the reason for the increase in cognitive load given talker variability may be that the listener must distribute attention over more cues in the signal than when there is a single talker.

More recently, we have found that listener expectations affect talker normalization processes as well. In an earlier study, we found that not all talker differences increase recognition time in a mixed-talker condition (Nusbaum & Morin, 1992; also see Johnson, 1990b). When the vowel spaces of talkers are sufficiently similar and their fundamental frequencies are similar, there may be no difference in recognizing targets when speech from these talkers is presented in separate blocks or in the same block of trials. Magnuson and Nusbaum (1993, 1994) carried out a study designed to investigate more specifically under what conditions talker variability increases recognition time. In this study, two sets of monosyllabic words were synthesized with two different mean F0s differing by 10 Hz. In one condition, a small passage was played to subjects in which two synthetic talkers, differing in F0 by 10 Hz, have a short dialogue. In a second condition, another group of subjects heard a passage in which one synthetic talker used a 10-Hz pitch increment to accent certain words. Both groups then listened to exactly the same set of single-pitch and mixed-pitch recognition trials using the monosyllabic stimuli. The subjects who listened to the dialogue between two talkers showed longer recognition times when there was a mix of the two different F0s in a trial compared to trials that consisted of words produced at a single F0. By comparison, subjects who expected that the 10-Hz pitch difference was not a talker difference showed no difference in recognition times or accuracy between the single-pitch and mixed-pitch trials. This demonstrates two things: First, the effect of increased recognition time in trials with a mix of F0s cannot be attributed to a simple contrast effect (see Johnson, 1990a) because both groups received exactly the same stimuli. Instead, the increased recognition times in the mixed-pitch trials seem to reflect processing specific to the attribution of the pitch difference to a talker difference and not something about the pitches themselves. Second, and perhaps more important for the present argument, the listeners' expectations affected whether or not they showed any processing sensitivity to pitch variability. This kind of processing flexibility cannot be accounted for by a simple passive computational system and argues strongly for an active perceptual mechanism (Nusbaum & Schwab, 1986).

Thus there are two different kinds of evidence regarding the nature of the mechanism that mediates perception when there is talker variability. It is difficult to see how to link the observed load sensitivity under talker variability and the processing flexibility unless it is through a single computational architecture. When there is talker variability, recognition appears to be carried out by a computational system with an active control mechanism. One implication of this is that it rules out simple filtering models of talker normalization. It seems unlikely that there is some passive transformation of the signal that is carried out to render acoustic pattern information into some normalized or talker-independent form (e.g., Syrdal & Gopal, 1986). A second implication is that if talker normalization is accomplished by an active control system, perhaps this may provide a more general solution to the problem imposed by lawful variation. If we consider briefly how such an active system might operate, it could suggest whether such a generalization is possible. To do this it is important to consider some of operating principles that constrain this system.

6.5 TOWARD AN ACTIVE THEORY OF TALKER NORMALIZATION

First and foremost, our view is that talker normalization is carried out as a consequence of the normative process of speech perception. In other words, talker normalization is not carried out by a separate module or computational system, but is a consequence of the basic computational structure of the normal operations of speech perception. This stands in sharp contrast to most previous approaches to talker normalization, which emphasized the problem of computing talker vocal tract limits and scaling vowel spaces. It may be more productive to treat the processing of lawful variation as a single perceptual problem and focus on the commonalties rather than separate these problems based on the specific sources of information and knowledge needed to support normalization and recognition.

Second, the effects of talker variability on perceptual processing directly reflect the computational operations needed to achieve phonetic constancy. Increased recognition times and interactions of varying cognitive load with recognition reflect the increased processing demands on capacity that are incurred by talker variability. Talker variability increases the number of possible alternative interpretations of the signal, thereby increasing the processing demands on the listener. As a corollary of our first point, we predict that the same kinds of processing demands will be observed whenever there is any nondeterministic relationship between acoustic cues and linguistic categories during perceptual processing. Furthermore, even though there may be some relationship between the information used in talker identification and talker normalization, we claim that the perceptual effects of talker variability are not a consequence of talker identification processes competing with speech understanding.

Third, in order to achieve phonetic constancy, given a nondeterministic relationship between acoustic cues and perceptual categories, different sources of information and knowledge, beyond the immediate acoustic pattern to be recognized, must be brought to bear on the recognition problem. For example, if the F1 and F2 extracted from an utterance could have been intended as either of two different vowels given talker variability, information about the vocal tract that produced the vowels (e.g., from F0 and F3) will be used to provide the context for interpretation. Whenever there is a one-to-many mapping between a particular acoustic pattern and linguistic categories, listeners will have to use information outside the specific pattern to resolve the uncertainty. This information could come from other parts of the signal, previous utterances, linguistic knowledge, or subsequent parts of the utterance.

In order to realize the kind of computational flexibility required for this approach, it is important to reconceptualize the basic process of speech perception. The standard view of speech perception is that phoneme recognition or auditory word recognition is a process of comparing auditory patterns extracted from an utterance with stored mental representations of pattern information associated with linguistic categories. Our view is that speech perception, as an active process, is basically a cognitive process as described by Neisser (1967) and is more akin to hypothesis testing than pattern matching (cf. Nusbaum & Schwab, 1986). Nusbaum and Henly (1992) have argued that linguistic categories need to be represented by structures that are much more flexible than have been previously proposed. They claimed that a particular linguistic category such as the phoneme /b/ might be better represented by a theory of what a /b/ is. This view is an extension of Murphy and Medin's (1985) argument regarding more consciously processed, higher order categories. From this perspective, a theory is a set of statements that provide an explanation that accounts for membership in a category. Rather than view a theory as a set of explicit verbal statements, our view is that a theory representation of a linguistic category is an abstract, general specification regarding the identity and function of that linguistic category. Although this could be couched as a set of features, it is more reasonable to think of a theory as something that would generate a set of features given particular contextual constraints.

Recognizing a particular phoneme or word is a process of generating a set of candidate hypotheses regarding the classification of the pattern structure of an utterance. Conjectures about possible categories that could account for a section of utterance are proposed based on the prior context, listener expectations, and information in the signal. Given a set of alternative classifications for a stretch of signal information, the perceptual system may then carry out tests that are intended to diagnose the specific differences among the alternative classifications. Cognitive load increases as a function of the number of alternatives to be considered and the number of diagnostic tests that must be carried out.

By this view, phonetic constancy is the result of a process of testing hypotheses that have been tailored to distinguish between alternative linguistic interpretations of an utterance. An active control system mediates this process of hypothesis formation and testing. An abstract representation of linguistic categories in terms of theories provides the flexibility to apply diverse forms of evidence to this classification process, allowing the perceptual system to resolve the nondeterministic structure produced by talker variability. These components taken together form a complex inferential system that has much in common with conceptual classification (Murphy & Medin, 1985) and other cognitive processes.

6.6 SUMMARY AND CONCLUSION

Rather than view talker normalization as a separate process that is added onto the front end of speech perception when there is talker variability, we propose that talker normalization is a consequence of normal recognition operations carried out by an active control system. Although the sets of knowledge or the cues listeners attend to may differ for different forms of lawful variability, it is entirely possible that the same kind of processing is carried out for rate normalization and talker normalization and coping with the effects of coarticulation. An active computational architecture provides both a means of resolving the nondeterministic relationship between acoustic cues and linguistic categories and an account of the behavior data showing load sensitivity and strategic flexibility in recognition under conditions of talker variability.

Moreover, Nusbaum and Henly (in press) have argued that the problem of lack of invariance is not special to phoneme perception. Even above the level of acoustic-phonetic mapping, there is a lack of invariance at all levels of pattern-interpretation mappings. Within the realm of talker differences, for example, there are phonological differences in different talkers idiolects and dialects that must be normalized during word recognition. Specialized filtering mechanisms cannot begin to account for the way listeners resolve this aspect of the spoken language comprehension problem. However, the kind of active, hypothesis-testing approach we have outlined here makes clear predictions that under conditions of increased variability there will be increased cognitive load during comprehension. By taking a cognitive approach to the problem of talker normalization and speech perception, this framework offers the prospect of providing a general account for aspects of spoken language understanding that share the same kind of nondeterministic computational structure.

ACKNOWLEDGMENTS

We thank Terry Regier for helpful discussions regarding computational theory. Preparation of this manuscript was supported in part by a grant from the Division of Social Sciences at the University of Chicago.

REFERENCES

Abbs, J. H., & Sussman, H. M. (1971). Neurophysiological feature detectors and speech perception: A discussion of theoretical implications. *Journal of Speech and Hearing Research, 14,* 23–36.

Ainsworth, W. (1975). Intrinsic and extrinsic factors in vowel judgments. In G. Fant & M. Tatham (Eds.), *Auditory analysis and perception of speech* (pp. 103–113). London: Academic Press.

Baddeley, A. D. (1986). *Working memory.* Oxford: Oxford Science Publications.

Barlow, H. B. (1972). Single units and sensation: A neuron doctrine for perceptual psychology? *Perception, 1,* 371–394.

Best, C. T. (1994). The emergence of native-language phonological influences in infants: A perceptual assimilation model. In J. C. Goodman & H. C. Nusbaum (Eds.), *The development of speech perception: The transition from speech sounds to spoken words* (pp. 167–224). Cambridge, MA: MIT Press.

Charniak, E. (1993). *Statistical language learning.* Cambridge, MA: MIT Press.

Chomsky, N. (1957). *Syntactic structures.* The Hague: Mouton.

Creelman, C. D. (1957). Case of the unknown talker. *Journal of the Acoustical Society of America, 29,* 655.

Delattre, P. C., Liberman, A. M., & Cooper, F. S. (1955). Acoustic loci and transitional cues for consonants. *Journal of the Acoustical Society of America, 27,* 769–773.

Dorman, M. F., Studdert-Kennedy, M., & Raphael, L. J. (1977). Stop consonant recognition: Release bursts and formant transitions as functionally equivalent, context-dependent cues. *Perception & Psychophysics, 22,* 109–122.

Elman, J., & McClelland, J. (1986). Exploiting lawful variability in the speech wave. In J. S. Perkell & D. H. Klatt (Eds.), *Invariance and variability in speech processes* (pp. 360–380). Hillsdale, NJ: Erlbaum.

Fant, G. (1973). *Speech sounds and features.* Cambridge, MA: MIT Press.

Fowler, C. A. (1989). Real objects of speech perception: A commentary on Diehl and Kluender. *Ecological Psychology, 1,* 145–160.

Fowler, C. A., & Smith, M. R. (1986). Speech perception as vector analysis: An approach to the problem of invariance and segmentation. In J. S. Perkell & D. H. Klatt (Eds.), *Invariance and variability in speech processes* (pp. 123–135). Hillsdale, NJ: Erlbaum.

Ganong, W. F. (1980). Phonetic categorization in auditory word perception. *Journal of Experimental Psychology, 6,* 110–125.

Gerstman, L. J. (1968). Classification of self-normalized vowels. *IEEE Transactions on Audio Electroacoustics, AU-16,* 78–80.

Gross, M. (1972). *Mathematical models in linguistics.* Englewood Cliffs, NJ: Prentice-Hall.

Grossberg, S. (1986). The adaptive self-organization of serial order in behavior: speech, language, and motor control. In E. C. Schwab & H. C. Nusbaum (Eds.), *Pattern recognition by humans and machines: Vol. 1. Speech perception* (pp. 187–294). San Diego, CA: Academic Press.

Hopcroft, J. E., & Ullman, J. D. (1969). *Formal languages and their relation to automata.* Reading, MA: Addison-Wesley.

Johnson, K. (1989). Higher formant normalization results from integration of F2 and F3. *Perception & Psychophysics, 46,* 174–180.

Johnson, K. (1990a). Contrast and normalization in vowel perception. *Journal of Phonetics, 18,* 229–254.

Johnson, K. (1990b). The role of perceived speaker identity in F0 normalization of vowels. *Journal of the Acoustical Society of America, 88,* 642–654.

Johnson, K. (1991). Differential effects of speaker and vowel variability on fricative perceptions. *Language and Speech, 34,* 265–279.

Klatt, D. H. (1977). Review of the ARPA speech understanding project. *Journal of the Acoustical Society of America, 62,* 1345–1366.

Klatt, D. H. (1979). Speech perception: A model of acoustic-phonetic analysis and lexical access. *Journal of Phonetics, 7,* 279–312.

Klatt, D. H. (1986). Comment. In J. S. Perkell & D. H. Klatt (Eds.), *Invariance and variability in speech processes* (pp. 381–382). Hillsdale, NJ: Erlbaum.

Levinson, S. E., Rabiner, L. R., & Sondhi, M. M. (1983). An introduction to the application of the theory of probabilistic functions of a Markov process to automatic speech recognition. *Bell System Technical Journal, 62,* 1035–1074.

Liberman, A. M., Cooper, F. S., Harris, K. S., & MacNeilage, P. F. (1962). *A motor theory of speech perception. Proceedings of the speech communication seminar* (Vol. 2). Stockholm: Royal Institute of Technology.

Liberman, A. M., Cooper, F. S., Harris, K. S., MacNeilage, P. F., & Studdert-Kennedy, M. (1967). Some observations on a model for speech perception. In W. Wathen-Dunn (Ed.), *Models for the perception of speech and visual form* (pp. 68–87). Cambridge, MA: MIT Press.

Liberman, A. M., Cooper, F. S., Shankweiler, D. P., & Studdert-Kennedy, M. (1967). Perception of the speech code. *Psychological Review, 74,* 431–461.

Liberman, A. M., Delattre, P. C., & Cooper, F. S. (1952). The role of selected stimulus variables in the perception of unvoiced stop consonants. *American Journal of Psychology, 65,* 497–516.

Liberman, A. M., & Mattingly, I. G. (1985). The motor theory of speech perception revised. *Cognition, 21,* 1–36.

Logan, G. D. (1979). On the use of a concurrent memory load to measure attention and automaticity. *Journal of Experimental Psychology: Human Perception and Performance, 5,* 189–207.

Lowerre, B., & Reddy, R. (1980). The Harpy speech understanding system. In W. A. Lea (Ed.), *Trends in speech recognition* (pp. 340–360). Englewood Cliffs, NJ: Prentice-Hall.

MacKay, D. M. (1951). Mindlike behavior in artefacts. *British Journal for the Philosophy of Science, 2,* 105–121.

MacKay, D. M. (1956). The epistemological problem for automata. In C. E. Shannon & J. McCarthy (Eds.), *Automata studies.* Princeton, NJ: Princeton University Press.

MacNeilage, P. F. (1970). Motor control of serial ordering of speech. *Psychological Review, 77,* 182–196.

Magnuson, J. S., & Nusbaum, H. C. (1993). *Talker differences and perceptual normalization. Journal of the Acoustical Society of America, 93,* 2371.

Magnuson, J. S., & Nusbaum, H. C. (1994). Some acoustic and nonacoustic conditions that produce talker normalization. *Proceedings of the Acoustical Society of Japan,* pp. 637–638.

Martin, C. S., Mullennix, J. W., Pisoni, D. B., & Summers, W. V. (1989). Effects of talker variability on recall of spoken word lists. *Journal of Experimental Psychology Learning, Memory, and Cognition, 15,* 676–684.

Massaro, D. W. (1972). Perceptual images, processing time, and perceptual units. *Psychological Review, 79,* 124–145.

Massaro, D. W. (1987). *Speech perception by ear and eye: A paradigm for psychological inquiry.* Hillsdale, NJ: Erlbaum.

Massaro, D. W., & Oden, G. C. (1980). Speech perception: A framework for research and theory. In N. J. Lass (Ed.), *Speech and language: Advances in basic research and practice* (Vol. 3, pp. 129–165). New York: Academic Press.

McClelland, J. L., & Elman, J. L. (1986). The TRACE model of speech perception. *Cognitive Psychology, 18,* 1–86.

Miller, G. A. (1962). Decision units in the perception of speech. *IRE Transactions on Information Theory, IT-8,* 81–83.

Miller, J. L., & Dexter, E. R. (1988). Effects of speaking rate and lexical status on phonetic perception. *Journal of Experimental Psychology: Human Perception and Performance, 14,* 369–378.

Minsky, M. (1975). A framework for representing knowledge. In P. H. Winston (Ed.), *The psychology of computer vision* (pp. 211–277). New York: McGraw-Hill.

Mullennix, J. W., & Pisoni, D. B. (1990). Stimulus variability and processing dependencies in speech perception. *Perception & Psychophysics, 47,* 379–380.

Mullennix, J. W., Pisoni, D. B., & Martin, C. S. (1989). Some effects of talker variability on spoken word recognition. *Journal of the Acoustical Society of America, 85,* 365–378.

Murphy, G. L., & Medin, D. L. (1985). The role of theories in conceptual coherence. *Psychological Review, 92,* 289–316.

Navon, D., & Gopher, D. (1979). On the economy of the human-processing system. *Psychological Review, 86,* 214–255.

Nearey, T. M. (1989). Static, dynamic, and relational properties in vowel perception. *Journal of the Acoustic Society of America, 85,* 2088–2113.

Neisser, U. (1967). *Cognitive psychology.* New York: Appleton-Century-Crofts.

Newell, A. (1975). A tutorial on speech understanding systems. In R. D. Reddy (Ed.), *Speech recognition* (pp. 4–54). New York: Academic Press.

Nusbaum, H. C., DeGroot, J., & Lee, L. (1995). Using speech recognition systems: Issues in cognitive engineering. In A. K. Syrdal, R. W. Bennett, & S. L. Greenspan (Eds.), *Applied speech technology* (pp. 127–194). Boca Raton, FL: CRC Press.

Nusbaum, H. C., & Henly, A. S. (1992). Listening to speech through an adaptive window of analysis. In B. Schouten (Ed.), *The processing of speech: From the auditory periphery to word recognition* (pp. 339–348). Berlin: Mouton-de Gruyter.

Nusbaum, H. C., & Henly, A. S. (in press). Understanding speech perception from the perspective of cognitive psychology. In J. Charles-Luce, P. A. Luce, & J. R. Sawusch (Eds.), *Theories in spoken language: Perception, production, and development.* Norwood, NJ: Ablex.

Nusbaum, H. C., & Morin, T. M. (1992). Paying attention to differences among talkers. In Y. Tohkura, Y. Sagisaka, & E. Vatikiotis-Bateson (Eds.), *Speech perception, production, and linguistic structure* (pp. 113–134). Tokyo: Ohmsha Publishing.

Nusbaum, H. C., & Pisoni, D. B. (1987). Automatic measurement of speech recognition performance: A comparison of six speaker-dependent recognition devices. *Computer Speech and Language, 2,* 87–108.

Nusbaum, H. C., & Schwab, E. C. (1986). The role of attention and active processing in speech perception. In E. C. Schwab & H. C. Nusbaum (Eds.), *Pattern recognition by humans and machines: Vol. 1. Speech perception* (pp. 113–157). San Diego, CA: Academic Press.

Nygaard, L. C., Sommers, M. S., & Pisoni, D. B. (1994). Speech perception as a talker-contingent process. *Psychological Science, 5,* 42–46.

Ohman, S. E. G. (1966). Coarticulation in VCV utterances: Spectrographic measurements. *Journal of the Acoustical Society of America, 39,* 151–168.

Palmeri, T. J., Goldinger, S. D., & Pisoni, D. B. (1993). Episodic encoding of voice attributes and recognition memory for spoken word. *Journal of Experimental Psychology: Learning, Memory, and Cognition, 19,* 309–328.

Peterson, G., & Barney, H. (1952). Control methods used in a study of the vowels. *Journal of the Acoustical Society of America, 24,* 175–184.

Pickles, J. O. (1982). *An introduction to the physiology of hearing.* London: Academic Press.

Pisoni, D. B. (1978). Speech perception. In W. K. Estes (Ed.), *Handbook of learning and cognitive processes: Vol. 6. Linguistic functions in cognitive theory* (pp. 167–234). Hillsdale, NJ: Erlbaum.

Rand, T. C. (1971). *Vocal tract size normalization in the perception of stop consonants.* Paper presented at the 81st meeting of the Acoustical Society of America, Washington, DC.

Roberts, L. G. (1965). Machine perception of three-dimensional solids. In J. T. Tippett (Ed.), *Optical and electro-optical information processing* (pp. 159–197). Cambridge, MA: MIT Press.

Samuel, A. G. (1986). The role of the lexicon in speech perception. In E. C. Schwab & H. C. Nusbaum (Eds.), *Pattern recognition by humans and machines: Vol. 1. Speech perception* (pp. 89–112). San Diego, CA: Academic Press.

Shankweiler, D., Strange, W., & Verbrugge, R. (1977). Speech and the problem of perceptual constancy. In R. Shaw & J. Bransford (Eds.), *Perceiving, acting, and knowing* (pp. 315–345). Hillsdale, NJ: Erlbaum.

Shiffrin, R. M., & Schneider, W. (1977). Controlled and automatic human information processing: II. Perceptual learning, automatic attending and a general theory. *Psychological Review, 84,* 127–190.

Stevens, K. N., & Blumstein, S. E. (1978). Invariant cues for place of articulation in stop consonants. *Journal of the Acoustical Society of America, 64,* 1358–1368.

Stevens, K. N., & Blumstein, S. E. (1981). The search for invariant acoustic correlates of phonetic features. In P. D. Eimas & J. Miller (Eds.), *Perspectives on the study of speech* (pp. 1–38). Hillsdale, NJ: Erlbaum.

Stevens, K. N., & Halle, M. (1967). Remarks on analysis by synthesis and distinctive features. In W. Walthen-Dunn (Ed.), *Models for the perception of speech and visual form* (pp. 88–102). Cambridge, MA: MIT Press.

Studdert-Kennedy, M., Liberman, A. M., Harris, K. S., & Cooper, F. S. (1970). Motor theory of speech perception: A reply to Lane's critical review. *Psychological Review, 77,* 234–249.

Summerfield, Q., & Haggard, M. (1975). Vocal tract normalization as demonstrated by reaction times. In G. Fant & M. Tatham (Eds.), *Auditory analysis and perception of speech* (pp. 115–141). London: Academic Press.

Syrdal, A. K., & Gopal, H. S. (1986). A perceptual model of vowel recognition based on the auditory representation of American English vowels. *Journal of the Acoustic Society of America, 79,* 1086–1100.

Treisman, A. M., & Gelade, G. (1980). A feature integration theory of attention. *Cognitive Psychology, 12,* 97–136.

Uhr, L. (1973). *Pattern recognition, learning, and thought: Computer-programmed models of higher mental processes.* Englewood Cliffs, NJ: Prentice-Hall.

Walley, A. C., & Carrell, T. D. (1983). Onset spectra and formant transitions in the adult's and child's perception of place of articulation in stop consonants. *Journal of the Acoustical Society of America, 73,* 1011–1022.

Wickelgren, W. A. (1969). Auditory or articulatory coding in verbal short-term memory. *Psychological Review, 76,* 232–235.

Wilpon, J. G. (1985). A study on the ability to automatically recognize telephone-quality speech from large customer populations. *AT&T Technical Journal, 64,* 423–451.

Woods, W. A. (1973). An experimental parsing system for transition network grammars. In R. Rustin (Ed.), *Natural language processing* (pp. 111–145). New York: Algorithmics Press.

7

Normalization of Vowels by Breath Sounds

D. H. WHALEN
SONYA M. SHEFFERT

Last night, the phone rang just before midnight, and only half awake, she answered it. There was only breathing on the other end, but instead of hanging up she lay there in the dark, listening to it. She was sure it was Philippe, but did she know the sound of his breathing that well? Could the sound of one person's breathing be that recognizable? Is it like fingerprints—no two breaths are the same? (Davis, 1994, p. 237)

7.1 INTRODUCTION

The acoustic realization of speech sounds depends greatly on the vocal tract that produces them. Adult speakers differ in their vocal anatomy, especially across the sexes, and every listener must take such differences into account. Additionally, every adult begins life as a child ("I started out as a child," as Bill Cosby used to say), and productive language begins as early as 1 year of age, well before the head has reached its full, adult size. So each speaker must be able to normalize his or her parents' speech in order to know what they are supposed to learn. And one's own speech must be normalized for the current size of the vocal tract, not to the size during the early stages of acquisition. Given such variation, humans have had to make use of a communicative system that allows listeners to make compensations for changes in speakers. Listeners clearly do make adjustments, most clearly in the case of vowels (Nearey, 1989), but also with stops (Rand, 1971) and fricatives (May, 1976; Strand & Johnson, 1996). Thus speaker normalization must be considered a feature of speech perception.

The sources of normalization have been found to be both intrinsic to the signal and extrinsic to it. Intrinsic factors include the ratio of the formants (F) (Chiba & Kajiyama, 1941; Potter & Steinberg, 1950), F0 of the vowel (Miller, 1989; Syrdal & Gopal, 1986), the spacing of F3 and F4 (Fujisaki & Kawashima, 1968), and the shape of the upper range of the spectral envelope (Kitamura & Akagi, 1994). Extrinsic factors include a speaker's overall range of formant values (Gerstman, 1968), presentation of point vowels (Ainsworth, 1975), the sentence preceding the item to be identified (Broadbent & Ladefoged, 1960; Remez, Rubin, Nygaard, & Howell, 1987), and even the assumed sex of the speaker as given visually (Strand & Johnson, 1996). As Nearey (1989) pointed out in his overview of this issue, the existence of intrinsic effects has often led to the insistence that only intrinsic effects should be considered, despite the experimental evidence of extrinsic effects. This tendency is heightened by the fact that the influence of extrinsic factors may be limited to ambiguous stimuli, in light of the lack of an effect of speaker information on error rates in identifying naturally produced vowels (Verbrugge, Strange, Shankweiler, & Edman, 1976). Intrinsic methods of normalization also have the advantage for computational treatments that they can be applied to any stretch of the speech signal without taking the rest into account. But the evidence is fairly clear that extrinsic factors must play a role, and so some combination of extrinsic and intrinsic normalization must occur.

A further question that remains unresolved is whether normalization is carried out on every vowel (and perhaps on accompanying consonants) or if the listener sets up a working model of the speaker in order to interpret what is heard. Recent evidence from short-term memory (STM) studies shows that it is more difficult to remember lists spoken by several speakers than those spoken by a single speaker (Goldinger, Pisoni, & Logan, 1991; Martin, Mullennix, Pisoni, & Summers, 1989). One possible interpretation of this effect is that the need to construct models of the different speakers is more time-consuming than constructing one for a single speaker, and thus the resources available for the memory task are reduced. More explicit testing for such "model construction" is necessary, including testing whether intrinsically ambiguous vowels (i.e., ones that cannot be classified without knowing which vocal tract produced them) are treated unambiguously in a single-speaker context, and whether the model can be retained for some length of time and reactivated either automatically or by explicitly cuing. The alternative to model construction is a more general set of context effects, in which speech is adapted to its current environment but in a way that relates various acoustic properties to each other, not to a proposed speaker. Such models would not predict that any gain would accrue from earlier exposure to a speaker.

Many of the normalization effects rely on features of the acoustics that are not available to consciousness on the part of the listener. The intensity differences due to vowel quality, for example, are fairly automatically taken into account in perception (Lehiste, 1970). Other features, such as speaker sex, are fairly easily reported, even if the exact effect of the normalization is still unavailable for listener report. If the model construction approach is correct, we would expect that it would be easy to manipulate the level of consciousness attainable by manipulating how much the listener "knows" about the speaker, including visual appearance, name, and "personal" facts (however fictitious!). Again, these experiments remain to be done, but there is an interesting discrepancy between what listeners can report and what they can actually do.

One interesting example of this discrepancy between performance and report is in the judgment of speaker height and weight based only on acoustic speech information. Listeners are quite willing to perform this task, and generally report a moderate level of confidence in their answers (Lass, Phillips, & Bruchey, 1980). Even novelists have noted the expectation of a correlation: "She walked past Sara with a quick 'Hi,' hugged Anthony, and said, 'Hello, darling,' in a voice that had more height than she did" (Davis, 1994, p. 263). However, subjects are terrible at the task. One reason for that poor performance, it turns out, is an almost complete lack of correlation between any measurable speech characteristic and height or weight (Künzel, 1989; Van Dommelen, 1995). The basis for this confidence is fairly clear. There are physical reasons to expect that large bodies will have large resonances and lower pitches, given the constraints on vibrating bodies. So there are ample opportunities for human listeners to associate low sounds with big bodies and vice versa. Within the species *Canis familiaris,* for example, there is a great tendency for large breeds (e.g., German shepherds) to have low fundamentals, while the smaller breeds (e.g., Chihuahuas) have high ones. However, those examples lead listeners astray in two ways. First, the size of the human body does not seem to be terribly well correlated with the size of the vocal tract, and especially so in the case of the vocal folds themselves. Although it is true that heavier folds (as seen, for example, in postpubescent males) result in a lower F0, the weight of the folds does not seem to correlate with body weight by itself. Nature is full of examples of creatures that have exploited the apparent connection between F0 and size to allow some species (certain frogs and toads, for example) to sound much larger than they are. The fact that this trick works is evidence of its abiding appeal to perceptual systems, even our own, in which we can learn from experience that the association is a weak one. We are fooled by the apparent link, and we continue to think that we can judge body size by voice quality.

We normalize successfully, even when we are misled about body size. This is due to the fact that vocal tract size is what is important, and we are better attuned to that feature than to other, irrelevant features. Vocal tract normalization is so important, in fact, that we must assume its operation for every act of speech perception. Speech perception itself has been found to be sensitive to virtually every acoustic property that covaries with speech production (Liberman & Mattingly, 1985; Lisker, 1986; Repp, 1982; Studdert-Kennedy, 1976). If speech perception makes use of all available information, as it seems to, and normalization is a normal part of speech perception, then we would expect that it too would make use of all information available, even if it is somewhat unusual.

With that thought in mind, we set out to see whether normalization could be affected by a nonspeech sound that nonetheless is a typical component of the speech process, namely, the sound of inspiration. Because speech is generated primarily by controlling the outgoing breath stream, it follows that inspiration is a necessary precondition to speaking. Sometimes that inspiration will be silent, or nearly so. But quite often it is easily audible. We have already found (Whalen, Hoequist, & Sheffert, 1995) that inclusion of such breath sounds can enhance the memorability of synthetic speech, although the exact mechanism of that improvement is unclear. One possibility is that the inspiration helps to normalize the speech, and thus makes the maintenance of the model of the speaker that much easier. However, we currently have no direct evidence that inspiration noise provides any information for normalization. The present study was designed to produce some of that evidence.

We looked for normalization effects of natural inspiration noises preceding synthetic utterances that formed two vowel continua. We made use of the speaker characteristic that has provided the most consistent normalization effects, namely, speaker sex. Would male and female breaths shift the boundary between the synthetic vowels? Additionally, we tested whether there is coarticulatory information in the inspiration noise. The noise is presumably generated primarily at the larynx and at various points in the lungs themselves, but it propagates through the vocal tract and thus will be shaped by it. If there is anticipation of the upcoming vowel in the vocal tract during the inspiration, then it may provide direct coarticulatory evidence of the vowel to be produced. If so, listeners might be able to use that information and so shift the boundary in the direction of the vowel that the breath was originally produced with.

7.2 EXPERIMENT

The experiment made use of natural inspiration noises, placed as a precursor to synthetic syllables (similar to Broadbent & Ladefoged, 1960). Two continua were used so that a variety of contexts could be tested.

7.2.1 Method

7.2.1.1 Stimuli

The inspiration noises were produced by two native speakers of English, one male and one female (the second author). Each read a randomized list containing five repetitions of the words *bead, bad,* and *bud.* They were instructed to be sure that they took a breath through the mouth before each utterance. From these, a good exemplar was chosen. They were roughly equivalent in duration and amplitude. Spectrograms of all six are presented in Figure 1. Although the spectral characteristics are quite weak, given the source of the noise, there are noticeable differences among the breaths. The male noises have a lower overall frequency than the female ones. The vowel context did not seem to give rise to different

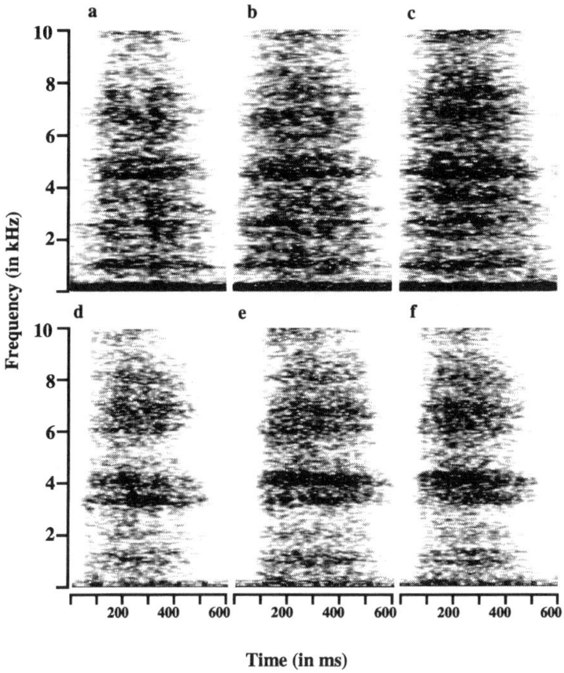

FIGURE 1 Spectrograms of the six inspiration noises used in the experiment. Panels (a–c) are for the male speaker, (d–f) for the female speaker. Panels (a) and (d) are from the "bud" utterances, (b) and (e) from the "bad" utterances, and (c) and (f) from the "bead" utterances.

resonances, but there were differences in the relative amplitude of the two main resonances, as can be seen in panels d and e of Figure 1.

We also included a speech precursor, namely, the phrase "And the next word is ______." One token of this phrase from each speaker was selected.

The synthetic speech stimuli were created on the serial resonance synthesizer SYN, written by Ignatius Mattingly. There were two continua, one going from /bæd/ to /bəd/ and the other going from /bɪd/ to /bɛd/. Formant values were intermediate between those of the male and the female speakers, as measured from their productions. (We also collected the speakers' productions of *bid* and *bed* for just this purpose.) For the /æ/ə/ continuum, F1 began at 300 Hz and F3 began at 2050 Hz. We found that shifting the onset of F2 along with the steady state value improved the intelligibility of the token. The onsets are listed in Table I. There was a short release burst simultaneous with the first 10–20 ms of the syllable, centered at 2000 Hz. The formant center frequencies, listed in Table I, were attained after 50 ms. There was a steady state of 250 ms, after which F1 changed linearly to 350 Hz and F2 changed to 1700 Hz. We had better results with a variable F3 ending frequency; those are listed in Table I. There was a small

TABLE I Formant Values for the æ/ə Continuum[a]

		F1	F2		F3	
Vowel	Cont. Number		Onset	Steady state	Steady state	Offset
ə	1	640	850	1450	2850	2900
	2	660	900	1530	2830	2825
	3	685	975	1610	2810	2750
	4	705	1015	1740	2790	2675
æ	5	725	1100	1875	2775	2600

[a]F, formant.

burst for the final stop simultaneous with the closure. Such "closure bursts" are seldom commented on in the literature, but are readily visible in the speech waveform for many utterances. Inclusion of a very weak closure burst greatly improved the perception of the final stop. F0 was a constant 160 Hz for the first 250 ms, then it fell linearly to 147 Hz. This value is midway between the F0 of the male and that of the female speaker.

For the /ɪ/ɛ/ continuum, the formants began at 250, 1200, and 2275 Hz for F1, F2, and F3 respectively. F3 was the same for all five stimuli, but it did rise from 2500 Hz to 2550 Hz during the "steady state" portion of the syllable (50–250 ms). There was a release burst simultaneous with the first part of the transitions, centered at 2000 Hz and lasting 10–20 ms. The steady state values for F1 and F2 are given in Table II. For the final stop, the transitions lasted 50 ms and ended at 175, 1850, and 2400 Hz for F1, F2, and F3 respectively. There was a small "closure" burst at the end of the syllable. As before, F0 was a constant 160 Hz for the first 250 ms, then it fell linearly to 147 Hz.

Because these formant and F0 values were based on the average of the actual formant and F0 values used by our two speakers, the sex of the synthetic "speaker" was maximally ambiguous, which would presumably allow the speaker information in the inspiration noise to have an effect. It would not be

TABLE II Formant Values for the Steady States of F1 and F2, ɪ/ɛ Continuum[a]

Vowel	Cont. #	F1	F2
ɪ	1	470	2280
	2	490	2260
	3	510	2240
	4	530	2220
ɛ	5	550	2200

[a]F, formant.

surprising if relative weak information, such as that presumably contained in the breath sound, would be unable to overcome more robust cues in the speech itself.

7.2.1.2 Procedure

Each of the five members of each continuum were combined with each of the precursors. For the /æ/ə/ continuum, the breaths produced before *bad* and *bud* were used. For the /ɪ/ɛ/ continuum, the breaths produced before *bead* and *bad* were used. The first case is therefore one in which the vowels at the endpoints of the continua were identical to the ones produced with the inspiration noise. The second case is one in which the vowels produced with the breath were more peripheral in the vowel space than the vowels of the test items. In this way, we might perhaps see a coarticulatory effect in the exaggerated case even if we did not find one in the case in which the exact items were used. The full speech precursors (male and female versions of "And the next word is _____") were the same for both continua.

The continua were recorded on digital audio tape (DAT) and presented to one subject at a time over headphones. Ten repetitions of each combination of synthetic syllable and precursor were randomized and presented for identification as *bad* and *bud* or, for the other continuum, *bid* or *bed.* There was a 200-ms pause between the precursor (speech or breath) and the syllable, and a 2.5-s pause in which the answer was written. There was a 5-s pause after every ten items, corresponding to the end of a line on the answer sheet. The order of presentation of the two continua was randomly selected for each listener.

7.2.1.3 Subjects

The subjects were 15 undergraduate students at the University of Connecticut, who received course credit for their participation, along with seven colleagues from Haskins Laboratories and the two authors. All were native speakers of English with no reported hearing problems.

7.2.2 Results

Our expectations for the directions of the shifts in identification were as follows. For the coarticulatory information in the breaths, we predicted that the identification would shift toward the vowel that the breath had been produced with. This was the same vowel of the response in the /æ/ə/ continuum, and the vowel that was nearest the endpoint vowel for the /ɪ/ɛ/ continuum (that is, /i/ for /ɪ/, and /æ/ for /ɛ/). Our expectations for the effects of speaker sex on the responses was based on the changes in the significance of F1 for the two speakers. With the smaller vocal tract, the female speaker should have higher F1s than the male. Thus this should lead to more /ə/ responses for a female breath or precursor in the /æ/ə/ continuum and more /ɪ/ responses for a female breath or precursor in the /ɪ/ɛ/ continuum.

TABLE III Percent "Bud" Responses to the /æ/ə/ Continuum[a]

	Speech	/æ/ Breath	/ə/ Breath	Marginal	Without speech
male	51.4	53.9	55.4	53.6	54.7
female	53.0	51.2	54.1	52.8	52.7
marginal	—	52.6	54.8	—	—

[a]The prediction was that the female speaker and the /e/ breath would elicit more "bud" responses.

The mean percentage of *bud* responses (across the whole continuum) to the /æ/ə/ continuum are shown in Table III. The mean percentage of "bid" responses (across the whole continuum) to the /ɪ/ɛ/ continuum are shown in Table IV. The effects were assessed with a series of analysis of variance (ANOVA), using the percentage of responses across the whole continuum. (With a small number of continuum steps and a relatively small number of judgments per step, our experience has been that PROBIT analysis overemphasizes random variation at the endpoints of the continuum.) For each continuum, three analyses were performed. The first, main analysis, included both the speech precursors and the breath precursors, with factors Sex of Speaker (two levels, male and female) and Precursor (three levels, speech and two phonetic contexts of breath). Because the breaths include two effects (speaker normalization and coarticulation), we can expect that this factor will need further elaboration without regard to the speech precursor. Thus the second analysis examined only the breath precursors, with the factors Sex and Precursor (two levels each). The third analysis was a one-way examination of Sex for the speech precursors.

For the /æ/ə/ continuum, Sex was not significant (n.s.) in the main analysis ($F(1,23) < 1$, n.s.). The Precursor factor just missed significance ($F(2,46) = 3.11$, $p = .054$), and the interaction was not significant ($F(2,46) = 2.07$, n.s.). In the analysis of just the breaths, Sex was again not significant ($F(1,23) = 2.38$, n.s.). The Precursor factor was significant ($F(1,23) = 6.30$, $p < .05$), while the interaction was not ($F(1,23) < .1$, n.s.). As can be seen from Table III, the /ə/ breaths elicited a significant 2.2% more *bud* responses, indicating that the coarticulatory information was effective in shifting the perception of these ambiguous synthetic

TABLE IV Percent *Bid* Responses to the /ɪ/ɛ/ Continuum[a]

	Speech	/æ/ Breath	/i/ Breath	Marginal	Without speech
Male	52.4	44.6	43.3	46.8	44.0
Female	51.5	45.1	48.0	48.2	46.6
Marginal	—	44.9	45.7	—	—

[a]The prediction was that the female speaker and the /i/ breath would elicit more "bid" responses.

vowels. In the analysis of just the speech precursors, Sex was not significant ($F(1,23) < .1$, n.s.). Thus the speaker characteristic of sex did not influence the perception of these stimuli.

For the /ɪ/ɛ/ continuum, Sex was not significant in the main analysis ($F(1,23) = 1.49$, n.s.). The Precursor factor was significant ($F(2,46) = 9.96$, $p < .001$), perhaps due to the overall difference between the speech and breath precursors. The interaction just missed significance ($F(2,46) = 3.05$, $p = .057$). In the analysis of the breaths alone, Sex was significant ($F(1,23) = 4.29$, $p < .05$). The Precursor factor was not significant ($F(1,23) < 1$, n.s.), whereas the interaction was marginal ($F(1,23) = 3.00$, $p < .10$). As can be seen from Table IV, the female breaths elicited 2.6% more *bid* responses than the male breaths, an effect in the direction predicted by the likely effect of normalizing for the speaker's vocal tract. Although the /i/ breaths elicited 0.8% more *bid* responses, as we would expect on coarticulatory grounds, this difference was not significant. In the analysis of just the speech precursors, Sex was not significant ($F(1,23) = 1.95$, n.s.), despite a 2.6% difference in the predicted direction. Thus the speaker characteristic of sex did not influence the perception of these stimuli when the precursor was speech, but it did do so when the precursor was an inspiration noise.

After the completion of the experiment, it seemed of interest to determine how much of the information in the breath sounds was consciously available to listeners. To test this, we ran a small study with eight members of the Speech Research Laboratory of Indiana University. They had not participated in the main experiment. These subjects listened to 10 repetitions of each of the six breath sounds to see whether they could identify the vowel it had preceded. We blocked the breaths into the same pairs that had been used in the perception test, so that subjects judged either /i/ or /æ/, or /ɔ/ or /æ/. Subjects were 49.5% correct on the first comparison, and 47.5% correct on the other. Neither of these figures differs from the chance level of 50%. Four of the subjects also made judgments of speaker sex. These judgments were 98.3% correct for both sets of breaths.

7.3 DISCUSSION

Although the sound produced by inspiration is nonlinguistic, it is nevertheless shaped by the vocal tract. Thus such breath sounds have the potential to provide information about the dimensions and configuration of that vocal tract. In the present experiment, we have found evidence that such information is used in the perception of synthetic speech, leading to the expectation that this information is available in more natural situations. Whether there will be instances in which the contribution of such sounds is apparent is a different question. But these results raise the possibility that they might be used in automatic speech recognition as a converging source of information about the speaker's characteristics. Additional research will be needed in order to determine the conditions that result in the contribution of such sounds.

The degree of conscious awareness of the information seemed to play no role in the effectiveness of that information. Speaker sex was readily perceived from the inspiration sounds, whereas vowel quality was not. Yet speaker sex influenced the judgments in one continuum, whereas coarticulatory vowel information affected the other. This indicates that the effect of the breath sounds is unlikely to be a strategic one, as might arguably be the case in the example of the specification of speaker sex by vision alone (Strand & Johnson, 1996).

Our findings suggest that the coarticulatory information in the breaths may need to match exactly the vowels that are to be perceived. In our data, the coarticulatory influence was present in the continuum in which the breaths were produced with just the vowels that constitute the endpoints of the continuum. In the other continuum, we used more peripheral vowel articulations, in the hopes that this might exaggerate the influence that the coarticulatory information would have. For that case, however, there was no significant influence of that information. Exactly appropriate information is perhaps more easily used in this context. We are currently conducting an experiment to test this further.

The natural speech precursors did not affect the perception of the continua, in contrast to results found with synthetic precursor sentences (Broadbent & Ladefoged, 1960; Remez et al., 1987). We suspect that this lack of an effect is due to the discrepancy between the natural speech and the synthesis. The previous studies used synthesis for both the precursor and the target. This may make it easier for the listeners to integrate the two into a single, coherent percept. The clear difference between the natural speech and the synthesis in the present experiment, on the other hand, may have led to a lack of integration and thus to a lack of an effect. Various manipulations of the stimuli, such as synthesizing the precursor or creating a more natural-sounding synthetic continuum, would be needed to fully resolve this issue.

The fact that speaker information extrinsic to the signal, as shown here and in Strand and Johnson (1996), can influence the perception of speech clearly indicates that normalization procedures should not be exclusively intrinsically based. There is enough evidence now to indicate that the listener may construct a "model" of the speaker as a means of perceiving speech, given the large number of differences in vocal tract size that any listener will confront in a lifetime. Such "model making" leads to the prediction that individual characteristics outside the speech realm (such as a personal name, a habitual gait, or even a well-known belonging) could influence perception of speech in a way appropriate to a known individual. As an alternative to making a model of an individual speaker, extrinsic effects might result from all the information available about a vocal tract as selected from among a range of vocal tract types that are not associated with individuals. In that case, only speech information would be expected to play a role. The present study shows, at least, that the sound of inspiration must be included in the range of speech-relevant information available to the listener.

ACKNOWLEDGMENTS

This research was supported by the National Institute of Child Health and Human Development (NICHD) grant HD-01994, to Haskins Laboratories. We thank Julia Irwin and Larry Brancazio for help with the experiments. Carol A. Fowler and Leigh Lisker provided helpful comments.

REFERENCES

Ainsworth, W. A. (1975). Intrinsic and extrinsic factors in vowel judgments. In G. Fant & M. Tatham (Eds.), *Auditory analysis and perception of speech* (pp. 103–111). New York: Academic Press.

Broadbent, D. E., & Ladefoged, P. (1960). Vowel judgments and adaptation level. *Proceedings of the Royal Society of London, 151,* 384–399.

Chiba, T., & Kajiyama, M. (1941). *The vowel: Its nature and structure.* Tokyo: Tokyo-Kaiseikan Publishing Co.

Davis, P. (1994). *Bondage.* New York: Pocket Books [1995].

Fujisaki, H., & Kawashima, T. (1968). The roles of pitch and higher formants in the perception of vowels. *IEEE Transactions on Audio and Electroacoustics, AU-16,* 73–77.

Gerstman, L. J. (1968). Classification of self-normalized vowels. *IEEE Transactions on Audio and Electroacoustics, AU-16,* 78–80.

Goldinger, S. D., Pisoni, D. B., & Logan, J. S. (1991). On the nature of talker variability effects on recall of spoken word lists. *Journal of Experimental Psychology: Learning, Memory, and Cognition, 17*(1), 152–162.

Kitamura, T., & Akagi, M. (1994). Speaker individualities in speech spectral envelopes. *Proceedings of the International Conference on Spoken Language Processing, Yokohama, Japan,* Vol. 3, pp. 1183–1186.

Künzel, H. J. (1989). How well does average fundamental frequency correlate with speaker height and weight? *Phonetica, 46,* 117–125.

Lass, N. J., Phillips, J. K., & Bruchey, C. A. (1980). The effect of filtered speech on speaker height and weight identification. *Journal of Phonetics, 8,* 91–100.

Lehiste, I. (1970). *Suprasegmentals.* Cambridge, MA: MIT Press.

Liberman, A. M., & Mattingly, I. G. (1985). The motor theory of speech perception revised. *Cognition, 21,* 1–36.

Lisker, L. (1986). "Voicing" in English: A catalogue of acoustic features signalling /b/ versus /p/ in trochees. *Language and Speech, 29,* 3–11.

Martin, C. S., Mullennix, J. W., Pisoni, D. B., & Summers, W. V. (1989). Effects of talker variability on recall of spoken lists. *Journal of Experimental Psychology: Learning, Memory, and Cognition, 15,* 676–684.

May, J. G. (1976). Vocal tract normalization for /s/ and /š/. *Haskins Laboratories Status Report on Speech Research, SR48,* 67–74.

Miller, J. D. (1989). Auditory-perceptual interpretation of the vowel. *Journal of the Acoustical Society of America, 85,* 2114–2134.

Nearey, T. M. (1989). Static, dynamic, and relational properties in vowel perception. *Journal of the Acoustical Society of America, 85,* 2088–2113.

Potter, R. K., & Steinberg, J. C. (1950). Towards the specification of speech. *Journal of the Acoustical Society of America, 22,* 807–820.

Rand, T. C. (1971). Vocal tract size normalization in the perception of stop consonants. *Haskins Laboratories Status Report on Speech Research, SR25/26,* 141–146.

Remez, R. E., Rubin, P. E., Nygaard, L. C., & Howell, W. A. (1987). Perceptual normalization of vowels produced by sinusoidal voices. *Journal of Experimental Psychology: Human Perception and Performance, 13,* 40–61.

Repp, B. H. (1982). Phonetic trading relations and context effects: New experimental evidence for a speech mode of perception. *Psychological Bulletin, 92,* 81–110.

Strand, E. A., & Johnson, K. (1996). Gradient and visual speaker normalization in the perception of fricatives. In *Proceedings of the 3rd KONVENS Conference.* Berlin, Mouton de Gruyter.

Studdert-Kennedy, M. (1976). Speech perception. In N. J. Lass (Ed.), *Contemporary issues in experimental phonetics* (pp. 243–293). New York: Academic Press.

Syrdal, A. K., & Gopal, H. S. (1986). A perceptual model of vowel recognition based on the auditory representation of American English vowels. *Journal of the Acoustical Society of America, 79,* 1086–1100.

Van Dommelen, W. A. (1995). Speaker and listener sex for speaker height and weight identification. In K. Elenius & P. Branderud (Eds.), *Proceedings of the 13th International Congress of Phonetic Sciences* (pp. 738–741). Stockholm: Stockholm University.

Verbrugge, R. R., Strange, W., Shankweiler, D. P., & Edman, J. R. (1976). What information enables a listener to map a talker's vowel space? *Journal of the Acoustical Society of America, 60,* 198–212.

Whalen, D. H., Hoequist, C. E., & Sheffert, S. (1995). The effects of breath sounds on the perception of synthetic speech. *Journal of the Acoustical Society of America, 97,* 3147–3153.

8

Speech Perception without Speaker Normalization

An Exemplar Model

KEITH JOHNSON

8.1 INTRODUCTION

Speaker normalization is a hypothesized perceptual process in which differences between speakers are reduced prior to identification of linguistic categories. There are a variety of conceptions of speaker normalization, all of which in one way or another involve a mapping from a speaker-specific representation to a relatively speaker-neutral abstraction, which is presumably an appropriate probe to linguistic memory.

For example, in Gerstman's (1968) range normalization, formant values are expressed relative to the speaker's range of produced formants. So, if a vowel has a first formant (F1) value of 500 Hz and the speaker's F1 in other vowels ranges from 300 Hz to 700 Hz, the normalized value of F1 is 0.5 because 500 is halfway between 300 and 700.

In the Joos (1948)/Potter and Steinberg (1950) approach, the formant values of a vowel are considered relative to each other. So, if a vowel has a second formant (F2) value of 1500 Hz and F1 of 500, one dimension of the normalized representation is the difference between them. In Syrdal and Gopal's (1986) and Traunmüller's (1981) implementations the differences are calculated after transforming the formant values to the Bark scale. J. D. Miller (1989) and Nearey (1978, 1989) calculated the differences of the log formant values. Bladon, Henton, and Pickering (1984) implemented this approach by sliding auditory spectra up or down (depending on the sex of the speaker) on the frequency scale.

What all of these models share is the basic property that the auditory representation of the speech signal must be modified in some way prior to recognition.

Gesture recovery models (Fowler, 1986; Liberman & Mattingly, 1985) appear at first to be very different from these acoustic normalization models. Although gesture recovery is principally concerned with the problem of contextual variation in speech (the flip side of speaker variation in the lack of invariance problem, see Perkell & Klatt, 1986), it can also be seen as a type of speaker normalization. This is because gestures are abstract speaking intentions, not actual articulator movements. With an understanding of gesture as a relatively speaker-neutral abstraction, the process of gesture recovery is by definition a speaker normalization process of the same sort as those mentioned in the preceding paragraphs.[1]

In this chapter I will outline a model of speech perception that unlike these approaches includes no speaker normalization process. The next section describes the model in rough conceptual terms. In the third section I discuss some elaborations of the basic model that address points of plausibility and implementation. The fourth section is a description of a small working exemplar model of vowel recognition and results of some simulations.

8.2 PERCEPTION BY EXEMPLARS

In exemplar models of perception (Estes, 1993; Hintzman, 1986; Nosofsky, 1986, 1988, 1991; Nosofsky, Kruschke, & McKinley, 1992) a perceptual category is defined as the set of all experienced instances of the category. That is, no abstract category prototypes are posited. The process of categorization then involves comparing the to-be-categorized item with each of the remembered instances of each category, and categorization is based on sums of similarity over each category. Hintzman (1986) demonstrated that a model of this sort behaves as if categorization is based upon category prototypes, although category abstraction is produced at decision time rather than during acquisition.

A pure exemplar model is obviously impossible because it is necessary to assume that the perceiver remembers too much (Neal Johnson, personal communication, calls this the "head-filling-up problem"). This will be discussed further in the next section, but at this point it should be mentioned that this apparent need

[1] I am not arguing against Fowler's (1986) characterization of speech perception as "direct" gesture recovery. She emphasizes that her Gibsonian brand of gesture recovery is nontranslational, in the sense that the gestural intentions of the speaker are directly perceived by the listener (or better, perceiver). The mechanism involved in deriving gestures from an acoustic signal, although a huge black-box in the theory, is not at issue here. I am suggesting that recovery of linguistic intentions from speech articulation involves some abstraction because gestural intentions vary from speaker to speaker for the same linguistic entities (Johnson, Ladefoged, & Lindau, 1993).

for unlimited memory is matched by the apparent availability of unlimited memory in picture recognition. Standing, Conezio, and Haber (1970) found that people could recognize thousands of previously seen pictures with surprising accuracy and over surprisingly long times. Goldinger (Chap. 3, this volume; 1992) also found that implicit memory for (instances of) words is strong and long-lasting (see also Palmeri, Goldinger, & Pisoni, 1993; Schacter & Church, in press). So, although an exemplar model seems to need unrealistic amounts of memory, people have a surprising ability to remember instances.

Figure 1 illustrates categorization in an exemplar model of speech perception. In this illustration, an exemplar is an association between a set of auditory properties and a set of category labels. The auditory properties are output from the peripheral auditory system, and the set of category labels includes any classification that may be important to the perceiver, and which was available at the time that the exemplar was stored—for example, the linguistic value of the exemplar, the gender of the speaker, the name of the speaker, and so on. The association between sound and category is indicated in the figure as an oval labeled "exemplar," with lines stretching off in one direction toward a vector of auditory properties and in another direction toward a vector of category labels. The stack of ovals stands for the set of all exemplars. Given an item to be categorized, its auditory properties are compared with each exemplar's auditory properties, and the similarity between the item and each exemplar determines the activation level of the exemplar. If the match is good, the activation level of the exemplar is high. The sum of activations over all of the exemplars of a category is taken as evidence that the unknown sound should be categorized as an instance of that category. This is true for each of the types of categories, and so in this way, the model performs speech and speaker recognition simultaneously, as do humans (Remez, Fellowes, & Rubin, 1995).

This type of model can be implemented as a set of formulas (following Nosofsky, 1988). Auditory similarity s_{ij} between exemplars i and j is calculated by (1), where the auditory property m of exemplar j is written x_{jm}, the Euclidian distance between exemplar j and item i is written d_{ij}, w_m is an attention weight given to property m, and c is a sensitivity constant.

$$d_{ij} = [\Sigma w_m(x_{im} - x_{jm})^2]^{1/2} \quad (1a)$$
$$s_{ij} = \exp(-cd_{ij}) \quad (1b)$$

The degree to which item i activates exemplar j in memory is calculated from similarity using formula (2) by assuming that each exemplar has a base activation level (N_j) and optionally that Gaussian noise is added.

$$a_{ij} = N_j s_{ij} + e_j \quad (2)$$

Evidence for category C_1 given item i is then the sum of the activations of exemplars j of C_1 as shown in formula (3).

$$E_{1,i} = \Sigma a_{ij}, j \in C_1 \quad (3)$$

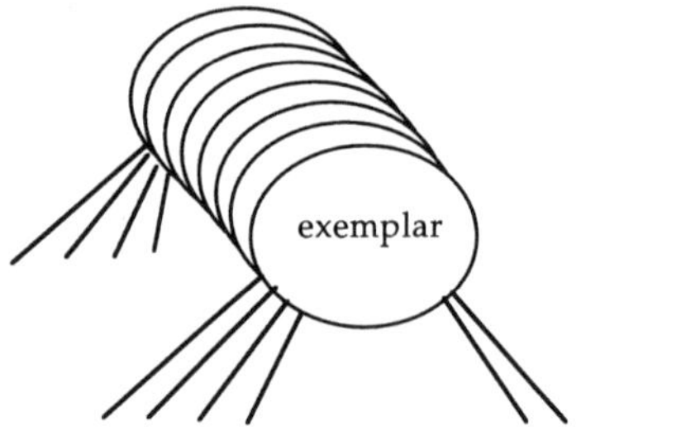

FIGURE 1 A set of exemplars relating auditory properties to category labels.

The weight parameters w_m allow the model to ignore variation on certain stimulus dimensions (and hence are called *attention weights*). As we will see in section 8.4, certain speaker normalization effects can be modeled with changes in the attention weights.

The sensitivity parameter c serves to limit the impact of distant exemplars. Because the function relating distance to similarity is exponential, the impact of distant neighbors on the calculation of total activation E can be reduced to almost nothing. So, the similarity function provides a sort of K nearest-neighbors classification, in which only nearby neighbors are considered.

The base activation levels N_j may vary as a function of some experimental manipulations. For example, a forced-choice identification task can be simulated by forcing the base activation levels of the available responses to be 1 and those of all other categories to be 0. This move forces the identification response to be one of the selected responses because the activations for the other categories are 0 (or, if e_j is used, hover around 0).

8.2.1 Compensation for Speaker Variability in an Exemplar Model

In this model of speech perception, the auditory properties that distinguish speakers are retained in the exemplars. The result of this is that the exemplars that are most similar to a to-be-categorized item are those exemplars that were spoken by the same or a similar speaker. By retaining speaker-specific information in the long-term category representation (the set of exemplars), the model makes it possible to categorize new items by reference to appropriate prior examples—a subset of exemplars that resemble the to-be-recognized item on speaker-specific dimensions.

In Johnson (1990a) I argued for an indirect model of speaker normalization in which cues for vowel identity are evaluated relative to the perceived identity of the speaker. The type of model that I envisioned was one in which the perceived identity of the speaker established (or guided the selection of) a frame of reference for the evaluation of linguistic cues (see also Nearey's [1978] sliding template model of vowel perception, and Whalen and Sheffert's [Chap. 7, this volume] discussion of speaker model construction). The exemplar model outlined here is an indirect model because categorization takes place by reference to items in memory that retain speaker information. That is, the frame of reference (a model of the speaker) is inherent in the set of exemplars, and the similarity calculation (formula 1, above) limits the comparison to items in memory that are sufficiently close to the to-be-categorized item.

8.2.2 Attention Weights

The model parameters w_m shrink or expand the perceptual space along each of the auditory dimensions. These parameters are called *attention weights* (Nosofsky, 1986) because they control the degree to which the categorization process is sensitive to particular auditory properties. For example, if a particular experimental task calls upon the listener to categorize a set of vowel stimuli (to take a relevant example) primarily upon the basis of their first formant frequencies, it is reasonable to expect that the listener will tune in to F1. This can be modeled by letting the weight for F1 (or the weights for the critical bands in the F1 region) be larger than the weights for other auditory properties.[2]

Of course, attention weights can be set so that speaker cues like fundamental frequency are ignored. In vowel perception this would lead to the vowel confusions that you might expect if perception depended solely on location in the F1/F2 plane (for example). However, in modeling the behavior of listeners, I have not found any situations in which this happens. That is, although the structure of the exemplar model makes it possible to ignore a speaker-specific dimension like F0 by setting its weight to 0, in practice this does not happen.

8.2.3 Base Activation Level N_j

Ganong (1980) observed that phonetic categorization is influenced by word frequency. The effect that he observed is reminiscent of the perceptual magnet effect (Kuhl, 1991) in that high-frequency words tended to attract listener's responses.[3] One way to account for this behavior (if the raw number of exemplars does not; see McQueen, 1991) is to assume that the activation parameters N_j tend

[2] I am being purposefully vague about several issues in this chapter. One of them is the definition of *auditory property*. At some points I consider formant values to be auditory properties and at other points I consider auditory properties to be critical-band activation levels, or even vector quantized spectral templates. In the simulations presented in section 8.4 I use measured formants, F0, and durations, but in earlier work (Johnson, 1990b) I used auditory-based spectra. For vowels, these seem to be interchangeable (Fant, 1960), but a more general model of speech perception will probably have to be based on spectra.

[3] Thinking about similarities between the Ganong effect and the perceptual magnet effect suggests an exemplar-based explanation of the perceptual magnet effect (assuming, as argued in the text, that word-frequency effects are related to exemplar coding). This topic is beyond the scope of this chapter.

to be larger for higher frequency words. Nosofsky et al. (1992) proposed that base activation level is subject to a time function such that recent exemplars have higher base activation than do past exemplars. On average then, more frequent words will have a greater number of recent exemplars and therefore higher aggregate base activation levels.

The base activation level parameter may also be a route for allowing higher level processing to have an influence on speech perception. If syntactic or semantic context leads to the prediction that a particular set of words is likely to occur, the base activation levels of the exemplars of these words could be increased. Manipulation of base activation in this way changes the recognition process directly, as opposed to the use of a language model as a filter on the output of recognition, as is done in automatic speech recognition. Whether this is a desirable property is open to debate (see the discussion in Norris, 1994).

In some of the simulations described below, I assumed that in the forced-choice paradigm listeners increase the base activations of exemplars of the permissible responses and decrease (to zero) the base activations of all other exemplars. Obviously, real listeners do not absolutely rule out impermissible alternatives, but this simplification made the models easier to implement.

Base activation level may also be manipulated to simulate a couple of types of context effects that occur in speech perception experiments. Contrast effects observed in selective adaptation and anchoring paradigms that seem to arise from "modifications of internal perceptual referents" (Fox, 1985, p. 1552) can be modeled as changes in base activation level. Fox (1985) proposed that contrast effects occur after speaker normalization. In the model proposed here, which has no speaker normalization stage, the contrast can be implemented as a base-level adjustment such that the base level for all exemplars of the contrasting category is increased by some amount.

Johnson (1991) found a type of speaker continuity effect, where it seemed that listeners expected the voice of the speaker to remain constant across time (and a silent gap of 4 s broke this expectation). To model this effect we can adjust the base activation level for all exemplars of a particular speaker's voice, or the set of similar-sounding speakers, so that future categorizations are more heavily influenced by exemplars from the same speaker. This type of speaker continuity mechanism might explain listeners' decreased word-recognition speed and accuracy for multiple-speaker listening as opposed to single-speaker listening (Mullennix, Pisoni, & Martin, 1989).

8.3 ELABORATIONS AND IMPLEMENTATION

This section explores some elaborations that must be considered if the basic exemplar model discussed in the previous section is to be taken seriously as a model of human speech perception. In addition, I discuss some issues that must be addressed if the model is to be implemented and tested. This section is more

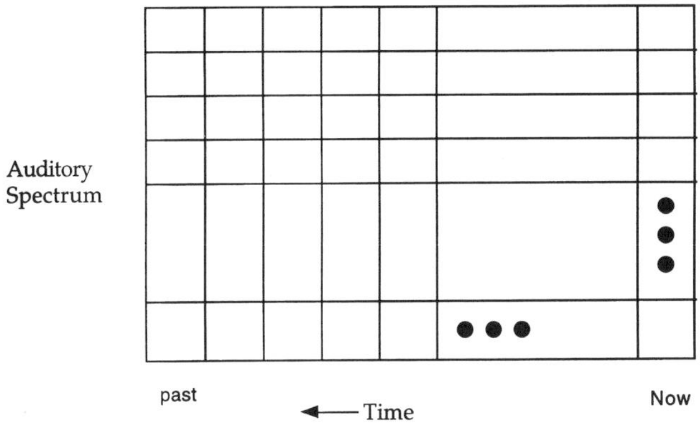

FIGURE 2 An auditory buffer for use in an exemplar model. A quantized auditory spectrum is represented in the vertical dimension with each row representing a frequency region, and time is represented on the horizontal dimension with time passing from right to left.

speculative than the last because I have not yet put together a working implementation of the elaborated model.

8.3.1 Incorporating Time in an Exemplar Model

Previous research on exemplar models has focused on the perception of simple novel visual figures. Consequently, perception of time-varying stimuli has not been considered. One way to incorporate time into an exemplar model is to add a buffer that retains auditory parameters over some interval of time. The model sketched in Figure 1 had a vector of auditory parameters representing the output of the auditory system at one instant in time. This can be extended by incorporating a short-term memory for auditory parameters (Figure 2).

The matrix in Figure 2 is a buffer for incoming speech signals, each column stands for a brief interval of time (on the order of 10 ms), and each row stands for an auditory property. As time passes, the columns shift to the left with the "now" column being filled with the newest set of auditory properties and the columns to the left constituting a veridical short-term memory of the signal (Crowder, 1981). Figure 1 showed connections between each exemplar and only four auditory properties. In this more complicated model each cell in the matrix in Figure 2 is connected to each exemplar.

Another complicating factor is that the similarity between the incoming matrix and the auditory patterns stored with each exemplar must be evaluated each time a new column is added to the matrix. This is obviously not an efficient way to process a speech signal in a serial computing architecture, in which similarity between exemplars and the incoming signal must be evaluated one after the other. But, this point is less problematic if similarity is calculated in parallel, assuming that each exemplar is an independent agent. Still, by including time in the model, with its consequent need for continuous evaluation of the matrix, we introduce a locus for implementing various approaches for temporal selective attention and segmentation strategies.

For example, a general segmentation routine could be implemented by a surprise detector. In this approach, the matrix is evaluated if the auditory vector added to the "now" column is quite different from the immediately preceding column. This is analogous to saying that attention is drawn to the matrix when something happens there. So, sudden acoustic changes such as those that occur at segment boundaries would trigger a recognition attempt.

Word-based segmentation is also possible. In this approach, if the contents of the matrix have been identified as a word, the system will delay further evaluations of the matrix until the "now" column has scrolled some distance into the past.

Rhythmic attention to the matrix (e.g., stress-based or syllable-based segmentation, Cutler & Norris, 1988) involves probing the matrix cyclically at a rate determined by the intervals between previous recognitions, or previous signal events. Note here that stress and syllable cycles correspond to intervals that might be established by the surprise detector, because stress locations and syllable boundaries are associated with signal events. So the choice of a language-specific segmentation strategy might be guided by attention to certain types of auditory changes.

8.3.2 The Head-Filling-Up Problem

The head-filling-up problem is one of the main weaknesses of an exemplar model of speech perception. It is simply not possible that each experienced auditory pattern is stored at a separate location in the brain. The patterns are too complicated (as suggested by the elaboration in Figure 2), and there are too many of them. So, in order to seriously consider an exemplar model we have to have a way to implement it without storing each exemplar.

Kruschke's (1992) connectionist exemplar model is appealing in this regard because a covering map takes the place of exemplars. Figure 3 illustrates a covering map representing a space of exemplars given two auditory properties and two categories (note that only a few of the many interconnections are illustrated). Each location in the map corresponds to a vector of possible auditory properties. Attention weights, as before, govern the mapping from each property to the map (one weight for each property), and association weights govern the mapping from locations in the map to category nodes (one weight between each location in the map and each category). In a richer representation with more auditory properties and categories, the covering map and hence the number of association weights becomes quite large, but unlike a literal exemplar model its size is bounded.

In Kruschke's approach, the weights, both attention weights and association weights, are learned (by a gradient descent learning procedure) by feedback on correct categorization. Consequently, exemplars are encoded in the model as weight modifications rather than through explicit storage.

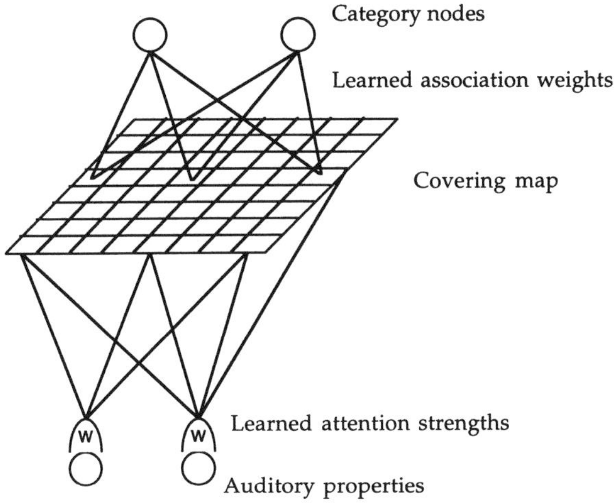

FIGURE 3 A covering map exemplar model of perception. Each input auditory property is connected to each location in the map of possible exemplars, and each location in the map is connected to a set of category nodes.

The covering map as illustrated is essentially a quantized perceptual space. Given the fact that there are limits on the perceivability of incremental changes in duration, pitch, and timbre (just noticeable differences), this assumption seems reasonable. For the sake of a working implementation we may want to take this a step further and use vector quantization (Linde, Buzo, & Gray, 1980).

8.3.3 The Production–Perception Link

Some speech experiences are of one's own speech, which presumably code not only auditory properties and categorical labels, but also articulatory properties. Therefore, an exemplar model can, in principle, also be used to give an account of the production–perception link.[4] This observation leads to some predictions.

In discussing the perception of speech produced by a glossectomee (a person whose tongue was surgically removed), Fowler (1990) invokes the notion *gestural mirage.* She says,

> For the deviant speech of the glossectomized speaker to be perceived as speech at all, the speaker must create acoustic signals that mimic those produced by normal articulations. When he succeeds, listeners hear the normal vocal-tract actions not the compensatory articulations that, in fact, occurred. That is, they hear a mirage. (p. 533)

[4] McGowan (Chap. 11, this volume) discusses some ways of characterizing the articulatory information that might be included in these exemplars.

In extreme cases, such as speech produced without a tongue, or speech produced by a mynah bird, articulatory impressions (the movements a listener would make to produce similar-sounding speech) are obviously imaginary. However, less extreme examples of gestural perception, such as speech produced by people who have slightly different articulatory strategies (Johnson et al., 1993), are no less imaginary. If, as I am suggesting here, the production–perception link is based on one's own speech, then the gestural knowledge derived or generated while listening to others is based on ego exemplars. Gestural mirages are the norm, not the exception.

Consider the perception of a different sort of intention in speech communication. When a person speaks he or she clearly intends to convey some meaning to the listener, but just as clearly we often understand each other only approximately. Our differing experiences of the conventions that link language to the world give us all somewhat different frames of reference for interpreting the utterances we hear. Using my own semantic–pragmatic frame of reference I construct mirages that encode "what I think you said."

An exemplar model that encodes the production–perception link in ego exemplars (but not exclusively so; McGurk & McDonald, 1976) provides a basis for gestural perception and for the imitation of another's speech, but these gestural mirages are not central to perception.

8.4 SOME MODELING RESULTS

This section returns to the unelaborated model set out in section 8.2, fills in some details, and reports the results of some simulations. These results demonstrate in a general way some of the properties discussed in section 8.2, as well as the use of an exemplar model to account for the presentation type effect reported in Johnson (1990b).

8.4.1 A Corpus of Vowel Exemplars

Thirty-nine native speakers of English (14 men and 25 women) read the words *aid, awed, had, head, heed, hid, hood, hud, odd, owed,* and *who'd* five times each (in random order). Five acoustic parameters were derived from each token—fundamental frequency, first, second, and third formant, and vowel duration. The frequency measurements were taken from the midpoint of the vowel.

These exemplars are obviously much simpler than the time-varying auditory spectra envisioned in section 3, but previous research has shown that these acoustic dimensions correlate well with perceptual dimensions for vowels. For example, multidimensional scaling (MDS) studies (Fox, 1981; Shepard, 1972; Singh & Woods, 1970; Terbeek, 1977) have found that vowel formant values and F0 correlate with derived dimensions of the perceptual vowel space. Strange, Jenkins,

TABLE I Model Parameters and Errors for Simulations of Vowel Identification, Sex Identification, and for Fits to the Blocked and Mixed Conditions in Johnson (1990b)[a]

	Vowel identification	Sex identification	Blocked	Mixed
c	0.105	0.36	0.137	0.255
w_{F0},	0.25	0.95	0.2	0.714
w_{F1},	0.25	0.048	0.226	0.012
w_{F2},	0.12	0.0	0.039	0.041
w_{F3},	0.27	0.003	0.415	0.17
w_{dur}	0.1	0.0	0.12	0.078
Error	20%	0.02%	0.047	0.069

[a] Error values for the identification simulations are given in percent incorrectly identified, and error values for the experiment simulations are given in root mean square deviation from the actual results.

and Johnson (1983; see also Strange, 1989) also found that vowel duration is used by English listeners to disambiguate spectrally similar vowels.

In addition to these acoustic properties, each exemplar was encoded with categorical labels indicating (a) the intended word, (b) the sex of the speaker, and (c) the identity of the speaker.

8.4.2 Vowel Identification

Each token in this corpus of exemplars was in turn removed from the corpus and treated as an unknown token to be identified using the remaining exemplars in formulas (1–3) (section 8.2). Base activation levels for all of the exemplars was fixed at 1, and no random noise e_j was added in the calculation of similarity.

The attention weights (w_{F0}, w_{F1}, w_{F2}, w_{F3}, w_{dur}) and the sensitivity parameter c were adjusted using a simulated annealing algorithm (Masters, 1995) to maximize percent correct vowel identification.

Overall percent correct achieved by the best-fitting model was 80%. The model parameters are shown in Table I. The values of the attention weights indicate that each of the five dimensions was important for this exemplar-based vowel classification task.[5] This level of vowel identification accuracy is comparable to human listeners' ability to identify vowels synthesized from midpoint formant values (Lehiste & Meltzer, 1973; Ryalls & Lieberman, 1982).

The vowel confusion matrix produced by the model is shown in Table II. This matrix is significantly correlated ($r = 0.988$), with the confusion matrix reported by Peterson and Barney (1952) for listeners' identifications of naturally

[5] One caution about interpreting these weights. They scale differences in Hz (or ms in the case of vowel duration) and variance on the dimensions is correlated with the mean. So, although the weights for F0 and F1 are the same, the contribution of F1 to vowel identification is larger because the variance of F1 is larger.

TABLE II Vowel Confusion Matrix Produced by an Exemplar Model of Vowel Perception[a]

	Response										
	aid	**awed**	**had**	**head**	**heed**	**hid**	**hood**	**hud**	**odd**	**owed**	**who'd**
aid	**85.34**	.52	.00	.00	10.99	2.09	.52	.00	.00	.52	.00
awed	.52	**68.06**	.52	.00	.00	.00	.00	1.57	22.51	6.81	.00
had	.00	1.06	**84.66**	9.52	.00	.00	.53	1.06	1.06	.53	1.59
head	.53	.00	3.68	**83.16**	.00	7.89	2.11	1.58	.53	.53	.00
heed	11.52	.00	.00	.00	**85.86**	.00	1.05	.00	.00	.00	1.5
hid	4.40	.00	.55	6.59	2.75	**84.07**	.55	.00	.00	.55	.55
hood	.00	.00	.00	.00	.53	.00	**78.42**	8.42	.53	10.00	2.11
hud	.53	2.14	4.28	2.67	.53	.53	11.76	**74.87**	.53	1.60	.53
odd	.00	25.93	1.59	.53	.00	.00	.53	1.59	**68.25**	1.59	.00
owed	.00	5.79	.00	.00	.00	.00	9.47	1.05	.00	**78.95**	4.74
who'd	.52	.00	.00	.00	.52	1.56	5.21	1.04	.00	3.13	**88.02**

[a]The speaker's intended vowel is listed down the left column and the model's identification response is listed in the first row. Percent correct identifications averaged across speakers are printed in boldface and confusions are indicated in the off-diagonals.

produced vowels (in a list comparable to the one used in this study), and the confusions—that is, the matrix without the diagonal—are also significantly correlated ($r = 0.716$) with the confusions in Peterson and Barney's study. This indicates that the acoustic measures used in this study are adequate for further model studies of vowel perception (i.e., without the elaborations mentioned in section 8.3). In addition, these results show that it is possible, using an exemplar model, to simulate human vowel perception without normalization.

8.4.3 Sex Identification

In a simulation that was analogous to the one just reported, the model was tuned to maximize correct sex identification. By giving greatest attention to F0 (the best-fitting parameters are shown in Table I), the model was able to achieve 99.8% correct sex identification for these tokens. But even with the model parameters that resulted in the best vowel identification (previous section) the sex of the speaker was correctly identified 96% of the time.

8.4.4 Twiddling Some Knobs

Formant values for the *hood–hud* continua that were used in Johnson (1990b) are shown in Table III. The vowel portions of those stimuli were 190-ms long and two continua were synthesized, one with F0 at 120 Hz and one with F0 at 240 Hz.

TABLE III Formant Values of the *Hood–Hud* Continuum Used in Johnson (1990b) and the Simulations Reported in this Chapter

Token #	1	2	3	4	5	6	7
F1	474	491	509	526	543	561	578
F2	1111	1124	1137	1150	1163	1176	1189
F3	2416	2424	2432	2440	2448	2456	2464

The vowel identification model described in section 8.4.2 (the set of model parameters that gave the best vowel identification) was used to identify these tokens in a forced-choice experiment. As mentioned earlier, I assumed that in a forced-choice experiment only exemplars of the permitted categories are used to evaluate the stimuli. The results from an open-class version of this simulation were comparable to the results reported here, but some of the stimuli in the middle of the high F0 continuum were identified as "owed."

In order to compare the results of this simulation with listeners' identification performance, I calculated the probability of a *hood* response for each token using Luce's (1963) choice rule—the probability of a *hood* response is equal to the similarity of the token to the *hood* category divided by the sum of the similarities of the token to the *hood* and the *hud* categories, where "similarity" is defined by formula (2) above.

Figure 4 shows probability of a *hood* response as a function of token number for both the high F0 and low F0 continua. These results show a clear speaker normalization effect. That is, as has been found with human listeners (Johnson, 1990b; R. L. Miller, 1953), tokens with high F0 were more likely to be identified as *hood.* Later paragraphs will discuss some ways that the exemplar model's parameters can be adjusted to quantitatively simulate listener performance. For now I want to emphasize the fact that the results shown in Figure 4 show that an exemplar model optimized for correct vowel identification over a corpus of naturally produced vowels shows a speaker normalization effect without any adjustment of the model parameters.

In section 8.2.2 I discussed the possibility that base activation levels of exemplars (N_j in formula 2) might be sensitive to word frequency, giving rise to the Ganong (1980) effect. Figure 5 shows a simulated Ganong effect produced by manipulating base activation level (Figure 5 shows results for the low F0 continuum; results for the high F0 continuum were comparable). As before, probability of a *hood* response to tokens from the *hood–hud* continuum were calculated using Luce's choice rule. In one simulation *hood* was treated as a more frequent word than *hud* by setting N_{hood} to 0.6 and N_{hud} to 0.4 (where N_{hood} indicates the N_j values associated with all of the exemplars of *hood*). Results of this simulation, using the vowel-identification model parameters and forced-choice identification, are labeled "greater *hood* base activation" in Figure 5. In a second simulation, *hud* was

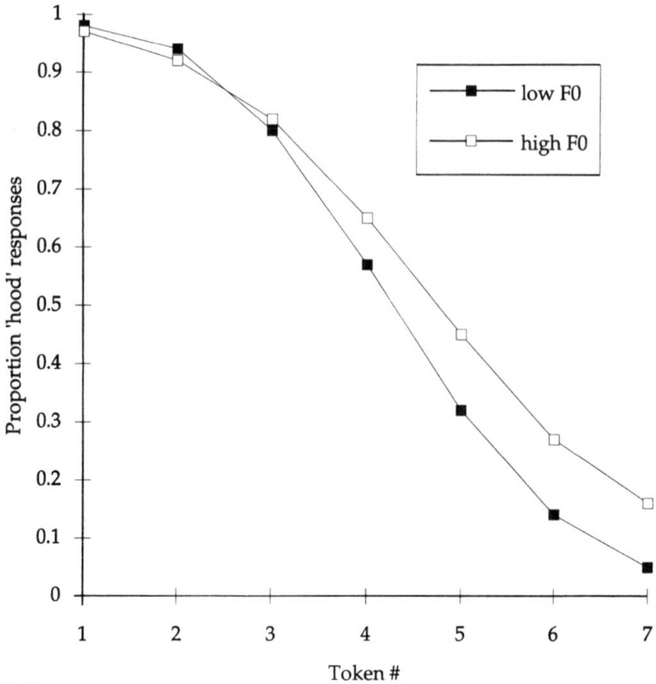

FIGURE 4 A simulated speaker normalization effect. The response is of a vowel identification exemplar model to a continuum ranging from *hood* to *hud*. One version of the continuum has an F0 value of 120 Hz (filled symbols) and another version has an F0 value of 240 Hz (open symbols).

treated as the more frequent word by reversing the N_j values. Results of this simulation are labeled "greater *hud* base activation" in Figure 5.

The boundary shift seen in this simulation is comparable to the boundary shift found by Ganong (1980) when word frequencies of the response alternatives were manipulated. He found a tendency for high-frequency words to be perceived more often (requiring less convincing acoustic cues) than low-frequency words. Similarly, in the exemplar model, when base activation of the exemplars of a category is high a stimulus is more likely to be categorized as belonging to that category than it would have been otherwise.

As mentioned above, the effect of syntactic and semantic expectations on speech perception can also be modeled by manipulating base activation. I could have said that Figure 5 shows a simulation of the perception of the *hood–hud* continuum in two semantic contexts, one that leads to the expectation that the word will be *hood* and one that leads to the expectation that the word will be *hud.* In this interpretation the N_j values reflect semantic priming rather than word frequency.

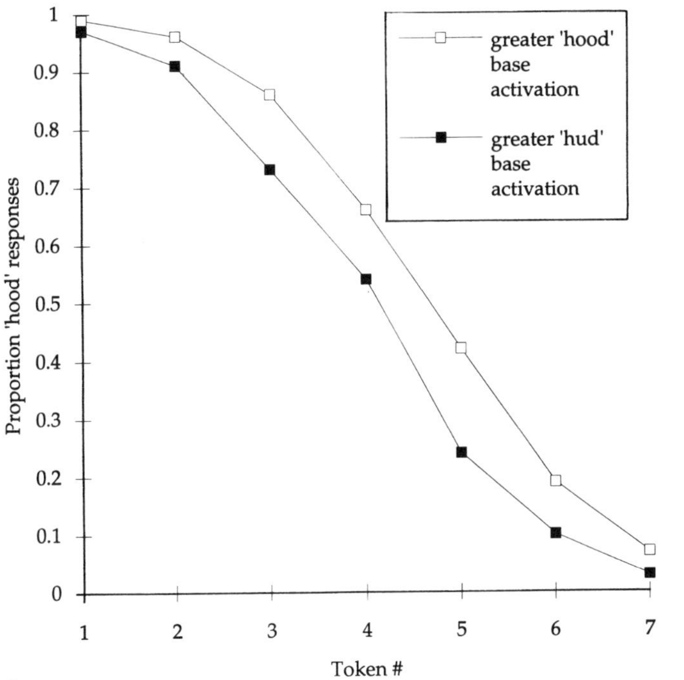

FIGURE 5 A simulated Ganong effect. The figure shows the response of a vowel identification exemplar model to a continuum ranging from *hood* to *hud* (low-F0 stimuli only). When the base activation levels of all *hood* exemplars were elevated there were more "hood" responses (open symbols), and when the base activation levels of all *hud* exemplars were elevated there were more "hud" responses (filled symbols).

8.4.5 Simulating the "Presentation Type" Effect

In Johnson (1990b) I reported that a speaker normalization effect (for the *hood–hud* continuum that we have been discussing) occurs when the stimuli are randomly intermixed, but disappears when the stimuli are blocked by F0. Analogous effects have been found in vowel identification (see Nearey, 1989, Tables 1 & 2) and auditory word recognition (Mullennix, et al., 1989). These studies have found that perceptual accuracy is reduced when words produced by different speakers are randomly intermixed, as compared to perception of the same stimuli blocked by speaker.

Nusbaum and Morin (1992) presented data suggesting that mixed-speaker presentation causes listeners to shift their attention to acoustic properties that are relevant for speaker identification (F0 and higher formants in their experiment). It makes sense to assume that listeners will tend to focus their attention to stimulus dimensions that vary from trial to trial, and thus that in a mixed-speaker presentation listeners will attend more to F0 than they do when stimuli are blocked by speaker. This predicts that in simulating the results of Johnson (1990b), the attention weight for F0 will be larger in the mixed condition than in the blocked condition.

Figure 6 shows the perceptual data from Johnson (1990b) plotted with light lines, and the results of an exemplar model simulation of the experiment plotted with dark lines. Figure 6A shows the blocked-speaker condition, and Figure 6B shows the mixed-speaker condition. Responses to stimuli with high F0 (240 Hz) are plotted with open squares and responses to stimuli with low F0 (120 Hz) are plotted with filled squares. The separation of the response functions for low and high F0 tokens in the mixed condition is similar to the "speaker normalization effect" simulated in section 8.4.4 (see Figure 4). However, the magnitude of the separation is much larger in the listeners' performance.[6]

To simulate this experiment the simulated annealing procedure was used to find model parameters that gave the best fit to the actual data in the blocked condition (assuming that the N_j for *hood* and *hud* exemplars were 1 and those for all other vowel categories were 0, and using Luce's choice rule as before). Then model parameters that provided the best fit to the actual data in the mixed condition were found. The model parameters and root mean square (RMS) error are shown in Table I.

The fits to the data are quite good; the predicted identification results are different from the actual data by only about 5% for each token on average. Also, as predicted by Nusbaum and Morin (1992), the attention weight for F0 was larger in the mixed condition than in the blocked condition. Note that the model parameters that gave the best fit in the blocked condition are very similar to the parameters that were found in the vowel identification task, and that the model parameters that gave the best fit in the mixed condition were similar to the parameters found to provide maximally accurate sex identification. This finding is consistent with the hypothesis that listeners focus their attention on the changing identity of the speaker in the mixed condition. Interestingly, this pattern of attention allocation may also be detrimental for vowel identification.

I tested this speculation by running the vowel identification simulation that was described in section 8.4.2, with the model parameters found in this simulation for the mixed F0 condition. Vowel identification accuracy was reduced from 80% (the best the exemplar model could do) to 72%. This result (as well as the experimental findings reported by Nusbaum & Morin, 1992) suggests that the talker variability effect found by Mullennix et al. may have been caused by a tendency for listeners' attention in the mixed condition to be drawn to acoustic properties that are more relevant for speaker identification than for word recognition.

[6] The lack of boundary shift in blocked condition may have resulted from the fact that the synthetic stimuli were more similar to male exemplars, or may have been the result of a Parducci (1975)-style response bias.

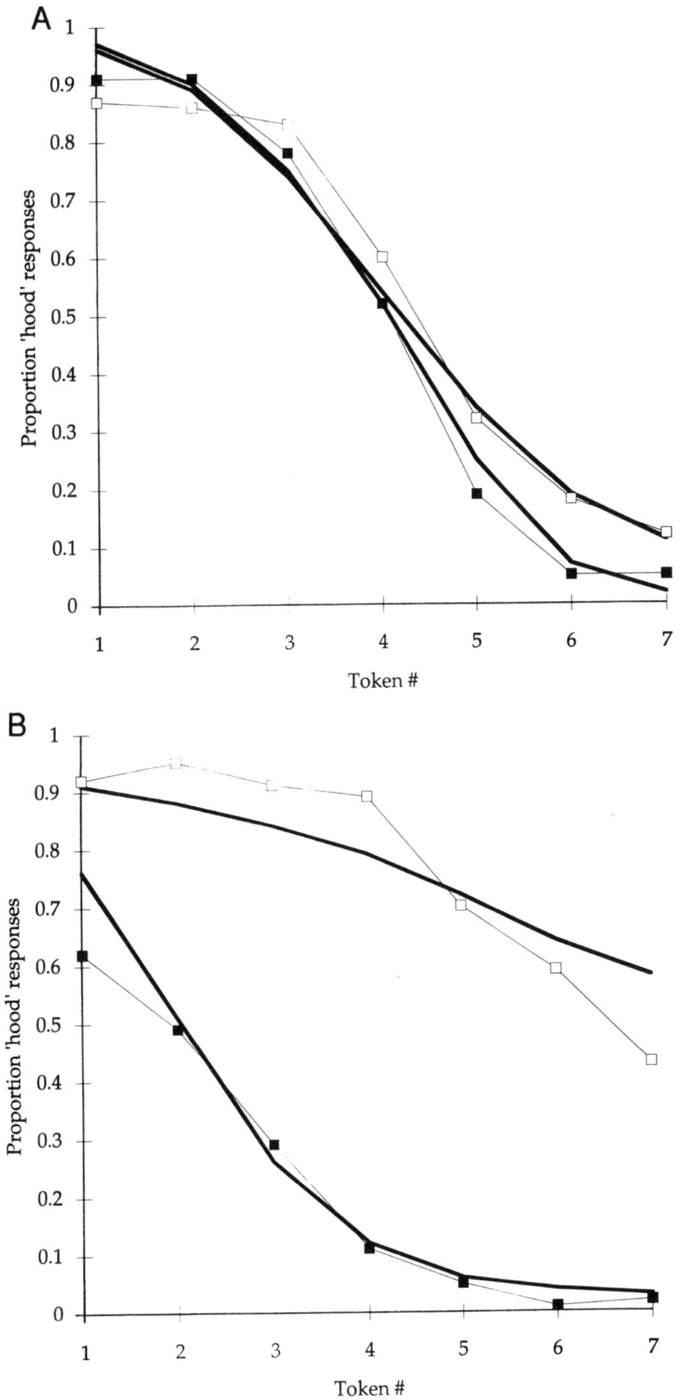

FIGURE 6 Model fits to the Johnson (1990b) presentation-type experiment. The actual data are shown with light lines and symbols (open for high F0 tokens, and filled for low F0 tokens). Model fits are shown with darker lines. (A) the data and model fits for the blocked condition; (B) the data and model fits for the mixed condition.

8.5 CONCLUSION

In this chapter I have outlined an exemplar-based model of speech perception, indicated some ways that the basic model can be elaborated, and presented results of several simulations showing that this model of speech perception mimics some aspects of human vowel perception performance and response to talker variability.

The picture of vowel normalization that emerges from this study is radically different from the traditional view. In this approach, speaker normalization behavior (both the ability to recognize vowels produced by different speakers and the presence of a boundary shift in the *hood–hud* continuum) is not caused by a representation changing process. Instead, these patterns of behavior emerge from the complex internal structure of linguistic categories. Because the model retains the variability encountered in speech it is able to cope with the variability that it encounters in new tokens. That is, the model *uses* talker variability in speech processing.

The title of this chapter, "Speech perception without speaker normalization" implies that I view speech perception as a passive process (see Nusbaum & Magnuson, Chap. 6, this volume). This is not the case. I have explicitly assumed that listeners may selectively shift their attention to different acoustic aspects of the speech signal, may cyclically focus attention on the signal, and may use top-down information to increase sensitivity to selected perceptual categories. All of these sources of flexibility in listener's behavior involve active response to the listening situation. However, I do not include among the active processes of speech perception representation-changing normalization routines of any sort. The model outlined here is an active, flexible model of speech perception without speaker normalization.

I have focused on one particular source of variability in the speech signal—acoustic differences between talkers. Here I would like to point out that I expect that the elaborated model outlined in section 8.3 will also be able to handle other sources of variability as well. For example, the model would compensate for dialect variation by using the dialect variability inherent in remembered exemplars. Some effects of dialect familiarity, for instance, would emerge naturally from this model without having to suppose that a dialect "normalization" rule is learned. Variation in the speech signal caused by changes in speaking rate would be handled in the same way (including vowel reduction and even resyllabification and extensive gestural reorganization). So, although I have focused on talker variability in this chapter, I am aiming for a general model that uses the same mechanism to handle many different sources of variability in the speech signal.

Although much remains to be specified, an exemplar-based approach offers an important alternative to the traditional view of speech perception. Future research needs to be devoted to fleshing out the elaborated model, and exploring control mechanisms that might be used to manage the flexibility of an exemplar model.

ACKNOWLEDGMENTS

This research was supported by the National Institute on Deafness and Other Communication Disorders under Grant No. 7 R29 DC01645-04. Elizabeth Strand recorded the speech database, and David Pimental made the acoustic measurements. Discussions with Rob Fox, Neal Johnson, John Mullennix, and the members of the Ohio State University Linguistics Lab were helpful as I worked on this chapter.

REFERENCES

Bladon, R. A. W., Henton, C. G., & Pickering, J. B. (1984). Towards an auditory theory of speaker normalization. *Language and Communication, 4,* 59–69.

Crowder, R. (1981). The role of auditory memory in speech perception and discrimination. In T. Meyers, J. Laver, & J. Anderson (Eds.), *The cognitive representation of speech* (pp. 167–179). New York: North-Holland.

Cutler, A., & Norris, D. (1988). The role of strong syllables in segmentation for lexical access. *Journal of Experimental Psychology: Human Perception and Performance, 14,* 113–121.

Estes, W. K. (1993). Concepts, categories, and psychological science. *Psychological Science, 4,* 143–153.

Fant, G. (1960). *Acoustic theory of speech production.* The Hague: Mouton.

Fowler, C. A. (1986). An event approach to the study of speech perception from a direct-realist perspective. *Journal of Phonetics, 14,* 3–28.

Fowler, C. A. (1990). Calling a mirage a mirage: Direct perception of speech produced without a tongue. *Journal of Phonetics, 18,* 529–541.

Fox, R. A. (1981). *Perceptual structure of English monophthongs and diphthongs.* Paper presented at the 17th regional meeting of the Chicago Linguistic Society, Chicago.

Fox, R. A. (1985). Auditory contrast and speaker quality variation in vowel perception. *Journal of the Acoustical Society of America, 77,* 1552–1559.

Ganong, W. F. (1980). Phonetic categorization in auditory word perception. *Journal of Experimental Psychology: Human Perception and Performance, 6,* 110–125.

Gerstman, L. (1968). Classification of self-normalized vowels. *IEEE, AU-16,* 78–80.

Goldinger, S. D. (1992). *Words and voices: Implicit and explicit memory for spoken words. Research on speech perception* (Tech. Rep. No. 7). Bloomington: Indiana University Speech Research Laboratory, Department of Psychology.

Hintzman, D. L. (1986). "Schema abstraction" in a multiple-trace memory model. *Psychological Review, 93,* 411–428.

Johnson, K. (1990a). The role of perceived speaker identity in F0 normalization of vowels. *Journal of the Acoustical Society of America, 88,* 642–654.

Johnson, K. (1990b). Contrast and normalization in vowel perception. *Journal of Phonetics, 18,* 229–254.

Johnson, K. (1991). Differential effects of speaker and vowel variability on fricative perception. *Language and Speech, 34,* 265–279.

Johnson, K., Ladefoged, P., & Lindau, M. (1993). Individual differences in vowel production. *Journal of the Acoustical Society of America, 94,* 701–714.

Joos, M. (1948). Acoustic phonetics. *Language, 24,* (Suppl. 2), 1–136.

Kruschke, J. K. (1992). ALCOVE: An exemplar-based connectionist model of category learning. *Psychological Review, 99,* 22–44.

Kuhl, P. K. (1991). Human adults and human infants show a "perceptual magnet effect' for the prototypes of speech categories, monkeys do not. *Perception & Psychophysics, 50,* 93–107.

Lehiste, I., & Meltzer, D. (1973). Vowel and speaker identification in natural and synthetic speech. *Language and Speech, 16,* 356–364.

Liberman, A. M., & Mattingly, I. G. (1985). The motor theory of speech perception revised. *Cognition, 21,* 1–36.

Linde, Y., Buzo, A., & Gray, R. M. (1980). An algorithm for vector quantizer design. *IEEE Transactions on Communication, COM-28,* 84–95.

Luce, R. D. (1963). Detection and recognition. In R. D. Luce, R. R. Bush, & E. Galanter (Eds.), *Handbook of mathematical psychology* (pp. 103–189). New York: Wiley.

Masters, T. (1995). *Advanced algorithms for neural networks: A C++ sourcebook.* New York: Wiley.

McGurk, H., & McDonald, J. (1976). Hearing lips and seeing voices. *Nature (London), 264,* 746–748.

McQueen, J. M. (1991). The influence of the lexicon on phonetic categorization: Stimulus quality and word-final ambiguity. *Journal of Experimental Psychology: Human Perception and Performance, 17,* 433–443.

Miller, J. D. (1989). Auditory-perceptual interpretation of the vowel. *Journal of the Acoustical Society of America, 85,* 2114–2134.

Miller, R. L. (1953). Auditory tests with synthetic vowels. *Journal of the Acoustical Society of America, 25,* 114–121.

Mullennix, J. M., Pisoni, D. B., & Martin, C. S. (1989). Some effects of talker variability on spoken word recognition. *Journal of the Acoustical Society of America, 85,* 365–378.

Nearey, T. M. (1978). *Phonetic feature systems for vowels.* Bloomington, IN: IU Linguistics Club.

Nearey, T. M. (1989). Static, dynamic, and relational properties in vowel perception. *Journal of the Acoustical Society of America, 85,* 2088–2113.

Norris, D. (1994). Shortlist: A connectionist model of continuous speech recognition. *Cognition, 52,* 189–234.

Nosofsky, R. M. (1986). Attention, similarity, and the identification-categorization relationship. *Journal of Experimental Psychology: General, 115,* 39–57.

Nosofsky, R. M. (1988). Exemplar-based accounts of relations between classification, recognition, and typicality. *Journal of Experimental Psychology: Learning, Memory, and Cognition, 14,* 700–708.

Nosofsky, R. M. (1991). Tests of an exemplar model for relating perceptual classification and recognition memory. *Journal of Experimental Psychology: Human Perception and Performance, 17,* 3–27.

Nosofsky, R. M., Kruschke, J. K., & McKinley, S. C. (1992). Combining exemplar-based category representations and connectionist learning rules. *Journal of Experimental Psychology: Learning, Memory, and Cognition, 18,* 211–233.

Nusbaum, H. C., & Morin, T. M. (1992). Paying attention to differences among talkers. In Y. Tohkura, E. Vatikiotis-Bateson, & Y. Sagisaka (Eds.), *Speech perception, production, and linguistic structure* (pp. 113–134). Tokyo: Ohmsha Publishing.

Palmeri, T. J., Goldinger, S. D., & Pisoni, D. B. (1993). Episodic encoding of voice attributes and recognition memory for spoken words. *Journal of Experimental Psychology: Learning, Memory, and Cognition, 19,* 1–20.

Parducci, A. (1975). Contextual effects: A range-frequency analysis. In E. C. Carterette & M. P. Friedman (Eds.), *Handbook of perception* (Vol. 2). New York: Academic Press.

Perkell, J. S., & Klatt, D. H. (Eds.) (1986). *Invariance and Variability in Speech Processes.* Hillsdale, NJ: Lawrence Erlbaum Associates.

Peterson, G. E., & Barney, H. L. (1952). Control methods used in a study of the identification of vowels. *Journal of the Acoustical Society of America, 24,* 175–184.

Potter, R., & Steinberg, J. (1950). Toward the specification of speech. *Journal of the Acoustical Society of America, 22,* 807–820.

Remez, R. E., Fellowes, J. M., & Rubin, P. E. (1995, September). *Talker identification is based on phonetic information* (Tech. Rep.). New York: Barnard College, Speech Perception Laboratory.

Ryalls, J., & Lieberman, P. (1982). Fundamental frequency and vowel perception. *Journal of the Acoustical Society of America, 72,* 1631–1634.

Schacter, D. L., & Church, B. A. (in press). Auditory priming: Implicit and explicit memory for words and voices. *Journal of Experimental Psychology: Learning, Memory, and Cognition.*

Shepard, R. N. (1972). Psychological representation of speech sounds. In E. E. David, & P. B. Denes (Eds.), *Human communication: A unified view.* New York: McGraw-Hill.

Singh, S., & Woods, G. (1970). Perceptual structure of 12 American vowels. *Journal of the Acoustical Society of America, 49,* 1861–1866.

Standing, L., Conezio, J., & Haber, R. N. (1970). Perception and memory for pictures: Single-trial learning of 2560 visual stimuli. *Psychonomic Science, 19,* 73–74.

Strange, W. (1989). Dynamic specification of coarticulated vowels spoken in sentence context. *Journal of the Acoustical Society of America, 85,* 2135–2153.

Strange, W., Jenkins, J. J., & Johnson, T. L. (1983). Dynamic specification of coarticulated vowels. *Journal of the Acoustical Society of America, 74,* 695–705.

Syrdal, A., & Gopal, H. (1986). A perceptual model of vowel recognition based on the auditory representation of American English vowels. *Journal of the Acoustical Society of America, 79,* 1086–1100.

Terbeek, D. (1977). A cross-language multidimensional scaling study of vowel perception. *UCLA Working Papers in Phonetics, 37,* 1–271.

Traunmüller, H. (1981). Perceptual dimension of openness in vowels. *Journal of the Acoustical Society of America, 69,* 1465–1475.

9

Speaker Modeling for Speaker Adaptation in Automatic Speech Recognition

NIKKO STRÖM

9.1 INTRODUCTION

The role of speaker adaptation in the speech perception process is still not completely understood. The phenomenon that first led researchers to investigate adaptation processes is the apparent overlap in the spectral representation of vowel sounds from different speakers (i.e., the same vowel sound is sometimes categorized differently by the listener when spoken by different speakers). Joos (1948) proposed that listeners utilize relational cues between vowels from the same speaker, and Ladefoged and Broadbent (1957) supported his theory by their famous experiment with controlled synthetic speech. They found that altering the formant frequencies in a precursor utterance resulted in different perceived identity of the target word. To account for the effect they postulated a psychological adaptation process and concluded that "unknown vowels are identified in terms of the way in which their acoustic structure fits into the pattern of sounds that the listener has been able to observe" (p. 2085). Although this view has been very influential in the vowel perception research, it has been challenged by researchers who argue that the effect is of minor importance in the perception of natural speech. In particular, the dynamic patterns of vowels in their consonantal context have been ascribed more importance (Strange, 1989; Verbrugge & Strange, 1976). Strange (1989) wrote,

Talker Variability in Speech Processing

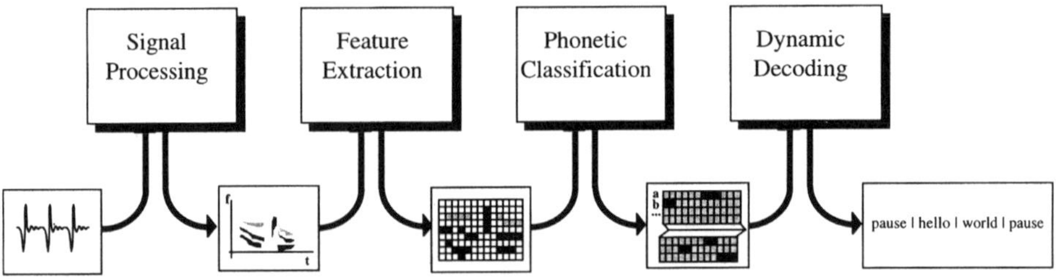

FIGURE 1 Schematic overview of automatic speech recognition. The processing is structured in blocks. A block takes one input stream and transforms it to an output stream. Blocks are organized in a linear chain, where each block produces an output stream with a representation closer to the final symbolic representation. The signal-processing block takes the speech signal and transforms it to the frequency domain. The feature-extraction block transforms further to a more compact representation of the spectra. The next block, the phonetic classification, is a pattern-matching device that classifies short-time spectra phonetically. Finally, the dynamic decoding block assembles the information from the phonetic classification and the lexical and grammatical constraints to find the most likely sequence of words for the utterance.

> If, as perceptual results suggest, there is sufficient information within single syllables to allow the listener to identify intended vowels, even when those vowels are coarticulated by different speakers in different consonantal contexts, then the need to postulate psychological processes by which the perceiver enriches otherwise ambiguous sensory input is eliminated. (p. 2085)

In the applied field of automatic speech recognition (ASR), the theoretical possibility that other sources of knowledge can make adaptation schemes redundant has received less attention than in the speech perception field. Certainly, the variation due to consonantal context is recognized as an important property of the speech signal. This variation is usually modeled by introducing context-dependent models (i.e., different models for the same phoneme in different phonetic contexts). Nevertheless, there is general agreement that speaker-adaptation schemes can further improve recognition performance significantly. The performance gap between speaker-independent (SI) and speaker-dependent (SD) systems provides strong support for this view (Huang & Lee, 1991).

In the next section, some of the main concepts of ASR are introduced very briefly, and in section 9.3 I continue by reviewing work done in speaker adaptation. Finally, in sections 9.4 and 9.5 I discuss the evolving general method of speaker adaptation based on an explicit model of the systematic variation among speakers.

9.2 AUTOMATIC SPEECH RECOGNITION

Obviously, it is impossible to cover the area of ASR in any detail in this chapter. I will only try to give enough background of the subject to be able to discuss speaker adaptation in its context. Therefore, the balancing of the amount of detail given for different aspects of ASR is biased towards areas most relevant for speaker adaptation. Readers interested in a more elaborate and general discussion of ASR are referred to a textbook on the subject, for example, K. F. Lee (1989), Huang, Ariki, and Jack (1990), Rabiner and Juang (1993) or Waibel and Lee (1990), and readers familiar with the terminology and main concepts of ASR may want to skip to the next section.

Figure 1 is a schematic view of the currently predominating structure of ASR systems. The processing is structured in blocks with one stream of input and one stream of output each. The blocks are arranged in a linear chain where each block feeds its output to the next. The streams are descriptions of an utterance at different levels, and the description changes from focusing on the acoustic aspects in the earlier streams to increasing symbolic representation in the later streams. I realize that Figure 1 is a very simplified view of ASR, but it contains the main components and will serve as a framework for further discussion.

9.2.1 Signal Processing

The first block of Figure 1 has its speech perception analog in the early processing at the cochlea (Greenberg, 1988; Seneff, 1988; von Békésy, 1960). Here, the time-domain speech signal is transformed to a representation in the frequency domain. The short-time spectrum of the signal is computed using the FFT (fast Fourier transform) or LPC (linear predictive coding) (Markel & Gray, 1976; Rabiner & Schafer, 1978). The transform is repeatedly applied to short time segments of the signal with the midpoint moved a constant time for each new spectrum. The resulting sequence of spectra, called *frames,* forms the output stream with the three dimensions time, frequency, and amplitude. This stream is similar to a spectrogram, important in acoustical phonetics (Potter, Kopp, & Green, 1947), but the time resolution, determined by the frame rate, is typically lower than in a spectrogram. The time resolution should be chosen high enough to capture all relevant fluctuations in the speech signal, but as low as possible to decrease the burden on subsequent stages of the decoding. Typically, the frame rate is about 100 frames per second. Thus, it is roughly one order of magnitude higher than the phoneme rate and the same order as the glottal-pulse rate of a male speaker.

Although this partitioning into frames is the dominating method today, it should be noted that other approaches have been studied and implemented in ASR systems (Stevens, 1995; Zue, Glass, Phillips, & Seneff, 1989).

9.2.2 Feature Extraction

In the second block, the so-called feature extraction, the short-time spectra of each frame are mapped to a more compact representation by a compressing transform. The most common transforms are filterbanks and cepstrum transforms (Rabiner & Schafer, 1978). The goal of this processing is not simply to reduce the amount of redundant information in the representation of the frames, but more important to transform the information to a representation that optimizes the performance of subsequent decoding. Therefore, as the next step in the recognition chain often has a relatively weak modeling of the short-time dynamics, it is common to compute also the first and second time derivative of the transformed spectra. For each frame, a concatenated vector is formed from the transformed spectrum and its derivatives. We call the resulting vector, typically 20–50 real numbers, the *observation* of the frame. The sequence of observations is the output stream of the block.

9.2.3 Phonetic Classification

The third block in our schematic ASR system is the mapping from acoustic observations to phonetic classes. The observations from the feature-extraction module are input to a pattern-matching device that we call a *phonetic classifier.* The classifier has one output for each phonetic class, and each output is related to the probability that the frame is part of an instance of that class. The output stream from this block is a vector of classifier outputs for each frame. Thus, the segmentation of the utterance into phonetic segments in time is left to the next block.

The relation between the output of the classifier and the probability is somewhat different in different systems. In the currently most popular variation of the Hidden Markov Model (HMM), continuous-density HMMs, the output is a probability density for the observation given the phonetic class (K. F. Lee, 1989). Artificial neural networks (ANNs) estimate the probability of the phonetic class given the acoustic observation (Bourlard & Morgan, 1993; Elenius & Takacs, 1990; A. J. Robinson, 1994; Watrous, 1990). However, it is possible to convert between the two types of probabilities using Bayes's rule.

The phonetic classes of ASR systems are not always coincident with those in the phonetic literature. Phonemes are usually further divided into subclasses depending on the phonetic context and the frame's temporal position in the phoneme. We also note that the assignment of a phonetic class to each frame implies a linear model of phonology where phonetic and linguistic units correspond to nonoverlapping segments in time (for an alternative model, see Browman & Goldstein, 1989; Clements & Herz, 1991; Lieberman & Pierrehumbert, 1984).

We mentioned that the classifier can be implemented by a probability density function (pdf). Consider the most popular pdf: a mixture of multivariate Gaussian pdfs. This is a combination (mixture) of a number of instances of the well-known, bell-shaped Gaussian (or Normal) pdf. By using a mixture of many Gaussians, virtually any pdf can be well approximated, and modeling is simplified by the fact that the mathematical properties of the Gaussians are well understood. The shape of the pdf is determined by its parameters: the mixture weights, the mean vectors, and the covariance matrices. In practice, the parameters are estimated using statistical methods from the observations of large databases of recorded speech. The data used to estimate the parameters are called the *training data,* and the estimation procedure is often called *to train* the model.

The number of free parameters can be varied by, for example, varying the number of mixtures or forcing subsets of parameters to have the same value (*parameter tying*). Increasing the number of free parameters to estimate leads to higher resolution in the modeling but less robust estimates because there is less estimation data per parameter. Thus, to optimize the performance of the classifier, it is necessary not only to find the optimal values for the parameters, but also to find the optimal number of free parameters. We will see in section 9.3 that the trade-off between modeling resolution and robustness of estimates is a critical issue in speaker adaptation because it typically involves estimation based on a small sample of speech from a new speaker.

9.2.4 Dynamic Decoding

The final block implements the search for a matching string of words for the sequence of phoneme probabilities generated by the phonetic classifier. Because the number of possible utterances are virtually infinite, the design of the search algorithm is very important. Typically, the lexical constraints are modeled by a finite state automaton, and the goal of the search is to find the most probable path through the automaton. The most prominent search concept is that of dynamic programming (DP). Both dynamic time warping (DTW) (Sakoe & Chiba, 1971) and the widely used Viterbi decoding algorithm (Viterbi, 1967) are founded on the concept of DP. This last block is certainly a very important part of the ASR system, but of the four steps of the ASR process, speaker adaptation has been applied mainly to the second and third (i.e., feature extraction and phonetic classification). In the next section, I review work done in those two blocks and discuss analogies with proposed adaptation processes in speech perception.

9.3 SPEAKER ADAPTATION

9.3.1 Speaker Normalization Methods

In response to the apparent overlap in the spectrum shapes of different phonemes, researchers in the field of speech perception have shown a large interest in physiologically motivated transformations of the spectral representation of the speech. Potter and Steinberg (1950) wrote that "within limits, a certain spatial pattern of stimulation on the basilar membrane may be identified as a given sound regardless of position along the membrane," (p. 812) (i.e., if the same frequency scaling as the one of the cochlea is used, then shifting the spectrum representation of a sound along the transformed frequency axis does not change the phonetic identity of the sound). Research in the speech production area reveals a complementary systematic variation due to varying vocal tract length (Fant, 1960). The perception and production are not completely complementary because the direct effect of prolonging the vocal tract is a linear scaling of all formants, different from the scaling of the cochlea. Furthermore, the scaling of the vocal tract is not linear between males, females, and children due to different proportions and compensatory articulation (Fant, 1975), but in the frequency range important for vowel perception, the two scalings share the same gross characteristics.

These findings suggest a normalization procedure where the spectrum is shifted up or down a speaker-specific distance in Bark-units (the Bark scale is approximately the same as the frequency scaling of the cochlea; Shroeder, Atal, and Hall, 1979). In a classic study, Peterson and Barney (1952) collected a database of vowels from different speakers and measured their formants. Their original data as well as other, later databases have been used extensively by researchers to evaluate the Bark scale normalization and other similar transforms. A good survey of these efforts can be found in Miller (1989). Results of Traunmüller (1981) indicate that the perception of fundamental frequency in relation to the formants, at least to some extent, follows the same pattern.

Frequency shifts are certainly not the only systematic variation among speakers. From a speech production point of view, frequency shifts can be explained by varying vocal tract dimensions, but we also expect variation to occur due to physiological differences of the glottal source. The most studied effect of this type of variation is spectral tilt. The spectrum of voiced speech sounds falls by roughly −6 dB/octave, but the slope is different for different speakers and different speaking styles (Gauffin & Sundberg, 1989). Much of the difference can be physiologically explained by varying speed of the vocal fold closure.

In an ASR system, it seems most natural to implement adaptation to this type of variation in the feature-extraction step. The transform from the short-time spectrum to the frame observation is then made dependent on the current speaker in order to normalize observations from different speakers. Hence, this technique is usually called *speaker normalization.*

Blomberg (1989, 1990) proposed a method for explicitly normalizing for spectral slope, and general frequency shifts can be implemented by so-called frequency warping (Blomberg & Elenius, 1986; Matsumoto & Wakita, 1979). Another popular class of normalizing transforms are linear transforms with a few free parameters in both the frequency and amplitude dimension. The parameters of such transforms can be estimated by statistical methods from available adaptation data. Cox and Bridle (1989) described an elegant example of this method, originally proposed by Hunt (1981), with a linear transform composed by a "spectrum-bias" transform and a "spectrum-shift" transform, basically covering the two major sources of variation of the spectrum of voiced sounds discussed in this section.

9.3.2 Model-Tuning Methods

Although normalization methods can model a large part of the speaker variation, they are limited by the fact that they operate early in the recognition chain. For example, a speaker normalization transform cannot, in our framework, be phoneme-dependent because the feature-extraction module is phoneme independent. But to model speaker variation independent of phonemes is too large a simplification. Even if it would be possible to find a transform that, with reasonable accuracy, normalizes variation in the production of vowels regardless of the phoneme identity, it is difficult to see how the same transform could normalize for speaker variation of fricatives or nasals. Even for the vowels alone, simple transforms of the type discussed in the previous section may have difficulties to handle variation of a more complex nature, such as variation due to different dialects. This has led researchers to introduce speaker adaptation mechanisms also in the higher levels of the ASR system and in particular in the phonetic classification.

When discussing speaker adaptation in the phonetic classification step, I run into the problem that proposed adaptation methods in the phonetic classification step tend to be more or less specific to the particular classifier architecture chosen. Generally, a phonetic classifier is a function from the acoustic observation to some classification score, but in my further discussion, I will sometimes assume that it has the form of a mixture of multivariate Gaussian pdfs—the example in section 9.2.

Various methods have been proposed to tune the parameters of a speaker-independent classifier (or a classifier trained on a reference speaker) to a new speaker (see, for example, Bamberg & Mandel, 1990). Here we call these methods *model-tuning methods.* One of the most well-known and perhaps the theoretically most attractive method is the maximum a posteriori (MAP) adaptation (Brown, Lee, & Spohrer, 1983; Gauvain & Lee, 1994; Lasry & Stern, 1984; C. H. Lee, Lin, & Juang, 1990; Necioglu, Ostendorf, & Rohlicek, 1992; Zavaliagkos, Schwarz, McDonough, & Makhoul, 1995). Given an estimation method, two different estimates can be computed for each parameter (p) of the phonetic classifier: p_{SI}, an estimate based on the large speaker-independent database and p_{SD}, an estimate based on the small sample available from the new speaker. MAP solves very elegantly the problem of weighting the two estimates. The MAP estimate is on the form: $p = (1 - \alpha)\, p_{SI} + \alpha\, p_{SD}$, where α is an increasing function of the number of tokens from the new speaker. Thus, the MAP estimate changes continuously from the speaker-independent estimate to the speaker-dependent as more data are available.

ASR systems typically have a very large number of parameters. To be able to get accurate estimates for all those parameters, the concept of parameter tying is important. This is based on defining subsets of parameters that are forced to have the same value. Thus, the number of degrees of freedom of the model is reduced, and therefore the remaining parameter values can be estimated more accurately.

The optimal degree of parameter tying depends both on the training data and on the model, and can only be determined empirically. Parameter tying poses a problem for model-tuning methods because the optimal degree of tying is different depending on the amount of training data and thus different for p_{SI} and p_{SD}. Furthermore, the optimal degree of tying for p_{SD} depends on the amount of speech available from the new speaker.

Vector field smoothing (VFS) (Ohkura, Sugiyama, & Sagayama, 1992) is a proposed partial solution to the problem of parameter tying in model-tuning methods. VFS is a method where the tuning of the mean vectors of the Gaussians is smoothed over acoustically similar vectors. This is a "soft tying" that can be continuously decreased as the system collects more data from the new speaker. The apparent problem with VFS is the requirement that the vectors are acoustically similar. Important correlations certainly exist also between speech sounds that are not similar.

9.3.3 Speaker Clustering

An often used adaptation technique is *speaker clustering.* The training speech data are divided into clusters corresponding to speakers with "similar speech," and the parameters of the speech-recognition system are trained for each cluster. Adapting to a new speaker is then a process of selecting the most appropriate cluster. This simple form of speaker clustering has a problem similar to the problem of parameter tying in model-tuning methods—the optimal number of clusters depends on the amount of adaptation data available. In response to this problem, the method has been extended to allow varying numbers of clusters in a hierarchical structure (Furui, 1989). Another problem is that the fragmentation of the training data makes the parameter estimates for each cluster less accurate. Thus, there is a trade-off between the amount of data necessary to learn other aspects of the speech, such as context dependency, and the resolution of the speaker clustering. In practice, this restricts the use of speaker clustering to only a preliminary, coarse adaptation to the speaker. A common, simple speaker-clustering method is to group males and females in two different clusters (Hwang, Huang, & Alleva, 1993).

9.3.4 Recognition Results

As we have seen, there are a great variety of different methods for adapting to the speaker and they all have individual strengths and weaknesses. However, it has been shown that by combining different methods, good results can be achieved when they complement each other. Tonomura, Kosaka, and Matsunaga (1995) reported that a coarse speaker characterization by a speaker clustering method, followed by MAP adaptation and VFS, is a promising approach. Zhao (1993) also mixed speaker normalization and MAP adaptation with good results.

It is difficult to compare the performance of different speaker-adaptation algorithms. The results depend not only on the adaptation algorithm, but also on the particular database used, what part of the database is used for training, and what part is used for adaptation and testing. Results of baseline experiments are often reported for a SI and a SD system. The word error rate of the SI system is typically two or three times higher than the SD system (see, for example, Huang & Lee, 1991). Depending on the amount of adaptation data, the results of speaker-adapting systems are somewhere in the range between that of SD and SI. For many applications, the rate of improvement is as important as the performance after many calibration sentences. Therefore, the performance of an adaptation algorithm is better described by a plot of amount of calibration speech versus error rate, than by any single number. With current technology, calibration speech of a few sentences (less than 10 sec) can be used to cut the word error rate on the order of 10% (Ahadi & Woodland, 1995; Tonomura et al., 1995; Zhao, 1993). The amount of calibration speech where the speaker-adapting system cuts the error rate by half as much as the SD system is a few minutes (Huang & Lee, 1991; Leggetter & Woodland, 1994).

9.4 SPEAKER MODELING

In this section I discuss explicit models of the systematic speaker variation. I call such models *speaker models.* The important feature is that the speaker model is conceptually separated from the rest of the speech-recognition system. For example, vocal tract length and gender are probably two variables that can be of importance in a speaker model, independent of the particular ASR system. Vocal tract length and gender are examples of *speaker parameters,* parameters that describe the speaker. All speaker models have a set of speaker parameters and a *speaker space,* the domain of the speaker parameters. Thus, individual speakers have positions in the speaker space, and adapting to a speaker involves estimating this position. The speaker parameters are not necessarily physiologically related as in the previous examples. The important aspect is that they are different from the parameters of the phonetic classifier of the ASR system. For several reasons, the number of free speaker parameters should be much lower than the number of free parameters of the phonetic classifier. First, the speaker parameters must be estimated from a small sample from the new speaker and therefore robust estimates of only a few parameters are possible. The parameters of the phonetic classifier, on the other hand, are estimated using a large database of training speech data. A second argument is based on intuition: the complexity of the speech code itself is greater than the complexity of the individual variations of it. If this were not the case, the most efficient method of learning to understand a new speaker would be to acquire a completely new language, contradicting most people's intuition about speech communication.

To illuminate the speaker modeling approach further, I compare it with the methods in the previous sections. Feature normalization, model tuning, and

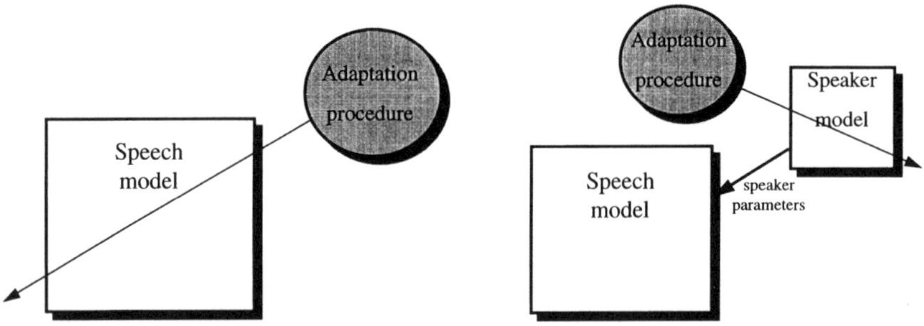

FIGURE 2 Adaptation methods. Left: Conventional adaptation scheme with a speech model and an adaptation procedure that tunes the parameters of the speech model to fit the characteristics of the current speaker. Right: The speaker-modeling approach—the speech model is conditioned by the speaker parameters and the adaptation procedure is tuning the speaker parameters of the speaker model.

speaker clustering are basically based on two components: a speech model and an algorithm to modify the speech model to fit a new speaker. A speaker-modeling method adds a model of the speaker and requires that the other modules of the system are sensitive to the speaker parameters (see Figure 2). Because the number of speaker parameters is small, robust estimation is possible. The particular influence of the speaker parameters on each of the large number of parameters of, for example, the phonetic classifier, is estimated during training using the training database.

Certainly, it is possible to identify speaker spaces and speaker parameters in other proposed methods, too. In the speaker normalization method of Cox and Bridle (1989), for example, one can identify the free parameters of the linear transformation with the speaker parameters, and in any speaker-clustering method one can define a discrete speaker space consisting of the speaker clusters. In a typical model-tuning method, the speaker space is the space of all parameters to tune. Also, algorithms have been proposed that reduce the number of free parameters of the speaker adaptation without explicitly introducing a speaker space (Ahadi & Woodland, 1995; Cox, 1995; Leggetter & Woodland, 1994). Thus, the difference between speaker-modeling methods and other methods is merely conceptual, but the explicit speaker model helps to focus on the modeling of speaker variation by decoupling it from the particular adaptation algorithm. In this way the very intuitive concept of a speaker model can help us to find efficient (low-dimensional) models of the systematic speaker variation. This is essential in the development of fast speaker-adaptation schemes for ASR.

Another possible advantage with an explicit model of the speaker is that it may provide an interface for coupling with higher levels of a human–machine interface. Consider the two possible speaker parameters, dialect and age, both known to affect the acoustic realization of speech. We know that speakers of differing dialects also have different lexical preferences (Shiel, 1993) and speak-

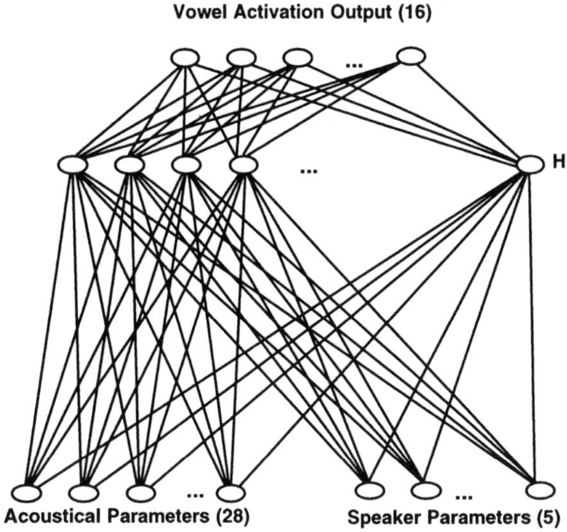

FIGURE 3 The structure of the context-independent artificial neural network in Carlson and Glass (1992a). The figures in parentheses are the numbers of units in each layer.

ers of different ages are interested in different subjects. Thus, the speaker model motivated by the acoustic speaker variation can be partially shared by modules at higher levels.

9.4.1 Speaker-Sensitive Phonetic Classifiers

In the speaker-modeling approach to speaker adaptation, the phonetic classification is conditioned by the speaker parameters. A *speaker-sensitive phonetic classifier* is a phonetic classifier that is dependent on the hypothesized speaker parameters. Thus, one can view the speaker parameters as an interface between the speaker model and the phonetic classification. An example of a speaker-sensitive phonetic classifier can be found in Carlson and Glass (1992a, 1992b) and Ström (1994, 1995), where the classifier is an ANN and the acoustic observations as well as the speaker parameters are input to the network. The activations of the output units estimates the phonetic class probabilities (see Figure 3). Cox and Bridle (1990) studied a similar model to tune the parameters introduced in Cox and Bridle (1989).

It is instructive to view the speaker parameters as the "source" of the variation. Changing a speaker parameter related to, for example, the vocal tract length, should alter the classification probabilities of all vowels. The ease of modeling such complex systematic variation, shared by different phonemes, is the strength of the explicit speaker modeling. It is a much more complicated task to include such dependencies in a model-tuning method, where the parameters of the different vowel models are tuned directly without an underlying model of the "source" of the variation. How about speaker normalization? The variation due to varying vocal tract length can be modeled by a frequency warping in the feature-extraction step, but it is not clear how to normalize for more complex types of variation due to, for example, dialect. On the other hand, a speaker model can simply be extended by a set of mutually exclusive binary speaker parameters for dialects.

Although very practical for modeling, I stress that the decoupling of the speaker model from the rest of the ASR system and in particular from the phonetic classifier is formal only. It is hardly possible to conceptualize a model of the variation without first having some framework for the description of the speech. From a pragmatic point of view, a speaker model is useful only if it models speaker variation that influences the phonetic classification. Furthermore, the resolution of the speaker model and the number of free-speaker parameters should be chosen to optimize the speech-recognition performance of the complete system. Thus, although the speaker model and the phonetic classification are formally decoupled, they cannot be considered two independent problems.

9.4.2 Knowledge-Based Speaker Spaces

So far I have exemplified the speaker parameters with vocal tract length, dialects, and so on. We call this type of speaker parameters knowledge-based, because they conform with the framework in which knowledge is represented in linguistic and speech research. Knowledge-based speaker parameters fall into three broad categories: (a) physical parameters, such as gender, age, vocal tract length, and so on (b) sociological parameters, such as dialect and sociolect, and (c) acoustic parameters, such as formant ratios, mean fundamental frequency, and spectral tilt.

Other than gender, knowledge-based parameters have not been used to any great degree in high-performing ASR systems. One reason can be that it is difficult to merge knowledge represented by the parameter estimates of the data-driven statistical models used with the high-level representation of the knowledge-based parameters. The speaker-modeling approach can change this, as it allows the influence of the speaker parameters to be trained, and therefore more complex dependencies can be implemented between the parameters and the acoustic realizations of the phonemes. Another difficulty with using knowledge-based parameters in a data-driven framework is that of labeling the data. Physical parameters of type (a) can sometimes be collected by simply asking the subject for the information. Sociological parameters (type b) could be labeled by a trained specialist, and acoustic parameters can be obtained semiautomatically by an analysis tool aided by a human expert labeler. In most cases the labor cost for accurately labeling large databases with knowledge-based parameters is high, but it may be the only way to achieve long-term improvement of the ASR technology.

Carlson and Glass (1992a, 1992b) investigated a few knowledge-based speaker parameters in a study of the TIMIT database (Zue, Seneff, & Glass, 1991).

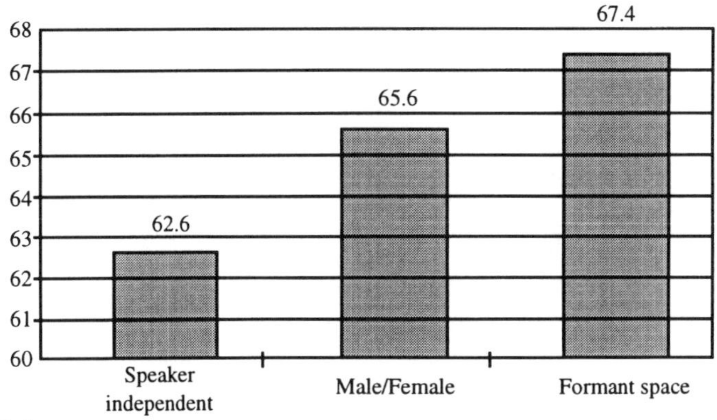

FIGURE 4 Some of the results for the context-independent case in Carlson and Glass (1992a). "Male/female" is the case of one binary speaker parameter for gender. "Formant space" is the continuous space of statistical measures of the speaker's formants described in the main text.

ANNs with different speaker parameters supplied in extra input units (Figure 3) were trained to classify vowel segments. The acoustic representation of the segments is based on the formant patterns (formant frequencies, amplitudes, and speed of frequency changes) computed automatically in an analysis-by-synthesis procedure. Figure 4 shows some of the classification results. We see that the binary parameter "gender" alone gives a substantial classification improvement. This should not be surprising, as it is well known that gender-dependent models can improve recognition performance (e.g., Hwang et al., 1993), but it shows how binary parameters can easily be incorporated in a speaker-modeling framework.

A continuous speaker space with speaker parameters related to the formant pattern representation was also investigated. Five parameters were defined as follows: mean values of the three lowest formants and standard deviation values of the first and second formant in the vowel segments. Speech production theory describes how the frequencies of the formants are related to the shape of the vocal tract (Fant, 1960), and Carlson and Glass reported that the gender information can be recovered quite reliably from the mean formant parameters. Thus, this representation is more informative than the single-gender parameter, and it accordingly gave an additional classification improvement (Figure 4).

9.4.3 Automatically Generated Speaker Spaces

In contrast to the knowledge-based speaker spaces discussed in the previous section, one can also define abstract speaker spaces, with speaker parameters with no obvious physical or linguistic interpretation. For example, the speaker spaces implicitly defined by speaker clustering and model-tuning methods are of this nature. In these frameworks, the speaker space is a product of the training of the

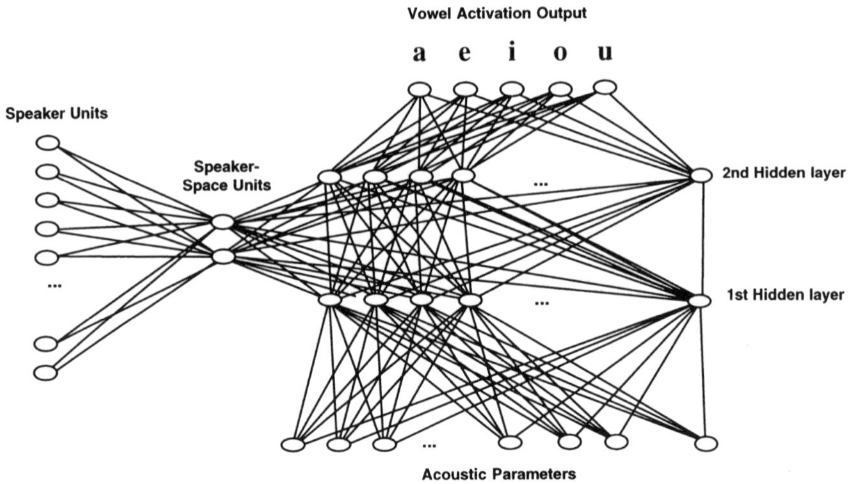

FIGURE 5 Structure of the artificial neural network used in Ström (1995). The two-speaker space units are connected to all hidden units. Therefore, complex, nonlinear speaker characteristics can be learned. See also Figure 6 and the main text for more details about the network.

ASR system. Labeling is not a big issue because the speaker space is effectively defined by the speakers of the training data. This is seen almost trivially in the case of speaker clustering, where speakers of the training data in a particular cluster define that cluster.

Most of the advantages of defining an explicit speaker space remain also for automatically generated spaces. Ström (1995) showed how to automatically generate a speaker space and a corresponding speaker-sensitive phonetic classifier in a speaker-modeling framework. Figure 5 shows the phonetic classifier of the study. The structure is similar to the ANN in the experiment of Carlson and Glass (1992a, 1992b), but the representation of the input data is different. In this experiment, a frame-based acoustic representation is used and the speaker space is two dimensional, with the speaker parameters defined by the activity of the two *speaker-space units* of the ANN. The classification task is to classify the vowel frames in read continuous Japanese speech.

A simple acoustic representation is used: FFT-based short-time spectra with a Hamming window of 25 ms, followed by a Bark-scaled, 16-channel filterbank (200–6000 Hz) is computed every 10 ms. The 16 output values from the filterbank are normalized to the range $(-1, +1)$ and copied to the input units of the ANN.

The ANN used in the study is rather complex and therefore Figure 5 is slightly simplified. To enhance the modeling of the temporal features of the vowels, a recurrent time-delay neural network (RTDNN) is used (Pearlmutter, 1990; T. Robinson & Fallside, 1991; Ström, 1992; Waibel, Hanazawa, Hinton, Shikano, & Lang, 1987). The hidden units of the first hidden layer are connected to the

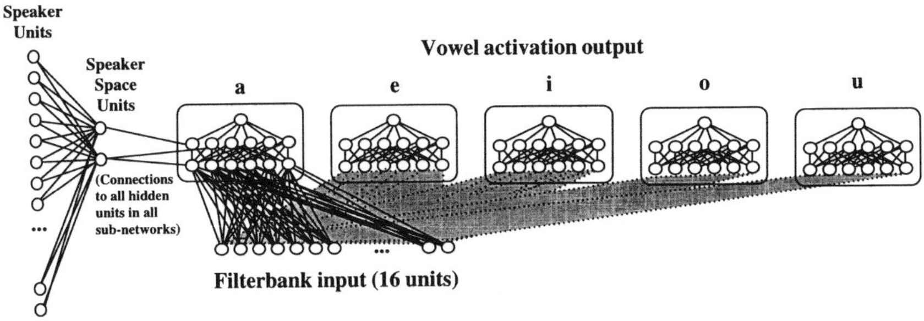

FIGURE 6 The modular structure of the network in Figure 5. A subnetwork with two hidden layers of six units each, is assigned for each of the five Japanese vowels. The filterbank acoustic representation is connected to the first hidden layer of all subnetworks. See text for details about the connections.

input units with time delays and look aheads so that they span a window of five consecutive frames. Similarly, the units of the second hidden layer span a window of three frames of the first, and the output units span a window of three frames of the second hidden layer. There are also recurrent connections: the hidden units of each layer are fully intraconnected with time delays of one and two frames. The enhanced modeling of temporal features is achieved at the cost of an increased number of connections. To reduce the number of connections, a modular architecture was chosen. Subnetworks with small hidden layers of only six units each are assigned to each of the five Japanese vowels. The structure of this modular network is shown in Figure 6.

Speaker sensitivity is introduced by connections from the two speaker-space units to all hidden units. The speaker space is defined by the connections from the special-purpose *speaker units* to the speaker-space units. There is one speaker unit for each speaker in the training data. The activity of a speaker unit is defined when the corresponding speaker is the current speaker and zero otherwise. The effect is that the activity of the two speaker-space units depends only on the two connections from the current speaker unit to the speaker-space units. This architecture has the advantage that all connections, including those from and to speaker-space units can be trained simultaneously by the back propagation through time algorithm (Pearlmutter, 1990).

Comparison with a speaker-independent RTDNN with identical structure except for the speaker-space units and the speaker units, showed that the frame-classification error rate decreased at least 25% with adaptation to short calibration speech (one sentence), indicating that the automatically generated speaker space actually models relevant speaker variation. However, frame-classification rate is not the ultimate measure of ASR performance, and no phoneme or word-recognition experiments are reported. Instead, the most interesting analysis of the speaker space of the study is the comparison with the knowledge-based F1/F2 space.

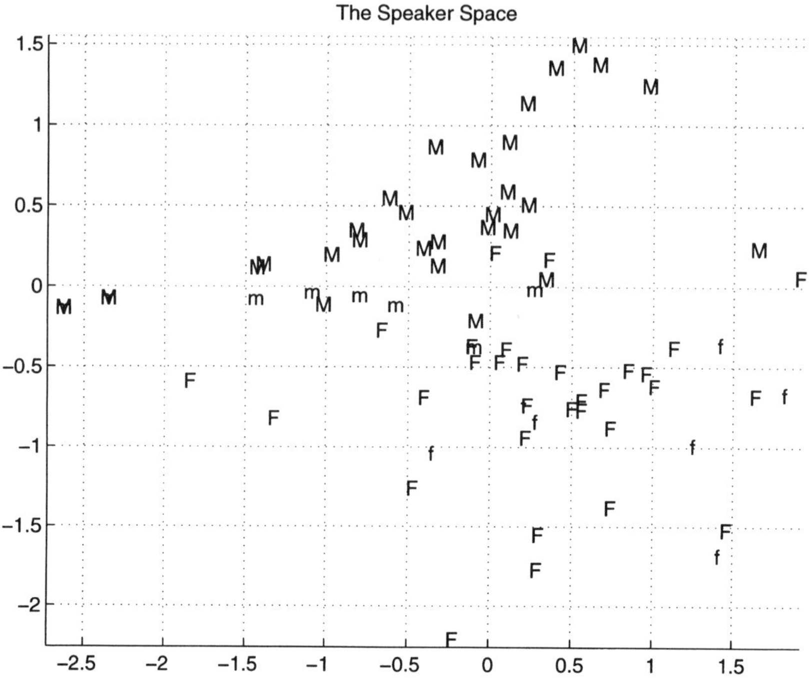

FIGURE 7 The automatically generated speaker space. Each letter in the plot represents one speaker. The x and y-axes are the connection strengths from the speaker unit to the two speaker-space units. "M" and "F" are male and female speakers respectively. (Figure originally from Advanced Telecommunications Research Institute International (ATR) technical report TR-IT-0116. Published with permission from ATR.)

The frequency of the first and second formant (F1, F2) are very strong cues to vowel identity (Fant, 1960; Peterson & Barney, 1952). With a formant synthesizer, it is easy to generate an ensemble of vowel sounds, differing only in F1 and F2, where all five Japanese vowels are represented. By feeding the speaker-sensitive RTDNN with such synthetic vowels, the decision regions in the F1/F2 space of the RTDNN can be determined. From speech perception and production research one expects the formants to be higher for female speakers as discussed in section 9.3. For that reason, I would like to compare the decision regions for males and females.

I mentioned that the activation of the speaker-space units (effectively the speaker parameters) are completely determined by the two connections from the current speaker unit. Figure 7 is a scatter plot of the strength of the connection from the speaker unit to the first speaker-space unit versus the strength of the connection to the second speaker-space unit for each speaker (i.e., Figure 7 shows the position in the speaker space for each speaker). I note that the male and female speakers are separated in the space, and to investigate further I select two points,

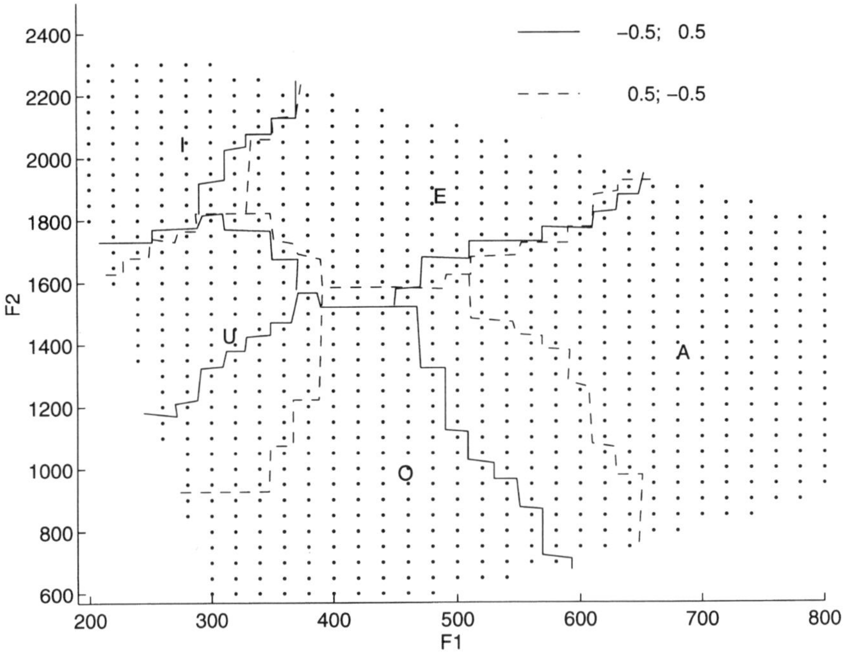

FIGURE 8 Decision regions in the F1/F2 space. Each dot represents one synthesized vowel. The synthetic vowels are input to the speaker-sensitive classifier together with one of two sets of speaker parameters. The dashed lines correspond to the decision regions of the female type parameters and the solid lines to the male type. (Figure is originally from Advanced Telecommunications Research Institute International (ATR) technical report TR-IT-0116. Published with permission from ATR.)

$(-0.5, 0.5)$ and $(0.5, -0.5)$, in the male and female regions of the speaker space, respectively.

The decision regions in the F1/F2 space are altered when the values of the speaker-space units are changed. Figure 8 shows the decision regions for the two points, and in agreement with theory, the decision boundaries corresponding to the point in the female region of the speaker space are higher both in F1 and F2. Thus, the technique with a bottleneck of a few speaker-space units compressing the speaker information automatically extracted a speaker space that shares at least some properties with the knowledge-based space.

9.5 SPEAKER ADAPTATION IN THE SPEAKER-MODELING FRAMEWORK

So far I have discussed how to model speaker variation and only touched on the subject of the adaptation procedure. This is not a coincidence—in fact, it is one of the advantages of the speaker-modeling framework that the adaptation procedure is not determined by the model of the variation. Different adaptation schemes may be the best choice in different situations. For example, the amount of adaptation speech available, text-dependent or independent adaptation speech, real-time requirements, and so on, poses different constraints on the adaptation algorithm. In contrast, the model of the speaker variation does not need to be altered for each new situation.

Intuitively, speaker adaptation is the process of estimating the speaker parameters and using the estimates to condition the phonetic classifier. Although this is the most common method, it does not make optimal use of the speaker model. I will try to show why this is the case by an analysis of the dynamic decoding block of the schematic ASR system of Figure 1.

The aim of the dynamic decoding block is to find the hypothesis, such as a word string or phoneme string, that maximizes the joint probability of the observed sequence of frames and the hypothesis, $P(hypothesis \wedge observation)$. The joint probability may look unfamiliar to readers with some experience with HMM, but applying Bayes's rule one sees that the hypothesis with the maximum probability in the HMM framework will be the same for the conditional probability used in HMMs. The details of the computation of the probability cannot be covered in this chapter, but typically it involves several approximations, the most severe of which is that the observations of frames are of independent stochastic variables. However, the given top-level description, $P(hypothesis \wedge observation)$, is enough to demonstrate the general properties of the adaptation scheme.

In the speaker-modeling framework, probabilities conditioned by the speaker parameters, $P(hypothesis \wedge observation \mid \lambda)$ are estimated, where λ is the vector of speaker parameters. Following the intuition that one should estimate the speaker parameters and use the estimate to condition the phonetic classifier, one would not take into account that the optimal speaker parameters depend on the phonetic classification. It is therefore natural to investigate the speaker-adaptation method of maximizing the probability with respect to both the hypothesis and the speaker parameters in a unified procedure. This resolves the problem that the hypothesis and the speaker parameters are mutually dependent. This technique was investigated by Cox and Bridle (1990) who termed it "simultaneous recognition and normalisation" (p. 161). Their results indicate that this is a promising method for fast unsupervised speaker adaptation, but no experiment with shorter adaptation data than three utterances is reported. The same general method was used by Ström (1994). Following up the work of Carlson and Glass reviewed in section 9.4, the same acoustic representation and the formant-based speaker space was used in an unsupervised speaker-adaptation experiment. The outcome was not completely satisfying. Some of the results are shown in Figure 9. Although the breakpoint for positive contribution of the adaptation to the recognition performance is about 10–20 adaptation vowels, which is not much, I cannot be satisfied with the behavior for shorter utterances where the adaptation degraded the performance significantly. The reason is the uncertainty in the speaker parameter

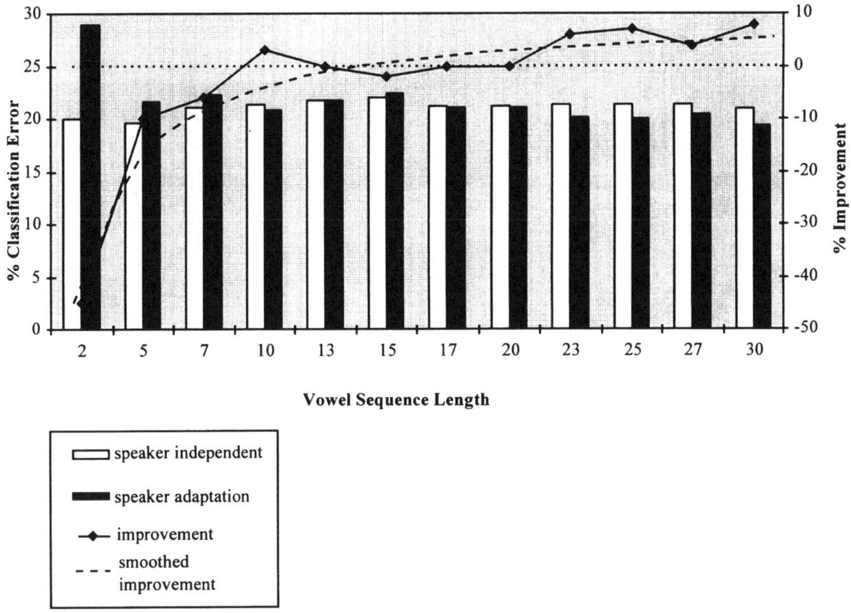

FIGURE 9 Results of the unsupervised fast speaker-adaptation experiment. A varying number of vowel tokens from the same speaker are presented to the classifier. In the speaker-adaptive mode, the classifier maximizes the probability for both the vowel classification sequence and the speaker parameters simultaneously. The speaker-independent classification is approximately constant, but the speaker-adaptive classification improves when more tokens are presented. "Improvement" in the figure is the relative change from speaker-independent to adaptive mode.

estimates. By expanding my original formula for the dynamic decoding, it is clear why the method fails when the uncertainty in the speaker parameter estimates is high.

$$P(hypothesis \wedge observation) = \int_{\Lambda} p(hypothesis \wedge observation \mid \lambda) p(\lambda) d\lambda,$$

where Λ is the speaker space.

We see that the maximization with respect to λ in the method is not equivalent to evaluating the integral for the joint probability, because it disregards the second factor of the integrand (the prior probability of the speaker parameters), and it replaces the integral by its maximum integrand. Both approximations are worse when the estimates of the speaker parameters are uncertain. Thus, to achieve better adaptation results for short utterances, the integral must be computed with other approximations. Some form of speaker clustering seems to be necessary for such a computation. This would be equivalent to a partitioning of the speaker space, and the integral could be approximated with a sum over the clusters. Some of the problems of speaker clustering discussed in section 9.3 are valid also for this type of clustering, but the important difference is that it is the speaker space that is partitioned—not the training data. Therefore, the speaker-sensitive phonetic classifier is still trained on all available data (i.e., there is no trade-off between the resolution of the clustering and the size of the training database). It is interesting that this evaluation of the integral without a maximization is not an adaptation procedure in the usual sense of a gradual tuning to the speaker. Instead, it simply represents the optimal use of the speaker model. In particular, it takes into account the trivial observation that the speaker is the same for the whole utterance. Adaptation in this framework is merely a computational matter (e.g., the granularity of the partitioning of the speaker space could be more coarse in areas that have previously had low probability).

9.6 SUMMARY AND FINAL REMARKS

Successful adaptation relies on some knowledge (implicit or explicit) of the possible variation. The speaker-modeling approach offers a framework for this knowledge. Although successful speaker-adaptation methods have been developed without explicit use of speaker modeling, there are always underlying constraints for the tuning of the models. I have argued that modeling these constraints explicitly in a speaker model is the best strategy in the search for better speaker adaptation.

In the examples of speaker modeling in ASR presented in this review, only adaptation in the phonetic classification module is investigated. However, the general framework can be applied to any part of the system; for example, in the dynamic decoding module, speaking rate could be an important speaker parameter (Siegler & Stern, 1995). In fact, speaking rate also affects the spectral characteristics of the phonemes (Lindblom, 1963) and could therefore be shared also with the phonetic classifier. Another limitation is that none of the examples are complete ASR systems. The closest is a phonetic classification of frames using a speaker-sensitive ANN. However, speaker modeling as I have described it is structurally compatible with existing systems, and I am convinced that explicit modeling of the speaker variation will be necessary for substantial further improvement of fast speaker adaptation in future ASR systems.

ACKNOWLEDGMENTS

The author wishes to acknowledge Rolf Carlson for fruitful discussions and valuable comments on this chapter.

REFERENCES

Ahadi, S. M., & Woodland, P. C. (1995). Rapid speaker adaptation using model prediction. *Proceedings ICASSP,* pp. 684–687.

Bamberg, P. G., & Mandel, M. A. (1990). Adaptation performance in a large-vocabulary recognizer. *Proceedings of the ESCA Workshop on Speaker Characterization in Speech Technology,* pp. 46–52, Edinburgh.

Blomberg, M. (1989). Voice source adaptation of synthetic phoneme spectra in speech recognition. *Proceedings EuroSpeech,* pp. 621–624.

Blomberg, M. (1990). Adaptation to a speaker's voice in a speech recognition system based on synthetic phoneme references. *Proceedings of the ESCA Workshop on Speaker Characterization in Speech Technology,* pp. 58–65, Edinburgh.

Blomberg, M., & Elenius, K. (1986). Nonlinear frequency warp for speech recognition. *Proceedings ICASSP,* pp. 2631–2634.

Bourlard, H., & Morgan, N. (1993). Continuous speech recognition by connectionist statistical methods. *IEEE Transactions on Neural Networks, 4*(6), 893–909.

Browman, C., & Goldstein, L. (1989). Articulatory gestures as phonological units. *Phonology, 6*(2), 201–251.

Brown, P. F., Lee, C.-H., & Spohrer, J. C. (1983). Bayesian adaptation in speech recognition. *Proceedings ICASSP,* pp. 761–764.

Carlson, R., & Glass, J. (1992a). *Vowel classification based on analysis-by-synthesis* (STL-QPSR 4/1992, pp. 17–27). Stockholm: Royal Institute of Technology (KTH), Department of Speech Communication and Music Acoustics.

Carlson, R., & Glass, J. (1992b). Vowel classification based on analysis-by-synthesis. *Proceedings ICSLP,* pp. 575–578.

Clements, G. N., & Herz, S. R. (1991). Nonlinear phonology and acoustic interpretation. *Proceedings ICPhS,* Vol. 1, pp. 364–373.

Cox, S. J. (1995). A speaker adaptation technique using linear regression. *Proceedings ICASSP,* pp. 451–454.

Cox, S. J., & Bridle, J. S. (1989). Unsupervised speaker adaptation by probabilistic spectrum fitting. *Proceedings ICASSP,* pp. 294–297.

Cox, S. J., & Bridle, J. S. (1990). Simultaneous speaker normalization and utterance labelling using Bayesian/neural net techniques. *Proceedings ICASSP,* pp. 161–164.

Elenius, K., & Takacs, G. (1990). *Acoustic-phonetic recognition of continuous speech by artificial neural networks* (STL-QPSR 2-3/1990, pp. 1–44). Stockholm: Royal Institute of Technology (KTH), Department of Speech Communication and Music Acoustics.

Fant, G. (1960). *Acoustic theory of speech production.* The Hague: Mouton.

Fant, G. (1975). *Non-uniform vowel normalization* (STL-QPSR 2-3/1975, pp. 1–19). Stockholm: Royal Institute of Technology (KTH), Department of Speech Communication and Music Acoustics.

Furui, S. (1989). Unsupervised speaker adaptation method based on hierarchial spectral clustering. *Proceedings ICASSP,* pp. 286–289.

Gauffin, J., & Sundberg, J. (1989). Spectral correlates of glottal voice source waveform characteristics. *Journal of Speech and Hearing Research, 32,* 556–565.

Gauvain, J. L., & Lee, C. H. (1994). Maximum a posteriori estimation for multivariate Gaussian observations of Markov chains. *IEEE Transactions on Speech and Audio Processing, 2*(2), 806–814.

Greenberg, S. (1988). Acoustic transduction in the auditory periphery. *Journal of Phonetics, 16*(1), 3–18.

Huang, X. D., Ariki, Y., & Jack, M. A. (1990). *Hidden Markov models for speech recognition.* Edinburgh: Edinburgh University Press.

Huang, X. D., & Lee, K. F. (1991). On speaker-independent, speaker-dependent and speaker-adaptive speech recognition. *Proceedings ICASSP,* pp. 877–880.

Hunt, M. J. (1981). Speaker-adaptation for word-based speech recognition systems [Abstract only]. *Journal of the Acoustical Society of America, 69,* S41–S42.

Hwang, M. Y., Huang, X., & Alleva, F. (1993). Recent progress in the SPHINX-II speech recognition system. *Proceedings of the IEEE Workshop on Automatic Speech Recognition, Snowbird, Utah,* pp. 24–25.

Joos, M. (1948). Acoustic phonetics. *Language, 24,* (Suppl. 2), 1–36.

Ladefoged, P., & Broadbent, D. E. (1957). Information conveyed by vowels. *Journal of the Acoustical Society of America, 29*(1), 99–104.

Lasry, M. J., & Stern, R. M. (1984). A posteriori estimation of correlated jointly Gaussian mean vectors. *IEEE Transactions on Pattern Analysis and Machine Intelligence, PAMI-6*(4), 530–535.

Lee, C.-H., Lin, C.-H., & Juang, B.-H. (1990). A study on speaker adaptation of continuous density HMM parameters. *Proceedings ICASSP,* pp. 145–148.

Lee, K. F. (1989). *Automatic speech recognition: The development of the SPHINX system.* Dordrecht, The Netherlands: Kluwer Academic Publishers.

Leggetter, C. J., & Woodland, P. C. (1994). Speaker adaptation of continuous density HMMs using multivariate linear regression. *Proceedings ICSLP,* pp. 451–454.

Lieberman, M., & Pierrehumbert, J. (1984). Intonational invariance under changes in pitch range and length. In M. Aronoff & R. T. Oehrle (Eds.), *Language sound structure* (pp. 157–233). Cambridge, MA: MIT Press.

Lindblom, B. (1963). Spectrographic study of vowel reduction. *Journal of the Acoustical Society of America, 35*(11), 1773–1781.

Markel, J. D., & Gray, A. H. (1976). *Linear prediction of speech.* New York: Springer-Verlag.

Matsumoto, H., & Wakita, H. (1979). Frequency warping for nonuniform talker normalization. *Proceedings ICASSP,* pp. 566–569.

Miller, J. D. (1989). Auditory-perceptual interpretation of the vowel. *Journal of the Acoustical Society of America, 85*(5), 2114–2134.

Necioglu, B. F., Ostendorf, M., & Rohlicek, J. R. (1992). A Bayesian approach to speaker adaptation for the stochastic segment model. *Proceedings ICASSP,* pp. I-437–I-440.

Ohkura, K., Sugiyama, M., & Sagayama, S. (1992). Speaker adaptation based on transfer vector field smoothing with continuous mixture density HMMs. *Proceedings ICSLP,* pp. 369–372.

Pearlmutter, B. A. (1990). *Dynamic recurrent neural networks* (Tech. Rep. CMU-CS-88-191). Pittsburgh, PA: Carnegie-Mellon University, Computer Science Department.

Peterson, G. E., & Barney, H. L. (1952). Control methods used in a study of the vowels. *Journal of the Acoustical Society of America, 24*(2), 175–184.

Potter, R. K., Kopp, A. G., & Green, H. C. (1947). *Visible speech.* New York: Van Nostrand.

Potter, R. K., & Steinberg, J. C. (1950). Toward the specification of speech. *Journal of the Acoustical Society of America, 22*(6), 807–820.

Rabiner, L. R., & Juang, B.-H. (1993). *Fundamentals of speech recognition.* Englewood Cliffs, NJ: Prentice-Hall.

Rabiner, L. R., & Schafer, R. W. (1978). *Digital processing of speech signals.* Englewood Cliffs, NJ: Prentice-Hall.

Robinson, A. J. (1994). An application of recurrent nets to phone probability estimation. *IEEE Transactions on Neural Networks, 5*(2), 298–305.

Robinson, T., & Fallside, F. (1991). A recurrent error propagation network speech recognition system. *Computer Speech and Language, 5*(3), 259–274.

Sakoe, H., & Chiba, S. (1971). A dynamic programming approach to continuous speech recognition. *Proceedings ICASSP,* Paper 20 C-13.

Schroeder, M. R., Atal, B. S., & Hall, J. L. (1979). Objective measure of certain speech signal degradations based on masking properties of the human auditory perception. In B. Lindbolm & S. Öhman (Eds.), *Frontiers of speech communication research* (pp. 217–229). New York: Academic Press.

Seneff, S. (1988). A joint synchrony/mean-rate model of auditory speech processing. *Journal of Phonetics, 16*(1), 55–76.

Shiel, F. (1993). A new approach to speaker adaptation by modelling pronounciation in automatic speech recognition. *Speech Communication, 13,* 281–286.

Siegler, M. A., & Stern, R. M. (1995). On the effects of speech rate in large vocabulary speech recognition systems. *Proceedings ICASSP,* pp. 612–615.

Stevens, K. N. (1995). Applying phonetic knowledge to lexical access. *Proceedings EuroSpeech,* pp. 3–11.

Strange, W. (1989). Evolving theories of vowel perception. *Journal of the Acoustical Society of America, 85*(5), 2081–2087.

Ström, N. (1992). *Development of a recurrent time-delay neural net speech recognition system* (STL-QPSR 2-3/1992, pp. 1–44). Stockholm: Royal Institute of Technology (KTH), Department of Speech Communication and Music Acoustics.

Ström, N. (1994). Experiments with a new algorithm for fast speaker adaptation. *Proceedings ICSLP,* pp. 459–462.

Ström, N. (1995). *A speaker sensitive artificial neural network architecture for speaker adaptation* (ATR Tech. Rep. TR-IT-0116). Kyoto, Japan: ATR.

Tonomura, M., Kosaka, T., & Matsunaga, S. (1995). Speaker adaptation based on transfer vector field smoothing using maximum a posteriori probability estimation. *Proceedings ICASSP,* pp. 688–691.

Traunmüller, H. (1981). Perceptual dimension of openness in vowels. *Journal of the Acoustical Society of America, 69*(5), 1465–1475.

Verbrugge, R. R., & Strange, W. (1976). What information enables a listener to map a talker's vowel space. *Journal of the Acoustical Society of America, 60*(1), 198–212.

Viterbi, A. J. (1967). Error bounds for convolutional codes and an asymptotically optimum decoding algorithm. *IEEE Transactions on Information Theory, IT-13,* 260–269.

von Békésy, G. (1960). *Experiments in hearing* (E. G. Wever, Ed. and Trans.). New York: McGraw-Hill.

Waibel, A., Hanazawa, T., Hinton, G., Shikano, K., & Lang, K. (1987). *Phoneme recognition using time-delay neural networks* (ATR Tech. Rep. TR-006). Kyoto, Japan: ATR.

Waibel, A., & Lee, K.-F. (1990). *Readings in speech recognition.* San Mateo, CA: Morgan Kaufmann.

Watrous, R. L. (1990). Phoneme discrimination using connectionist networks. *Journal of the Acoustical Society of America, 87*(4), 1753–1772.

Zavaliagkos, G., Schwarz, R., McDonough, J., & Makhoul, J. (1995). Adaptation algorithms for large scale HMM recognizers. *Proceedings EuroSpeech,* pp. 1131–1134.

Zhao, Y. (1993). A new speaker adaptation technique using very short calibration speech. *Proceedings ICASSP,* pp. II-562–II-565.

Zue, V., Seneff, S., & Glass, J. (1991). Speech database development: TIMIT and beyond. *Speech Communication, 9*(4), 351–356.

Zue, V., Glass, J., Phillips, M., & Seneff, S. (1989). Acoustic segmentation and phonetic classification in the SUMMIT system. *Proceedings ICASSP,* pp. 389–392.

10

Overcoming Speaker Variability in Automatic Speech Recognition

The Speaker Adaptation Approach

YUNXIN ZHAO

10.1 INTRODUCTION

Interspeaker variability is one of the most important variation sources in speech that challenge today's automatic speech recognition (ASR) technology (Cole et al., 1995). The differences among speakers lie in the anatomy of vocal tracts and vocal cords, dialects, speaking idiosyncracies, and so on, which are manifested as variations in speech signals produced by men, women, and children that come from different dialect regions or social backgrounds. Interspeaker variability also interacts with other variabilities such as allophonic contextual dependency, intraspeaker speech variation, recording environment mismatch, which together make human speech a very rich and complex signal. Although significant progress has been made in speaker-independent ASR, the technology remains rather fragile under a wide range of speaker conditions. Therefore, many research efforts are currently concentrated on developing speaker-robust techniques that overcome the variability across speakers.

This work is partially supported by the National Science Foundation, Grant No. IRI 95-02074.

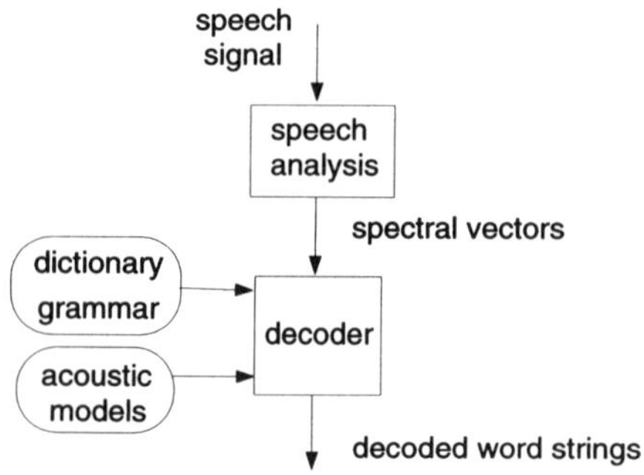

FIGURE 1 A block diagram of an automatic speech-recognition system.

Interspeaker variability is exhibited at various feature levels of speech signals: long-term (voice quality), segmental (vowels, consonants), and suprasegmental (stress, duration, intonation, etc.) (Ladefoged, 1993). Robust speaker characterization involves almost all the components of an ASR system: feature representation, acoustic modeling, lexicon representation, and even language modeling, where achieving speaker invariance remains a very challenging task. In this chapter, the focus is on an alternative approach, namely, speaker adaptation, which adapts an existing ASR system for a new speaker based on his or her speech characteristics. This chapter consists of four sections. An overview on speaker adaptation is given in section 10.2; the details of a self-learning speaker-adaptation system are provided in section 10.3, and a summary is made in section 10.4.

10.2 OVERVIEW

A block diagram of a subword unit-based ASR system is shown in Figure 1. A speech utterance is digitized into samples via an A/D sampler, from which the feature-analysis module produces a sequence of spectral (or cepstral) feature vectors. The acoustic models describe the distributions of the speech spectra for each of the subword units, often the phone units; the dictionary describes the composition of words by the subword units, and the grammar describes the syntax constraints on the composition of sentences or phrases from words. The decoding module produces a word string or multiple word strings for each utterance via a decoding algorithm that is based on certain principles of mathematical optimization.

Current speaker-adaptation techniques mainly address the adaptation on the acoustic models. Speaker-dependent acoustic models are trained from a single speaker. If such a system is used for a new speaker, speaker adaptation is necessary because the acoustic models are very specific to the training speaker. Speaker-independent acoustic models are trained from a large speaker population. However, the spectral distributions described by Gaussian densities often exhibit large variances within phone units, causing cross-unit overlaps and hence recognition errors. In general, the spectral distributions are multimodal; therefore, the Gaussian mixture densities (details are given in section 10.3) are much more accurate and are widely used for modeling speaker-independent speech (Rabiner, Juang, Levinson, & Sondhi, 1985). The acoustic models can also be refined by partitioning the training data according to speaker groups and then estimating separate models for individual groups. The partitions have been made according to the conventions of male and female voices, dialects, or via automatic clustering of speakers from the training data (Mathan & Miclet, 1990). At the recognition stage, the appropriate acoustic models are chosen based on the speaker's group identity. The trade-off is that the more refined the speaker groups are, the less training data are available for each group that could lead to unreliable models.

Because the speaker-independent or the refined models have the shortcoming of not generalizing well for significantly different speakers and not characterizing individual speakers accurately (compared to speaker-dependent models), speaker adaptation is attractive in its capacity to use speech utterances from a new speaker to reduce the mismatch between the trained models and the speaker's characteristics, which could improve the recognition accuracy to the level of speaker-dependent systems. Speaker adaptation has been indispensable in commercial ASR systems that are extensively used by single speakers. In the next section, speaker-adaptation techniques are categorized by the requirement on adaptation data and the adaptation methods.

10.2.1 Adaptation Data

Supervised and *unsupervised* adaptation differ in that supervised adaptation requires the text content of the adaptation speech be known, and unsupervised adaptation does not; given the text content, the adaptation speech can be accurately labeled into phone units using an automatic segmentation algorithm (often the Viterbi algorithm). *Off-line* and *on-line* adaptation differ in the way that the adaptation data are acquired: the off-line mode requires a new speaker to provide enrollment speech before starting a task, whereas the on-line mode takes the speaker's task speech as the adaptation data and hence does not require enrollment speech. The supervised on-line adaptation is achieved by asking users to provide feedback whenever recognition errors occur, such feedback can be naturally made in tasks such as dictation. When a speaker-dependent system is used for a new speaker, the starting recognition accuracy is often very low, and off-line adaptation is generally needed. Unsupervised on-line adaptation utilizes an automatic feedback mechanism to self-improve the ASR system for a new speaker (Paul & Necioglu, 1993; Zhao, 1993c). In order to ensure convergence for self-learning, the initial recognition accuracy of the ASR system should not be too low. The adaptation technique is suitable for tuning a speaker-independent ASR system for a new speaker.

10.2.2 Adaptation Methods

The adaptation methods are categorized as those that make assumptions on the transformation relations between the speech spectra of a new speaker and the training speakers and those that do not make such assumptions. Let x denote a speech spectrum from a new speaker and y a spectrum from the training speakers. Let Ω_x be the acoustic space of x and its models be characterized by the parameters Λ_x; similarly let Ω_y be the acoustic space of y and its models be characterized by the parameters Λ_y. In the method of *data transformation,* a function $f(.)$ is assumed that maps x to y (i.e., $f(x) \rightarrow y$). Based on a function $f(.)$, certain functions $g(.)$ can be derived that map the parameters Λ_y of the trained models to the parameters Λ_x for the new speaker's models (i.e., $g(\Lambda_y) \rightarrow \Lambda_x$). When the mapping functions $g(.)$ are used instead of $f(.)$, the adaptation methods are referred to as *model transformation.* Commonly used mapping functions are as follows:

1. Cepstral bias (Cox & Bridle, 1989; Zhao, 1993a)
   $f(x) = x + b$
2. Linear transform
   $f(x) = ax + b$
3. Piecewise-linear transform (Bellegarda et al., 1992)
   $f(x) = a_i x + b_i$, *if* $x \in \Omega_{x,i}$, $\cup\, \Omega_{x,i} = \Omega_x$, where the $\Omega_{x,i}$'s are subspaces of Ω_x (e.g., the subspaces representing phone units).
4. Neural-net-based nonlinear transform (Huang, 1992).

The parameters in the transformation functions $f(.)$ and $g(.)$ (a, b, etc.) can be estimated by the least-mean-square-error method using supervised adaptation data, or by the expectation maximization (EM) method (Dempster, Laird, & Rubin, 1977) using unsupervised adaptation data and the existing acoustic models (Cox & Bridle, 1989; Digalakis & Neumeyer, 1995). Model transformation can also handle random parameters in the mapping functions (Sankar & Lee, 1994).

In *model adaptation,* the individual parameters of the acoustic models $\lambda_y \in \Lambda_y$ are modified based on the statistics of a new speaker's speech $x \in \Omega_x$ (i.e., $\lambda_y \rightarrow \lambda_x \in \Lambda_x$). Bayesian estimation provides a well-defined statistical framework for supervised model adaptation (Gauvain & Lee, 1994). Although adaptation on model parameters can be performed on-line as more speech data come in, transformations on data or models commonly require the mapping relations be learned off-line. When the transformation relation is simple, such as the cepstral bias, the parameters can be reliably estimated from each utterance before it is recognized; as such, on-line transformation is achievable.

Model adaptation can be further distinguished into data-specific and relational methods. In a data-specific method, each model is adapted only by the data belonging to the speech unit that the model represents. Because the acoustic models used in ASR systems contain many parameters, a large amount of data is required to cover all the speech units. In relational adaptation, the interrelationship between speech units in the acoustic space is taken into account so that the adaptation data of one unit could affect the models of the related units. The hierarchical adaptation method explores the top-down relationship among the acoustic models (Furui, 1989); the predictive adaptation method explores the lateral relationship among phone units via statistical regression (Cox, 1995); the interpolation method explores the neighboring relationship among the model mean vectors (Shinoda, Iso, & Watanabe, 1991); the context-modulation method explores the relationship between the mixture components within each Gaussian mixture density (Zhao, 1994).

10.3 SELF-LEARNING SPEAKER ADAPTATION

10.3.1 Adaptation Principle

The self-learning adaptation technique is based on a decomposition of the speech spectral variation sources into two categories: one acoustic and the other phone-specific (Zhao, 1993c, 1994). The acoustic source is attributed to speakers' physical individualities and linear channel distortions that cause spectral variations independent of phone units; the phone-specific source is attributed to speakers' idiosyncrasies and piecewise linear channel distortions that cause spectral variations dependent on phone units.

The acoustic and phone-specific variation sources are modeled as two cascaded linear transformations on the spectra of a standard speaker. Considering a speaker q, let $H^{(q)}$ and $L_i^{(q)}$ be the linear transformations representing the acoustic and the ith phone-specific sources, respectively, for $i = 1,2, \cdots, K$. Let $X_{i,t}^{(q)}$ and $X_{i,t}^{(o)}$ be a pair of spectra of a phone unit i, at time t, from the speaker q and the standard speaker o. The composite mapping from the two linear transformations is

$$X_{i,t}^{(q)} = H^{(q)} L_i^{(q)} X_{i,t}^{(o)}, \ \forall i,t. \tag{1}$$

In the logarithmic spectral domain, using lower-case variables, the multiplicative mappings become additive biases, for example,

$$x_{i,t}^{(q)} = h^{(q)} + l_i^{(q)} + x_{i,t}^{(o)}, \ \forall i,t. \tag{2}$$

In the adaptation method, the acoustic bias $h^{(q)}$ is explicitly estimated, whereas the phone-specific biases $l_i^{(q)}$ are implicitly handled via the adaptation of phone model parameters. The subtraction of $h^{(q)}$ from $x_{i,t}^{(q)}$ is called the acoustic normalization, which yields the acoustically normalized spectra $\tilde{x}_{i,t}^{(q)} = x_{i,t}^{(q)} - h^{(q)}, \ \forall i,t$. For unmatched recording conditions, a linear transformation distortion D in the logarithmic domain, d, is absorbed by the bias vector $\tilde{h}^{(q)} = h^{(q)} + d$, and the higher order distortions are absorbed by the phone-specific biases $\tilde{l}_i^{(q)} = l_i^{(q)} + d_{i.}$ In the following discussions, channel-induced spectral variations are not distinguished from speaker-induced variations for notational simplicity.

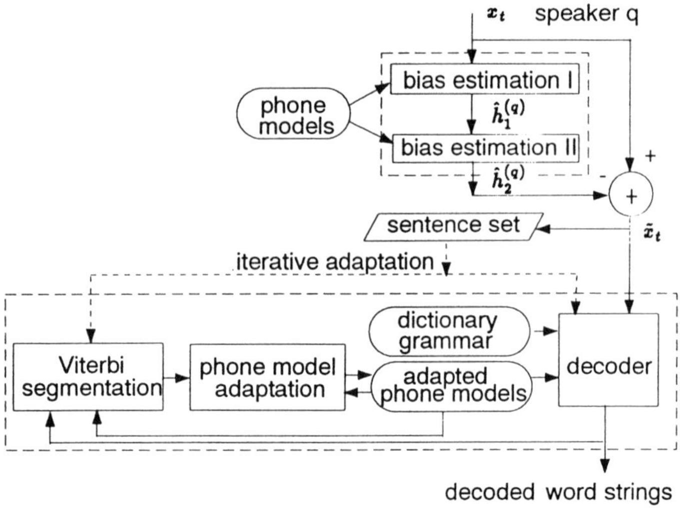

FIGURE 2 A block diagram of the self-learning speech-recognition system.

The speech-recognition system uses both instantaneous and dynamic spectral features. From Eq.(2) one can observe that the dynamic spectral features are not affected by the additive spectral bias $h^{(q)}$, due to the computation of spectral difference in the dynamic features. On the other hand, the dynamic features could be affected by the phone-specific biases $l_i^{(q)}$ at the boundaries of phone units. In the current study, the normalization and adaptation are performed only on the instantaneous spectral features and models. This separate treatment of the instantaneous and dynamic spectral models is facilitated by the block-diagonal covariance structure defined for the Gaussian densities: one block for the instantaneous features, the other for the dynamic features (Zhao, 1993b).

10.3.2 Adaptation System

A block diagram of the self-learning speech-recognition system is shown in Figure 2. Assuming the speaker q speaks one sentence at a time, the adaptation is implemented in two sequential steps for each sentence: the first step is based on data transformation, and the second step is based on model adaptation, both using the on-line unsupervised data. The first step is performed before decoding the sentence, where the spectral bias is estimated from the current sentence and the utterance spectra sequences are subsequently normalized. The second step is carried out after decoding the sentence, where the parameters of the phone models are adapted via Bayesian estimation. In the second step, the adaptation data are prepared via the Viterbi segmentation of the sentence into phone segments according to the recognized word string. The adapted phone models are then used to recognize the next sentence utterance. When delaying the decoding output is permissible, at the completion of a session, the recorded sentences are reused to iteratively adapt the phone model parameters and to recognize the sentences until the recognition results are converged.

The speaker-independent continuous speech-recognition system is based on the Hidden Markov Models (HMM) of phone units: each phone-unit HMM has three tied states; each state is modeled by a Gaussian mixture density. For each mixture density, the basis Gaussian densities are context-independent; the mixture weights are triphone context-dependent; the mixture size and the Gaussian density parameters are determined via a bottom-up merging algorithm. The phone models were trained from a subset of 717 sentences in the TIMIT database, with a total of 62 units as defined in TIMIT (excluding "h#") (Lamel, Kassel, & Seneff, 1986). The average mixture size per mixture density is approximately 19, and the total number of triphone contexts is about 4500. Further details of the background materials can be found in Zhao (1993b, 1994).

10.3.3 Adaptation Algorithm

10.3.3.1 Acoustic Normalization

Assuming the phone model parameters of a standard speaker are estimated from the speech data in a speaker-independent training set, the phone models are unimodal Gaussian densities $\mathcal{N}(\mu_i, C_i)$, $i = 1,2, \cdots, K$. For a speaker q, the spectral sequence of a sentence utterance is denoted as $x^{(q)} = (x_t^{(q)}, t = 1,\cdots, T^{(q)})$. In the context of the EM algorithm, the spectral vectors $x_t^{(q)}$ are called the observable data, and their phone labels i_t are the unobservable data. The complete data set consists of both the observable and unobservable data $(x_1^{(q)}, x_2^{(q)},\cdots, x_T^{(q)}, i_1, i_2,\cdots, i_T)$. Using uppercase variables $X^{(q)}$ and I to denote the random variables for the observable and unobservable data, respectively, the spectral bias $h^{(q)}$ is estimated through the iterative maximization of the expected value of the conditional log likelihood of the complete data. Assuming an initial value $\hat{h}_0^{(q)}$, the iterative estimation formula is

$$\begin{aligned}\hat{h}_{n+1}^{(q)} &= \arg\max_{h^{(q)}} E_{\hat{h}_n^{(q)}}\left[\log f\left(X^{(q)}, I \mid h^{(q)}\right) \mid X^{(q)} = x^{(q)}\right] \\ &= \arg\max_{h^{(q)}} \sum_{t=1}^{T^{(q)}} \sum_{i=1}^{K} P\left(i_t = i \mid x_t, \hat{h}_n^{(q)}\right) \log f\left(x_t^{(q)} \mid i_t = i, h^{(q)}\right) P(i_t = i)\end{aligned} \tag{3}$$

with

$$\begin{aligned}P\left(i_t = i \mid x_t^{(q)}, \hat{h}_n^{(q)}\right) &= \frac{f\left(x_t^{(q)} \mid i_t = i, \hat{h}_n^{(q)}\right) P(i_t = i)}{\sum_{i=1}^{K} f\left(x_t^{(q)} \mid i_t = i, \hat{h}_n^{(q)}\right) P(i_t = i)} \\ f\left(x_t^{(q)} \mid i_t = i, h^{(q)}\right) &\sim \mathcal{N}\left(\mu_i + h^{(q)}, C_i\right) \\ P(i_t = i) &= \frac{N_i}{N},\end{aligned} \tag{4}$$

where N_i is the sample size of the ith phone unit, and $N = \sum_{i=1}^{K} N_i$.

The initial bias $\hat{h}_0^{(q)}$ is unknown at the first iteration $n = 0$. Under good recognition conditions, it is reasonable to assume $\hat{h}_0^{(q)} \approx 0$, (i.e., the spectral bias is small). Under severely mismatched recording conditions, the spectral bias could be rather large, where initializing the EM with $\hat{h}_0^{(q)} = 0$ could lead to a local maximum point that is far from the true bias. Taking into account the unknown distortion $\hat{h}_0^{(q)}$ under mismatched conditions, the likelihoods $f(x_t^{(q)} | i_t = i, \hat{h}_0^{(q)})$ are computed from a uniform distribution, which leads to

$$P\left(i_t = i \,|\, x_t^{(q)}, \hat{h}_0^{(q)}\right) = P(i_t = i) = \frac{N_i}{N}. \tag{5}$$

The estimate $\hat{h}_1^{(q)}$ is derived as

$$\hat{h}_1^{(q)} = \frac{1}{T^{(q)}} \sum_{t=1}^{T^{(q)}} x_t^{(q)} - \sum_{i=1}^{K} \frac{N_i}{N} \mu_i = \bar{x}^{(q)} - \bar{\mu}, \tag{6}$$

where $\bar{x}^{(q)}$ is the mean spectrum of the sentence utterance, and $\bar{\mu}$ is the mean spectrum of the entire training set. In Figure 2, the estimation of $\hat{h}_1^{(q)}$ is shown as "bias estimation I."

For $n \geqslant 1$, the likelihood functions $f(x_t^{(q)} | i_t = i, \hat{h}_n^{(q)})$ are computed from the Gaussian densities as defined in Eq. (4). In order to simplify the computations, the posterior probabilities $P(i_t = i | x_t^{(q)}, \hat{h}_n^{(q)})$ are approximated by the decision operation

$$i_n^*(t) = \arg\max_i P(i_t = i \,|\, x_t^{(q)}, \hat{h}_n^{(q)}), \tag{7}$$

where the decision index $i_n^*(t)$ is the phone unit label for the spectrum x_t. If the covariance matrices are taken as the unit matrix, the spectral bias becomes

$$\hat{h}_{n+1}^{(q)} = \frac{1}{T^{(q)}} \sum_{t=1}^{T^{(q)}} \left(x_t^{(q)} - \mu_{i_n^*(t)}\right), \tag{8}$$

where $\mu_{i_n^*(t)}$ is the mean vector of the phone unit labeled for x_t. From the computed $\hat{h}_1^{(q)}$, one iteration is carried out using Eq. (8), which yields the refined bias estimate $\hat{h}_2^{(q)}$. In Figure 2, the estimation of $\hat{h}_2^{(q)}$ is shown as the "bias estimation II."

It has been shown previously (Zhao, 1993a, 1994) that it is advantageous to perform acoustic normalization on both training and test data, where removing spectral biases from the training spectra makes the phone models more effective in capturing the statistical variations of allophones. To construct phone models characterizing the standard speaker, the training data are first used to estimate a set of unimodal Gaussian density phone models. Using these models as reference, a spectral bias vector is estimated for each sentence utterance from each speaker, and the estimated spectral bias is subsequently removed from the sentence spectra. Gaussian mixture density phone models are estimated from such acoustically normalized training data.

10.3.3.2 Phone Model Adaptation

For phone model adaptation, the acoustically normalized speech spectra $\tilde{x}_t^{(q)}$ are segmented into states of phone units according to the recognized word string and the phonetic transcriptions of the words. For each Gaussian mixture density of a state of a phone unit, the parameters of the basis Gaussian densities are adapted via Bayesian estimation (Lee & Gauvain, 1993; Zhao, 1994), and the mixture weights are not adapted.

Bayesian estimation of Gaussian mixture density parameters Considering a size-M Gaussian mixture density, the mean vectors and covariance matrices of the component densities are denoted by $\theta_i = (\mu_i, C_i)$, $\forall i$. The mixture weights are $\alpha_i \geqslant 0$, $\forall i$ and $\sum_{i=1}^{M} \alpha_i = 1$. Denoting $\Theta = \{\theta_1, \theta_2, \cdots, \theta_M\}$, $A = \{\alpha_1, \alpha_2, \cdots, \alpha_M\}$, and assuming the feature dimension is L, the likelihood of a feature vector x_t (here x_t stands for $\tilde{x}_t^{(q)}$ for the simplicity of notation) is computed as

$$f(x_t|\Theta, A) = \sum_{i=1}^{M} \alpha_i f(x_t|\theta_i) \tag{9}$$

with $f(x_t|\theta_i) \sim \mathcal{N}(\mu_i, C_i)$, $\forall i$. The prior distributions of θ_i, $i = 1,2,\cdots, M$ are assumed to be independent, and the mixture weights α_i are taken as constant. The prior mean and covariance, $\mu_o^{(i)}$ and $C_o^{(i)}$, are estimated from a speaker-independent training set with a sample size n_i. Defining the precision matrix $r_i = C_i^{-1}$, the joint distribution of the mean and the precision matrix (μ_i, r_i) is taken as a conjugate prior distribution (Degroot, 1970). Specifically, the conditional distribution of μ_i given r_i is Gaussian with the mean $\mu_o^{(i)}$ and the precision matrix νr_i, ν being a scaling constant; the marginal distribution of r_i is a Wishart distribution with ρ degrees of freedom and a scaling matrix $\tau_i = n_i C_o^{(i)}$, namely,

$$\begin{aligned} p(\mu_i, r_i) \propto |r_i|^{1/2} \exp\left(-\frac{1}{2}\mathrm{tr}\left(\nu r_i(\mu_i - \mu_o^{(i)})(\mu_i - \mu_o^{(i)})'\right)\right) \\ \times |r_i|^{(\rho-L-1)/2} \exp\left(-\frac{1}{2}\mathrm{tr}(\tau_i r_i)\right), \end{aligned} \tag{10}$$

where $\propto$ signifies "proportional to." Because the prior mean $\mu_o^{(i)}$ and the prior covariance $C_o^{(i)}$ are estimated from n_i data samples, the precision scale ν and the degree of freedom ρ are both assigned the value of the training size n_i (Degroot, 1970).

Similar to the scenario of section 10.3.1, there is a set of observable feature data $x = \{x_1, x_2, \cdots, x_T\}$ and a set of unobservable data $\{i_1, i_2, \cdots, i_T\}$, i_t being the mixture index for x_t, $\forall t$. The estimation of Θ is, therefore, again formulated in the framework of the EM algorithm. The difference to the EM formulation in section 10.3.1 is that the conditional expectation is taken with respect to the posterior likelihood of the complete data set (X, I), i.e.,

$$\begin{aligned} \hat{\Theta}^{(n+1)} &= \arg\max_{\Theta} E_{\hat{\Theta}^{(n)}}\left[\log f(\Theta|X,I,A)|X = x\right] \\ &= \arg\max_{\Theta} E_{\hat{\Theta}^{(n)}}\left[\log(f(X,I|\Theta, A)p(\Theta))|X = x\right] \\ &= \arg\max_{\Theta} \left\{\sum_{t=1}^{T}\sum_{i=1}^{M} P(i_t = i|x_t, \theta_i^{(n)}) \log f(x_t, i_t = i|\theta_i) + \sum_{i=1}^{M} \log p(\theta_i)\right\}. \end{aligned} \tag{11}$$

The initial $\hat{\Theta}^{(0)}$ is the set of speaker-independent model parameters. The maximization of the expectation is decoupled for individual θ_i's, and it leads to the posterior estimate of the mean

$$\hat{\mu}_i^{(n+1)} = \left(1 - \lambda_i^{(n)}\right)\mu_o^{(i)} + \lambda_i^{(n)}\mu_x^{(i)(n)} \tag{12}$$

and the posterior estimate of the covariance (with approximation $\rho - L \approx n_i$)

$$\hat{C}_i^{(n+1)} = \left(1 - \lambda_i^{(n)}\right)C_o^{(i)} + \lambda_i^{(n)}C_x^{(i)(n)} + \lambda_i^{(n)}\left(1 - \lambda_i^{(n)}\right)\left(\mu_x^{(i)(n)} - \mu_o^{(i)}\right)\left(\mu_x^{(i)(n)} - \mu_o^{(i)}\right)', \tag{13}$$

where $\lambda_i^{(n)}$ is the interpolation parameter, $\mu_x^{(i)(n)}$ and $C_x^{(i)(n)}$ are the sample mean and sample covariance of the adaptation data. Denoting the posterior probabilities by $\gamma_{t,i}^{(n)}$, that is,

$$P\left(i_t = i \mid x_t, \theta_i^{(n)}\right) = \gamma_{t,i}^{(n)} = \alpha_i f\left(x_t \mid \theta_i^{(n)}\right) \Big/ \sum_{j=1}^{M} \alpha_j f\left(x_t \mid \theta_j^{(n)}\right), \tag{14}$$

the parameters $\lambda_i^{(n)}$, $\mu_x^{(i)(n)}$, and $C_x^{(i)(n)}$ are computed as

$$\begin{aligned}
\lambda_i^{(n)} &= \sum_{t=1}^{T}\gamma_{t,i}^{(n)} \Big/ \left(\sum_{t=1}^{T}\gamma_{t,i}^{(n)} + n_i\right) \\
\mu_x^{(i)(n)} &= \sum_{t=1}^{T}\gamma_{t,i}^{(n)} x_t \Big/ \sum_{t=1}^{T}\gamma_{t,i}^{(n)} \\
C_x^{(i)(n)} &= \sum_{t=1}^{T}\gamma_{t,i}^{(n)}\left(x_t - \mu_x^{(i)(n)}\right)\left(x_t - \mu_x^{(i)(n)}\right)' \Big/ \sum_{t=1}^{T}\gamma_{t,i}^{(n)}.
\end{aligned} \tag{15}$$

Iterative phone model adaptation Denote the recorded sentences in one session as $\{S_k, k = 1, 2, \cdots, K\}$ and the decoded word strings as $\{A_k^{(1)}, k = 1, 2, \cdots, K\}$, with k the sequential index on the sentences. In the sequential adaptation, the phone models that are used to recognize the jth sentence are adapted from the previous sentences $\{S_1, S_2, \cdots, S_{j-1}\}$, and the Viterbi segmentations are constrained by the word strings $\{A_1^{(1)}, A_2^{(1)}, \cdots, A_{j-1}^{(1)}\}$. In the iterative phone model adaptation, the word strings that are generated in the first iteration are denoted as $A_k^{(2)}$, and those generated in the nth iteration as $A_k^{(n+1)}$. When recognizing the jth sentence, the phone models are adapted from all the available sentences excluding the jth sentence, namely, $\{S_1, \cdots, S_{j-1}, S_{j+1}, \cdots, S_K\}$, and in the first iteration, the Viterbi segmentations are constrained by the word strings $\{A_1^{(2)}, \cdots, A_{j-1}^{(2)}, A_{j+1}^{(1)}, \cdots, A_K^{(1)}\}$, for $j = 1, 2, \cdots, K$. As such, the sentences that were uttered before the jth sentence are segmented according to the newly decoded word strings, and those after the jth sentence are segmented according to the word strings generated from the sequential adaptation. To generalize, at the nth iteration, when adapting the phone models for recognizing the jth sentence, the Viterbi segmentations are constrained by the word strings $\{A_1^{(n+1)}, \cdots, A_{j-1}^{(n+1)}, A_{j+1}^{(n)}, \cdots, A_K^{(n)}\}$.

10.3.4 Experimental Results

Experiments were performed on the TIMIT database and on the speech data collected at the Speech Technology Laboratory (STL), Santa Barbara, California.

The baseline speaker-independent HMM phone models were trained from 325 speakers and 717 sentences from the TIMIT database, where the TIMIT data were collected using the Sennheiser close-talking microphone. The TIMIT speech data were down-sampled from 16 kHz to 10.67 kHz. The cepstrum coefficients of the Perceptually based Linear Prediction (PLP) analysis (8th order) (Hermansky, Hanson, & Wakita, 1985) and log energy were taken as instantaneous features, and their first-order 50-ms temporal regression coefficients as dynamic features. The task vocabulary size was 853, and the grammar perplexities were 104 and 105 for the TIMIT and STL test sets, respectively. The TIMIT test set had 50 males and 25 females; each speaker spoke 2 or 3 sentences for a total of 186 sentences. The STL data were collected from one female (F) and one male (M); each speaker read 198 TIMIT SX sentences, which were simultaneously recorded via two microphones: a Sennheiser close-talking (CT) microphone and a Ramsa dynamic (RD) microphone. The combination of the two speakers and the two microphones generated four test sets: F-CT, M-CT, F-RD, and M-RD. Compared to the TIMIT data, the STL data were collected under a higher level of ambient noise (approximately 15 dB higher); the anti-aliasing filter characteristics were also not well matched to that used in the TIMIT database.

In order to evaluate the effectiveness of the proposed adaptation methods, recognition experiments were performed for the following cases:

1. Speaker-independent continuous-speech recognition (baseline)
2. Acoustic normalization assuming $\hat{h}_0^{(q)} = 0$ and using Eq. (8) (acu0)
3. Unsupervised sequential phone model adaptation after acu0 (USPA-acu0)
4. Supervised sequential phone model adaptation after acu0 (SSPA-acu0)
5. Acoustic normalization using the bias estimate $\hat{h}_1^{(q)}$ from Eq. (6) (acu1)
6. Acoustic normalization using $\hat{h}_2^{(q)}$ from the two-step bias estimation using Eqs.(6) and (8) (acu2)
7. Unsupervised sequential phone model adaptation after acu2 (USPA-acu2)
8. Iterative unsupervised phone model adaptation after acu2 (one iteration) (IPA-acu2)
9. Supervised sequential phone model adaptation after acu2 (SSPA-acu2).

As seen from Eq.(14), the computation of the posterior probabilities requires the evaluation of the Gaussian density likelihoods for individual data samples. In order to limit the amount of computation, only one iteration of EM was used in the Bayesian estimation of the phone model parameters, where the initial parameters were speaker-independent estimates.

The average recognition word accuracies for the cases (1) through (4) are summarized in Table I, and for the cases of (5) through (9) are summarized in Table II. For the STL speakers, the recognition word accuracy as a function of the on-line speech data are further illustrated in Figure 3 for the female speaker and Figure 4 for the male speaker, where (A) and (B) show the results on the data

TABLE I The Recognition Word Accuracies (%) Using Adaptation Methods 2 through 4

Type[a]	Baseline[b]	acu0[c]	USPA-acu0[d]	SSPA-acu0[e]
TIMIT	86.9	88.1	88.3	88.3
F-CT	74.6	83.0	86.1	86.1
M-CT	56.5	77.6	85.2	85.7
F-RD	44.2	64.4	72.8	76.3
M-RD	−0.3	54.5	73.3	78.1

[a] F, female; M, male; CT, close-talking microphone; RD, Ramsa dynamic microphone.
[b] Baseline, speaker-independent continuous-speech recognition.
[c] acu0, acoustic normalization assuming $\hat{h}_0^{(q)} = 0$ and using Eq. (8).
[d] USPA-acu0, unsupervised sequential phone model adaptation after acu0.
[e] SSPA-acu0, supervised sequential phone model adaptation after acu0.

collected from the Sennheiser microphone, and (C) and (D) show the results on the data collected from the Ramsa dynamic microphone. In (A) and (C) of the Figures 3 and 4, the word accuracies were averaged over the number of sentences (n) indicated on the horizontal axis, (i.e., if $n = 20$, the result was averaged over the past 20 sentences, and if $n = 40$, the result was averaged over the past 40 sentences, etc.); these results are referred to as the cumulative-averaged results. In (B) and (D) of the Figures 3 and 4, the word accuracies were averaged within each 20-sentence blocks (i.e., for $n = 20$, the result was averaged over the sentences 1 through 20; for $n = 40$, the result was averaged over the sentences 21 through 40, etc.); these results are referred as the interval-averaged results. The effects of the acoustic normalization and the phone model adaptation are discussed next.

TABLE II Recognition Word Accuracies Using Adaptation Methods 5 through 9

Type[a]	acu1[b]	acu2[c]	USPA-acu2[d]	IPA-acu2[e]	SSPA-acu2[f]
TIMIT	85.3	86.6	—	—	—
F-CT	81.1	81.9	84.0	85.2	84.3
M-CT	82.8	84.5	86.9	89.4	87.2
F-RD	69.9	70.7	78.2	81.0	80.6
M-RD	75.1	77.9	83.1	85.2	84.3

[a] F, female; M, male; CT, close-talking microphone: RD, Ramsa dynamic microphone.
[b] acu1, acoustic normalization using the bias estimate $\hat{h}_1^{(q)}$ from Eq. (6).
[c] acu2, acoustic normalization using $\hat{h}_2^{(q)}$ from the two-step bias estimation using Eqs. (6) and (8).
[d] USPA-acu2, unsupervised sequential phone model adaptation after acu2.
[e] IPA-acu2, iterative unsupervised phone model adaptation after acu2 (one iteration).
[f] SSPA-acu2, supervised sequential phone model adaptation after acu2.

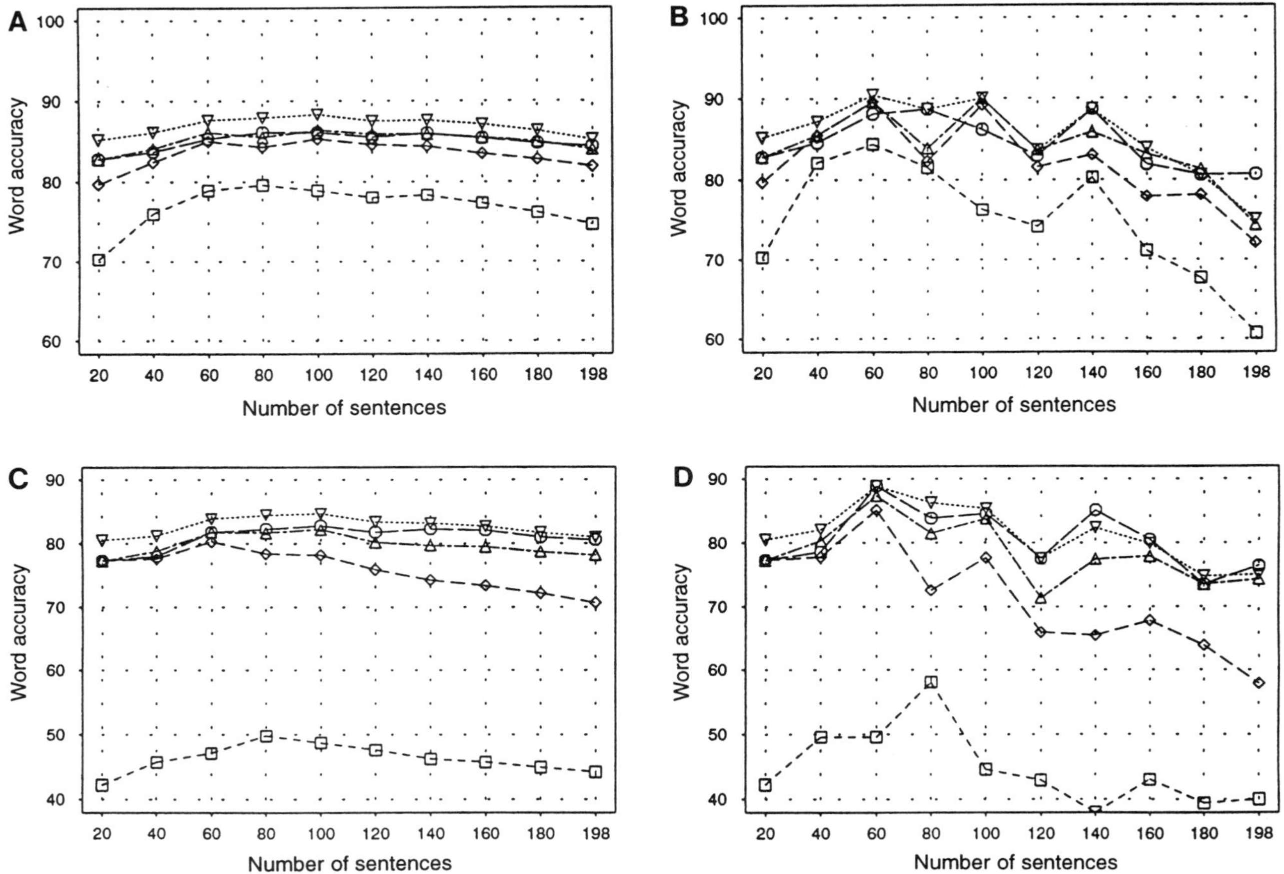

FIGURE 3 Recognition word accuracies for the female Speech Technology Laboratory (STL) speaker: □—baseline (case 1); ◇—acoustic normalization using $\hat{h}_2^{(q)}$ (case 6); △—unsupervised sequential phone model adaptation (case 7); ▽—iterative phone model adaptation (case 8); ○—supervised sequential phone model adaptation (case 9). (A) Cumulative average, Sennheiser microphone data; (B) Interval average, Sennheiser microphone data; (C) Cumulative average, Ramsa microphone data; (D) Interval average, Ramsa microphone data.

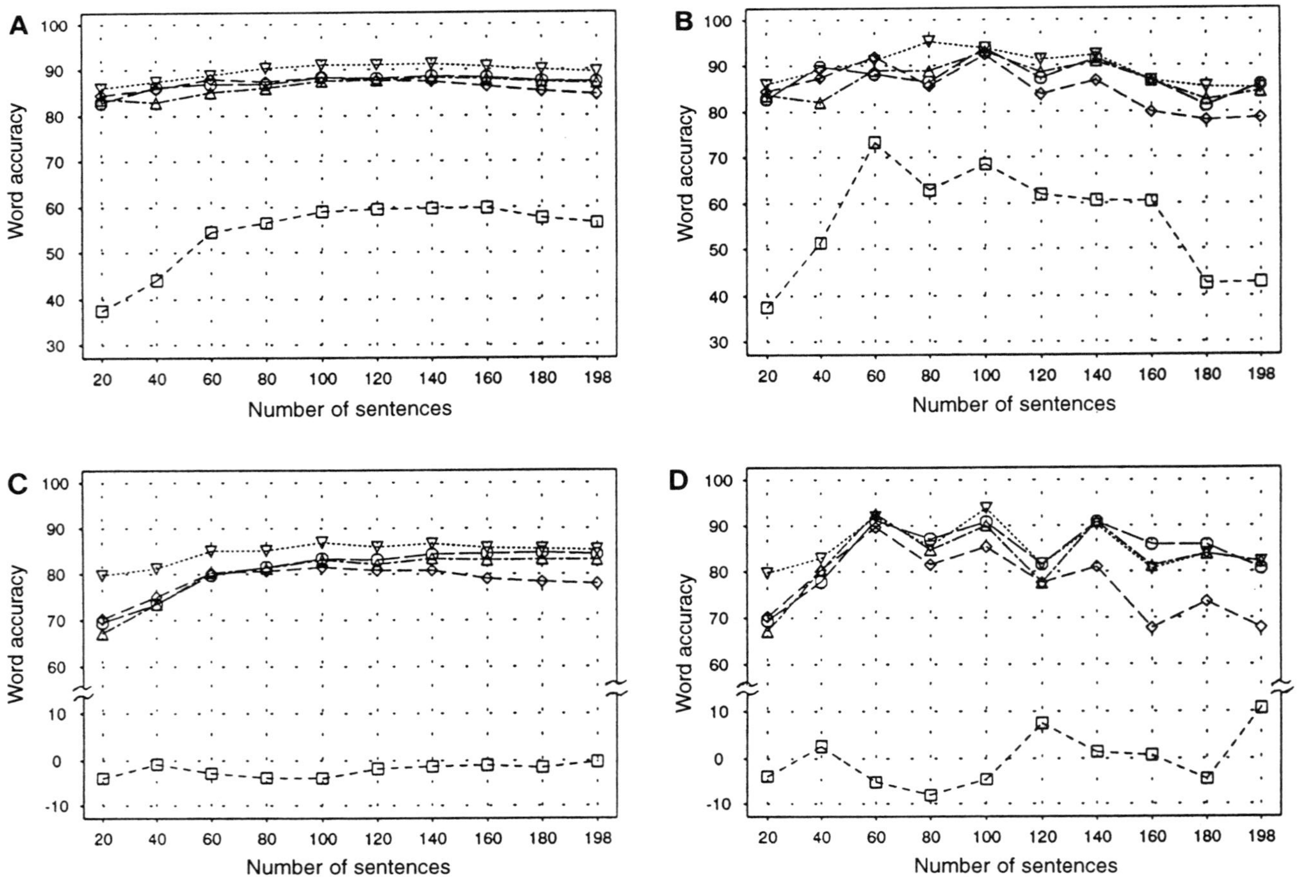

FIGURE 4 Recognition word accuracies for the Speech Technology Laboratory (STL) male speaker: □—baseline (case 1); ◇—acoustic normalization using $\hat{h}_2^{(q)}$ (case 6); △—unsupervised sequential phone model adaptation (case 7); ▽—iterative phone model adaptation (case 8); ○—supervised sequential phone model adaptation (case 9). (A) Cumulative average, Sennheiser microphone data; (B) Interval average, Sennheiser microphone data; (C) Cumulative average, Ramsa

10.3.4.1 Acoustic Normalization

On the TIMIT test set, due to the small amount of data available from each speaker, only acoustic normalization produced a significant effect. For the STL data, the baseline recognition word accuracies were much lower than that of the TIMIT set due to the mismatch of recording conditions, where acoustic normalization produced significant performance improvements. The relative strengths between the three methods of acoustic normalization (i.e., acu0, acu1, and acu2), depend on the baseline recognition condition. Under good baseline conditions (i.e., the TIMIT test set and the test set F-CT), with the respective baseline word accuracies of 86.9% and 74.6%, using the method acu0 produced the best results, whereas using the method acu1 led to decreased accuracy on the TIMIT test set. Under poor baseline conditions (i.e., the test sets of M-CT, F-RD, and M-RD, with the respective baseline accuracies of 56.5, 44.2, and −0.3%), the method acu1 is more effective than the method acu0, and using the method acu2 further improved the results from acu1 in all the three cases. The extremely poor decoding accuracy on the set M-RD was due to the fact that in addition to the unmatched microphone, the speaker put the microphone too close to his mouth, which caused a significant boost to the low-frequency components of speech (the negative accuracy was due to insertion errors).

These results can be interpreted from the relative effects between the spectral correlations within an utterance and the labeling accuracy of the posterior probabilities. From Eq. (6) one can observe that performing the acoustic normalization by removing $\hat{h}_1^{(q)}$ is a special form of cepstral mean removal, where a method of cepstral mean removal was proposed by Atal in his work of speaker identification (Atal, 1974), and cepstral mean removal has subsequently been used in various speech-recognition systems. An obvious problem with the cepstral mean removal is that if the spectra within an utterance are highly correlated, subtracting out the mean from all these spectra could lead to a loss of phonetic content in the speech spectra. Examining the errors from using acu1 confirms such a problem. For example, the erroneously decoded sentences from using acu1 are like "where were you while we were away," "a roll of wire lay near the wall," and so on, where using the method acu2 improved the decoding accuracy on these sentences significantly. On the other hand, when the baseline condition is very poor, the unreliable posterior probabilities produced erroneous phone labels on the speech spectra, which led to inaccurate estimate of spectral bias, and in this situation the acu0 method is inferior to the acu1 method.

10.3.4.2 Phone Model Adaptation

Comparing the results achieved after acoustic normalization, both the supervised and unsupervised sequential phone model adaptation (i.e., the SSPA and the USPA) further improved the recognition word accuracies. The trend is that the longer the learning period, the larger the gain of accuracy from the phone model adaptations. When the amount of speech data is small, the unsupervised phone model adaptation could deteriorate the decoding accuracy slightly. It is observed that the supervised adaptation yields higher average word accuracies than the unsupervised adaptation, where the difference between the two depends on the decoding condition after the acoustic normalization. If the word accuracy after the acoustic normalization is high, as in the case of F-CT after acu0 in Table I or M-CT after acu2 in Table II, the SSPA and the USPA produced similar effects; if the decoding accuracy remains low after acoustic normalization, as in the case of M-RD after acu0 in Table I or F-RD after acu2 in Table II, the SSPA yielded noticeably better results than the USPA. The case of M-RD after acu0 in Table I also demonstrated that even when the word accuracy was about 50%, the unsupervised phone model adaptation did not diverge but produced rather strong positive effect.

The results in Table II demonstrate that the iterative unsupervised adaptation further improved the decoding accuracy for each case. As illustrated in Figures 3 and 4, the main effect of the iterative adaptation is on the beginning subsets of sentences where the amount of adaptation data was too small in the sequential adaptation. Although more iterations could be carried out, only the first iteration produced significant effect in improving the word accuracy. For example, an additional iteration of phone model adaptation on the test set M-RD yielded the word accuracy of 85.4%, corresponding to only a 0.2% increase to the accuracy 85.2% achieved from the first iteration. One iteration of an iterative supervised phone model adaptation was also carried out on the test set M-RD, which yielded the word accuracy of 87.3%. Because in the supervised adaptation only one iteration is necessary, the figure 87.3% sets the limit of accuracy achievable from the unsupervised adaptation. In the current case, the accuracy from the unsupervised adaptation on the M-RD set is 2.1% lower than the limit accuracy.

Comparing the results in Tables I and II, one observes that the decoding accuracy from the phone model adaptation depends on the decoding accuracy achieved from the acoustic normalization, where a higher accuracy from the acoustic normalization leads to a higher accuracy from the phone model adaptation, and vice versa. The interval-averaged results in Figures 3B, D and 4B, D indicate that the relative effects between the acoustic normalization and the phone model adaptation varied considerably among subsets of sentences. For example, in Figure 3D, when $x = 60$, the difference between the word accuracies from the acu2 and the USPA-acu2 is only 2.2%, whereas when $x = 80$, the difference between the two methods becomes 8.9%. In contrast, the cumulative-averaged results in Figures 3A, 3C, 4A, and 4C are rather smooth, which reflects the general trend of the adaptation effects.

In order to fix the idea on the effects of acoustic normalization and phone model adaptation, several figures of relative error reductions on the STL test sets are summarized in Table III: the cepstral mean removal versus the baseline (column 1); the two-step bias removal versus the cepstral mean removal (column 2); the unsupervised sequential phone model adaptation versus the two-step bias removal (column 3); the iterative phone model adaptation versus the unsupervised

TABLE III Relative Error Reductions on the Speech Technology Laboratory Test Set

Type[a]	acu1[b] versus baseline[c]	acu2[d] versus acu1[b]	USPA-acu2[e] versus acu2[d]	IPA-acu2[f] versus USPA-acu2	IPA-acu2[f] versus baseline[c]
F-CT	25.59	4.23	11.60	7.50	41.73
M-CT	60.46	9.88	15.48	19.08	75.63
F-RD	46.06	2.66	25.60	12.84	65.95
M-RD	75.17	11.24	23.53	12.43	85.24

[a] F, female; M, male; CT, close-talking microphone: RD, Ramsa dynamic microphone.
[b] acu1, acoustic normalization using the bias estimate $\hat{h}_1^{(q)}$ from Eq. (6).
[c] baseline, speaker-independent continuous-speech recognition.
[d] acu2, acoustic normalization using $\hat{h}_2^{(q)}$ from the two-step bias estimation using Eqs. (6) and (8).
[e] USPA-acu2, unsupervised sequential phone model adaptation after acu2.
[f] IPA-acu2, iterative unsupervised phone model adaptation after acu2 (one iteration).

sequential phone model adaptation (column 4), and finally the iterative phone model adaptation versus the baseline (column 5). As seen from the table, the progressive error reductions from the first column to the fourth column are 26% ~ 75%, 3% ~ 11%, 12% ~ 26%, 8% ~ 19%, and the total relative error reductions as shown in the fifth column is 42% ~ 85%.

10.4 SUMMARY

This chapter has presented an overview of speaker-adaptation techniques and a detailed discussion of a self-learning adaptive ASR system. The self-learning speaker-adaptation technique significantly improved the performance of a speaker-independent continuous speech-recognition system. A general concern regarding the feasibility of self-learning in continuous speech recognition is that a poor baseline accuracy could lead to divergent adaptation results. The technique described in section 10.3 demonstrates that through spectral variation source decomposition, by first removing a phone-independent spectral variation source, which accounted for a severely degraded recognition performance, the errors in the unsupervised segmentation of phone units could be significantly reduced and thus facilitate phone model adaptation. Furthermore, even when the recognition word accuracy was only about 50% after acoustic normalization (the baseline accuracy was below 0%), the unsupervised phone model adaptation improved the recognition performance without divergence. Further theoretical studies are needed on the convergence conditions in self-learning.

Humans are capable of accurate identification of phonetic categories of speech sounds while ignoring speaker-induced variations. The ultimate solution to interspeaker variability might lie in the full discovery of the human mechanism, which still requires long-term research efforts. Speaker-adaptation techniques need to be improved based on models of interspeaker variability, and adaptation should cover both the spectral and phonological domains. In general, different adaptation strategies are required depending on the applications and underlying ASR systems; the bottom line is to reduce burdens on users. Unsupervised on-line adaptation is a direction for developing intelligent, dynamic ASR systems, where the knowledge sources of lexicon, syntax, and semantics should be better utilized in order to provide automatic feedback to the self-learning process. The combination of fast off-line adaptation with unsupervised on-line adaptation could be a solution for practical, robust ASR systems.

REFERENCES

Atal, B. S. (1974). Effectiveness of linear prediction characteristics of the speech wave for automatic speaker identification and verification. *Journal of the Acoustical Society of America, 55*(6), 1304–1312.

Bellegarda, J. R., de Souza, P. V., Nadas, A. J., Nahamoo, D., Picheny, M. A., & Bahl, L. R. (March, 1992). Robust speaker adaptation using a piecewise linear acoustic mapping. *Proceedings of IEEE International Conference on Acoustics, Speech, & Signal Processing,* pp. 445–448, San Francisco, CA.

Cole, R., Hirschman, L., Atlas, L., Beckman, M., Biermann, A., Bush, M., Clements, M., Cohen, J., Garcia, O., Hanson, B., Hermansky, H., Levinson, S., McKeown, K., Morgan, N., Novick, D. G., Ostendorf, M., Oviatt, S., Price, P., Silverman, H., Spitz, J., Waibel, A., Weinstein, C., Zahorian, S., & Zue, V. (1995). The challenge of spoken language systems: Research directions for the nineties. *IEEE Transactions on Speech and Audio Processing, 3*(1), 1–21.

Cox, S. J., & Bridle, J. S. (May, 1989). Unsupervised speaker adaptation by probabilistic fitting. *Proceedings of IEEE International Conference on Acoustics, Speech, & Signal Processing,* pp. 294–297, Glasgow, Scotland.

Cox, S. J. (May, 1995). A speaker adaptation technique using linear regression. *Proceedings of IEEE International Conference on Acoustics, Speech, & Signal Processing,* pp. 700–703, Detroit, MI.

Degroot, M. H. (1970). *Optimal statistical decisions.* New York: McGraw-Hill.

Dempster, A. P., Laird, N. M., & Rubin, D. B. (1977). Maximum likelihood estimation from incomplete data via the EM algorithm. *Journal of the Royal Statistical Society, B, 39*(1), 1–38.

Digalakis, V., & Neumeyer, L. (May, 1995). Speaker adaptation using combined transformation and Bayesian methods. *Proceedings of IEEE International Conference on Acoustics, Speech, & Signal Processing,* pp. 680–683, Detroit, MI.

Furui, S. (May, 1989). Unsupervised speaker adaptation method based on hierarchical spectral clustering. *Proceedings of IEEE International Conference on Acoustics, Speech, & Signal Processing,* pp. 286–289, Glasgow, Scotland.

Gauvain, J.-L., & Lee, C.-H. (1994). Maximum a posteriori estimation for multivariate Gaussian mixture observations of Markov chains. *IEEE Transactions on Speech and Audio Processing, 2*(2), 291–298.

Hermansky, H., Hanson, B. A., & Wakita, H. J. (March, 1985). Perceptually based linear predictive analysis of speech. *Proceedings of IEEE International Conference on Acoustics, Speech, & Signal Processing,* pp. 509–512, Tampa, FL.

Huang, X. D. (March, 1992). Speaker normalization for speech recognition. *Proceedings of IEEE International Conference on Acoustics, Speech, & Signal Processing,* pp. 465–468, San Francisco, CA.

Ladefoged, P. (1993). *A course in phonetics* (3rd ed.). Harcourt Brace College Publishers, Troy, MO.
Lamel, L. F., Kassel, R. H., & Seneff, S. (1986). Speech database development: Design and analysis of the acoustic-phonetic corpus. *Proceedings of the Speech Recognition Workshop (DARPA).*
Lee, C.-H., & Gauvain, J.-L. (April, 1993). Speaker adaptation based on MAP estimation of HMM parameters. *Proceedings of IEEE International Conference on Acoustics, Speech, & Signal Processing,* pp. 558–561, Minneapolis, MN.
Mathan, L., & Miclet, L. (April, 1990). Speaker hierarchical clustering for improving speaker-independent HMM word recognition. *Proceedings of IEEE International Conference on Acoustics, Speech, & Signal Processing,* pp. 149–152, Albuquerque, NM.
Paul, D. B., & Necioglu, B. F. (April, 1993). The Lincoln large-vocabulary stack-decoder HMM CSR. *Proceedings of IEEE International Conference on Acoustics, Speech, & Signal Processing,* Vol. 2, pp. 660–664, Minneapolis, MN.
Rabiner, R. L., Juang, B. H., Levinson, S. E., & Sondhi, M. M. (1985). Recognition of isolated digits using hidden Markov models with continuous mixture densities. *AT&T Technical Journal, 64*(6), 1211–1233.
Sankar, A., & Lee, C.-H. (1994). Stochastic matching for robust speech recognition. *IEEE Signal Processing Letters, 1*(8), 124–125.
Shinoda, K., Iso, K., & Watanabe, T. (May, 1991). Speaker adaptation for demi-syllable based continuous density HMM. *Proceedings of IEEE International Conference on Acoustics, Speech, & Signal Processing,* pp. 857–860, Toronto, Canada.
Zhao, Y. (April, 1993a). A New speaker adaptation technique using very short calibration speech. *Proceedings of IEEE International Conference on Acoustics, Speech, & Signal Processing,* pp. 562–565, Minneapolis, MN.
Zhao, Y. (1993b). A speaker-independent continuous speech recognition system using continuous mixture Gaussian density HMM of phoneme-sized units. *IEEE Transactions on Speech and Audio Processing, 1*(3), 345–361.
Zhao, Y. (Sept. 1993c). Self-learning speaker adaptation based on spectral variation source decomposition. *Proceedings of the 4th European Conference on Speech Communication and Technology,* pp. 359–362, Berlin, Germany.
Zhao, Y. (1994). An acoustic-phonetic based speaker adaptation technique for improving speaker-independent continuous speech recognition. *IEEE Transactions on Speech and Audio Processing, 2*(3), 380–384.

11

Vocal Tract Normalization for Articulatory Recovery and Adaptation

RICHARD S. MCGOWAN

11.1 INTRODUCTION

The problem of intertalker variability of acoustic output caused by anatomical differences in vocal tracts is a long-standing problem in speech perception research. In this chapter the problem will be considered in the particular case where an analysis-by-synthesis procedure is employed for recovering articulatory movement. The problem arises because the vocal tract model used in the analysis (i.e., that of the synthesizer) does not necessarily match that of any particular talker. Speaker adaptation in automatic speech recognition (ASR) will also be considered in light of the recovery problem.

A normalization procedure is proposed as a solution to the problem of anatomical variability and some aspects of motor variability, in the context of articulatory recovery. When the idea of using normalization has been used in the past, it is often stated in terms of how to scale, or map, aspects of an individual's utterance so that, if it falls within a given phonetic category, it will "look" like, or be mapped to another's utterance of the same category, or, equivalently, to a standard utterance of that category. These normalization procedures are usually applied to the acoustic speech signal. In the normalization procedure proposed here for analysis-by-synthesis, a talker's vocal tract will be mapped onto a *standard vocal tract* (the vocal tract model used in the analysis-by-synthesis procedure), while simultaneously adjusting the acoustic output of the standard vocal

Talker Variability in Speech Processing

tract to match the talker's acoustic output. The vocal tract mapping for each talker is known here as a *normalizing map* (*NM*). The NM for a talker maps any possible vocal tract shape of the talker onto a vocal tract shape for the standard vocal tract. Thus, the domain of an NM is the set of points in the space of the talker's possible vocal tract shapes, and the range is the set of points in the space of possible shapes for the standard vocal tract. Instead of mapping acoustically disparate signals representing the same phonetic category onto a standard signal, as has been the case in some previous normalization procedures, the normalization procedure described here maps disparate vocal tracts onto a standard vocal tract, while requiring, as much as possible, that the acoustic output of the standard vocal tract match that of the human talker.

Why are such NMs useful for articulatory recovery? Assume that for a given talker that an NM and its inverse have been constructed. To recover the articulation of an utterance of that talker, the acoustic signal of that utterance would be submitted to the analysis-by-synthesis procedure that employed the standard vocal tract to synthesize speech for comparison with the acoustics of the utterance. The analysis-by-synthesis procedure subsequently would obtain an articulation for the standard vocal tract, and the human articulation would be obtained by applying the inverse of the NM to this articulation (see Figure 5 for a summary).

The problem of defining an NM is first discussed when it is possible to measure articulation and acoustic output simultaneously for, at least, a limited set of utterances. This situation is known as *laboratory recovery* in this chapter. For example, it will be assumed that simultaneous x-ray microbeam data (Westbury, 1994) and acoustic speech data are available for a talker over a limited set of utterances. In this case the problem will be to construct an NM so that articulation can be inferred from new acoustic data. In the remainder of the chapter, speaker adaptation in ASR will be discussed in terms of vocal tract characterization and its relation to constructing an NM for laboratory recovery. This will lead to a revision of the method proposed for constructing the NM in the laboratory to suit the purposes of ASR.

The ideas presented regarding vocal tract recovery and characterization are intended to set a logical framework for handling variability of vocal tract anatomy and some aspects of motor behavior. They are speculative insofar as they have not been implemented; however, prior to implementation, a clear idea of what a particular application requires is necessary. Although the considerations on how an NM could be constructed are valid for any analysis-by-synthesis, there is a particular program of research that can be used as a concrete example, and this is the recovery of task-dynamic parameters using a genetic algorithm as an optimizing routine (McGowan, 1994; McGowan & Lee, in press). Task dynamics is a computational model of articulatory coordination (Saltzman & Munhall, 1989) with end effectors in the Haskins articulatory synthesizer (ASY) (Mermelstein, 1973; Rubin, Baer, & Mermelstein, 1981). The task-dynamic parameters are dynamical parameters specifying the movement dynamics of constriction degree and location pairs, such as tongue-body constriction degree and location and tongue-tip constriction degree and location in the midsagittal plane. The constriction degrees and locations are known as *tract variables,* and they can be related to the midsagittal geometry of the ASY vocal tract, and, hence, to the articulatory coordinates of the ASY vocal tract (Figures 1 and 2). Because the ASY vocal tract is the vocal tract used in the analysis-by-synthesis, it will serve as an example of a standard vocal tract.

11.2 NORMALIZING MAPS FOR LABORATORY RECOVERY

11.2.1 Properties of a Normalizing Map

The recovery procedure envisioned above requires certain properties of the NMs. Recall that recovery is to be done first by finding the standard vocal tract's best imitation of the human's speech via analysis-by-synthesis. Once the standard vocal tract has found a way to mimic the speech signal of a human vocal tract, the NM must be inverted to find the movements of the human talker. To be invertible, the NM must be injective or one-to-one. In practice, this requirement is equivalent to the one of robustness. (This is analogous to the distinction between small singular values relative to the largest and zero singular values for a linear transformation.) This means that, given a vocal tract shape in the domain of the NM, one needs to be confident that a small perturbation will not produce a large change in the range of the NM, and similarly, for the inverse of the NM. Furthermore, the scope of the recovery procedure is restricted to be one in which vocal tract gestures or articulatory movements are found by analysis-by-synthesis with a physically realistic model of a vocal tract and not an abstract representation of one. The possibility of using more abstract representations should not be excluded, but this may be easier to do after the more concrete procedure is outlined. Not only will the standard vocal tract behave like a real vocal tract, at least in the aspects that will be captured in this recovery procedure, but the NM from a human to the standard vocal tract will be required to approximate biological homology by mapping homologous points to one another. That is, lips must map to lips and alveolar ridges must map to alveolar ridges, and so on. It should be noted that the homology requirement may subsume the robustness requirement, and whether it does is an empirical question that should be answered in the future. Finally, as discussed above, the accessory condition on the NM is that the standard vocal tract produce output acoustics very similar to that of the human for shapes that correspond under the NM. In order for this to occur the NM cannot completely determine the standard vocal tract, and this will force a decision on what constitutes articulatory recovery.

The requirements that each NM take homologous points to each other, that it be robust, and that the acoustic outputs of the standard vocal tract and the human must match closely are, taken together, quite stringent. Thus, to limit the scope of the recovery procedure, only the recovery of the midsagittal aspects of articulatory

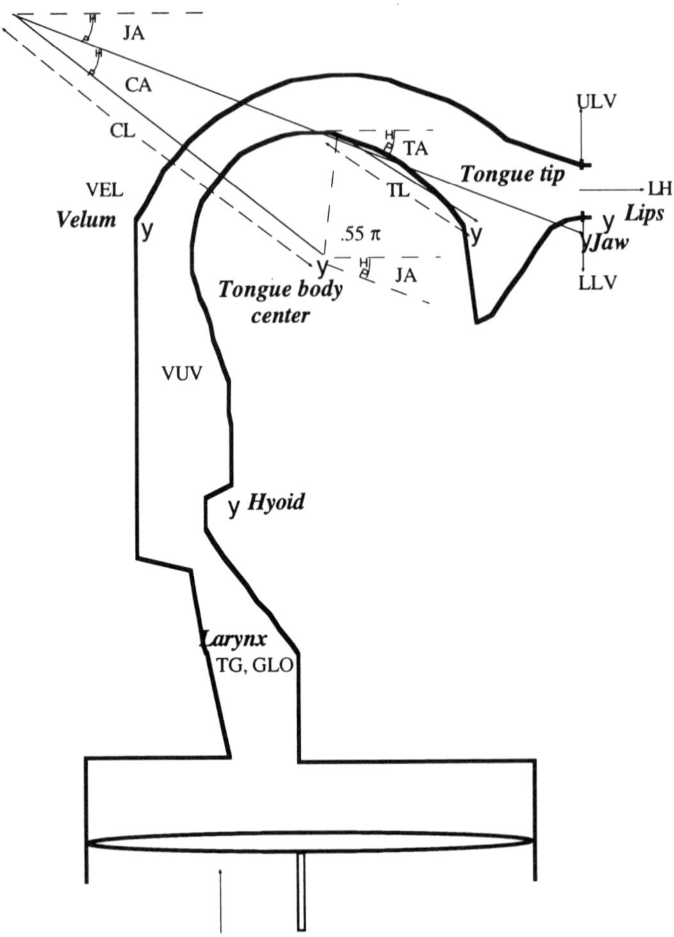

FIGURE 1 The midsagittal section and articulatory coordinates of the Haskins articulatory synthesizer, (ASY).

motions will be considered. (These should also be the most important aspects of articulation for ASR, as will be discussed below.) This will mean that the NMs will be restricted to the midsagittal plane, so that they need only map homologously and robustly in this plane. In fact, because much of the empirical data that can be obtained in the laboratory to construct the NMs will not have complete information about the midsagittal section of the pharynx, the NM will only be required to possess the robustness and homology properties in certain regions of the midsagittal section (e.g., the mouth). This will leave many degrees of freedom in the standard vocal tract to be adjusted for each individual's vocal tract so that a close acoustic matching between the standard vocal tract and the individual will

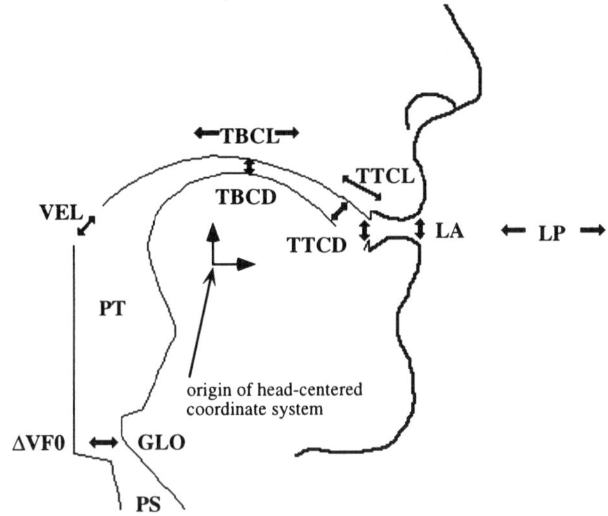

FIGURE 2 Tract variables used in task dynamics.

be possible, even after parts of its midsagittal section are fixed by the NM. These degrees of freedom are known as parameters orthogonal to the (range of) the NM (PONMs). They include, among others, the midsagittal distance-to-area function, the radiation impedance function, and the ratio of pharynx length-to-mouth cavity length, if this is not determined by the NM. The PONMs will be adjusted so that the standard vocal tract's output acoustics match, *as closely as possible,* that of the human talker over several different utterances simultaneously. If this adjustment is carried out over a sufficiently representative set of utterances, then the acoustic output of the standard vocal tract should closely match the acoustic output of the human for all possible utterances. The proposed procedure is reminiscent of the methods proposed by Beautemps, Badin, and Laboissière (1995) for finding midsagittal distance-to-area functions in vowels and fricatives by requiring acoustical matching for particular midsagittal shapes (see also Badin, Beautemps, Laboissière, & Schwartz, 1995).

The problem of intertalker variability caused by differences in vocal tract anatomy and mechanical properties must be confronted if an analysis-by-synthesis procedure is to work. The construction of NMs is one possible solution to this problem.

11.2.2 Construction of a Normalizing Map

As an example of laboratory recovery of articulatory movement, it is supposed that a database of simultaneous acoustic and x-ray microbeam utterances exists for the talker for which the analysis-by-synthesis procedure is to be run

(Westbury, 1994). In particular, it is assumed that there exists a set of static frames of simultaneous articulatory and acoustic data. The set is supposed to range over a set of phones that covers the articulatory and acoustic spaces well. Such a set, known as *initializing utterances* might include vowels and consonants such as /i, ɪ, e, ɛ, æ, ʌ, ɑ, ɔ, o, ʊ, u/ and /s, ʃ, z, ʒ, b, p, d, t, g, k/, as well as representative laterals and nasals. Given this data and the standard vocal tract in the form of an articulatory synthesizer, the proposed steps for the construction of an NM will be described. Recall that it is only those portions of the vocal tract where articulatory data actually exists where the NM will act. In the case of x-ray microbeam this is from the lips to the furthest back pellet on the tongue. Thus, large portions of pharyngeal articulation are not acted on by the NM.

The steps in constructing an NM are as follows: (1) Choice of representation: Choose representations or parameterizations of the human vocal tract and the standard vocal tract. These representations will specify particular portions of midsagittal shapes for which there are human articulatory data with n-tuples for the human and m-tuples for the standard vocal tract; (2) Construct samples of the NM: Make a choice as to what constitutes an equivalent configuration with a set of initializing utterances to designate the *initial corresponding vocal tracts.* For each pair of initial corresponding vocal tracts, the pairs of n-tuples (representing portions of the human midsagittal) and m-tuples (representing portions of the corresponding standard vocal tract midsagittal) are designated as samples of the complete NM, that is, the NM restricted to the initial corresponding vocal tracts (Figure 3); (3) Adjust for acoustic match: Adjust PONMs of the standard vocal tract so that the acoustics of the synthesizer and the human match, as closely as possible, over the set of initializing utterances. This choice of PONMs remains fixed for this human (Figure 3); (4) Generalize to the complete NM: Use nonlinear regression via a neural net to generate the complete NM from these samples. That is, any possible configuration for the human vocal tract (i.e., a possible n-tuple) should map to a possible configuration for the standard vocal tract (i.e., a possible m-tuple). The inverse NM would also be constructed using neural networks (Figure 4).

11.2.2.1 Step 1: Choice of Representations

The human and the standard vocal tract's midsagittal section can be represented in many different ways. One possible representation for a human vocal tract would be in terms of flesh point positions defined by pellet images from the x-ray microbeam. Here the x–y coordinates of all the pellets would be combined into an n-tuple of real numbers. Another representation would be in terms of tract variables or constriction degrees and locations (Figure 2). Again, all the constriction location-degree pairs would be combined into an n-tuple of real numbers.

Both of these representations will have corresponding representations in the standard vocal tract. Corresponding to the flesh-point representation of the human vocal tract could be the ASY articulatory coordinates (Figure 1). These coordinates would be combined into an m-tuple of real numbers. If a tract variable

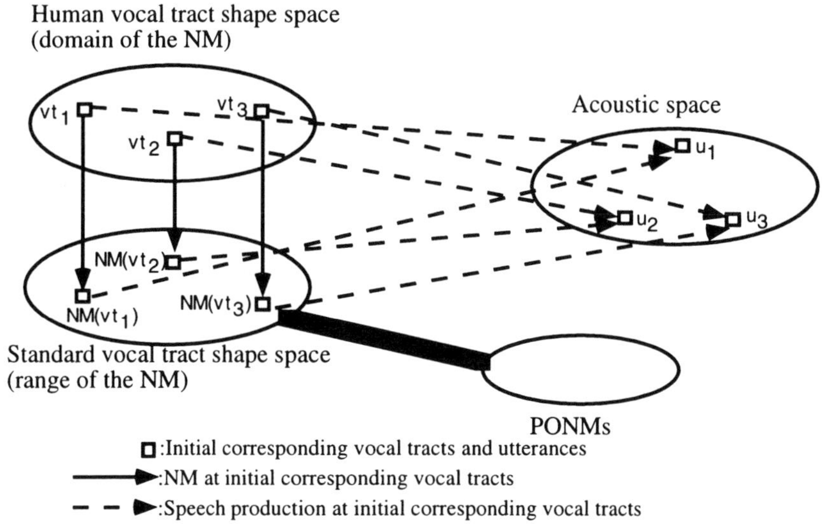

FIGURE 3 The normalizing map (NM) at initial corresponding utterances and the adjusted parameters orthogonal to the NM (PONMs) for near acoustic matching. vt, vocal tract.

representation is chosen for the human vocal tract, each set of tract variable coordinates for the human vocal tract would be paired with a set of tract variable coordinates for the standard vocal tract (Figure 2). The first pair of representations will be referred to as the *pellet-articulator representation pair,* and the second as the *tract variable representation pair.*

11.2.2.2 Step 2: Construct Samples of the NM

Next, using the initializing utterances from the human talker and the standard vocal tract, human vocal tract shapes (n-tuples) and standard vocal tract shapes (m-tuples) will be designated as initial corresponding vocal tracts (Figure 3). These vocal tract pairs will map to one another according to the NM under construction, and, thus, form a sampling of the NM. As with assigning representations, there are many ways of designating initial corresponding vocal tracts for the NM. Two possible methods of designating initial corresponding vocal tracts will be discussed, and both could apply to either example of representation pairs given in step 1.

The first initialization method requires that a set of realizations of initializing utterances from the human correspond to a set of realizations of the same initializing utterances produced by the standard vocal tract. The utterances produced by both the human and standard vocal tracts would be judged to be correct realizations by human listeners. For the pellet-articulator representation pair, the pellet positions and ASY articulator coordinates would be paired at each of the designated initializing utterances, for a sampling of the NM. For the tract variable representation pair, the tract variable coordinates of the human would be paired with the tract variable coordinates of ASY for each of the designated initializing utterances.

A second way that vocal midsagittal sections of humans could be designated as equivalent to midsagittal sections of the standard vocal tract is by visual fitting over the set of initializing utterances. For each of the designated initializing utterances, the positions of the tongue body, tongue tip, jaw, and lips of the articulatory synthesizer would be varied in software to fit the human pellet data as closely as possible. Again, the pellet positions and articulatory coordinates would be paired, or human tract variables and ASY tract variables would be paired, depending on the choice made in step 1, at each of the designated initializing utterances.

The purpose of trying different representation and initialization schemes is to find out how stringently defined the relations between the initial corresponding vocal tracts have to be in order to obtain a good NM. The required accuracy of the recovery will depend on the application; therefore, the method by which the NM is constructed depends on the application. The application dependence of the recovery process will become clearer when articulatory recovery is discussed with regard to speech recognition applications. Note that during either of the initialization procedures, positions of articulators are equated during some part of the initializing utterances. Therefore, this normalization procedure accounts for some aspects of motor control, as well as anatomy.

11.2.2.3 Step 3: Adjust PONMs for an Acoustic Match

The PONMs of the standard vocal tract need to be adjusted so that there is as much matching of the acoustic output as possible, simultaneously over the set of pairs of the initial corresponding vocal tracts (Figure 3). The acoustic measures over which matching would be judged is an issue that will need to be considered in more detail. Just a few possibilities are mentioned here. For example, in the case of a vowel, the central portion could be used for spectral analysis from which the first four formant frequencies and amplitudes and overall root-mean-square (RMS) amplitude measures could be measured. For a fricative, a window surrounding the middle of the noise production could be used to compute magnitude spectra, overall RMS amplitude, and formant frequencies, where possible. For a stop, a short window surrounding each release burst could be used to compute its magnitude spectra and overall RMS amplitude. To obtain the best set of PONMs for a given individual talker, an algorithm (e.g., a genetic algorithm) would be used to match the acoustic measures of the standard vocal tract with those of the human talker, simultaneously over the set of initial corresponding vocal tracts.

The PONMs that could be used to fit the acoustic data over the set of pairs of initial corresponding vocal tracts depends on the particular articulatory synthesizer used. Here, ASY is used as an example. The parameters of the midsagittal distance-to-area function are a part of the set of PONMs. The form of this function depends on the region of the vocal tract. Initially, the midsagittal distance-to-area functions in the soft and hard palate regions would be varied for good acoustic

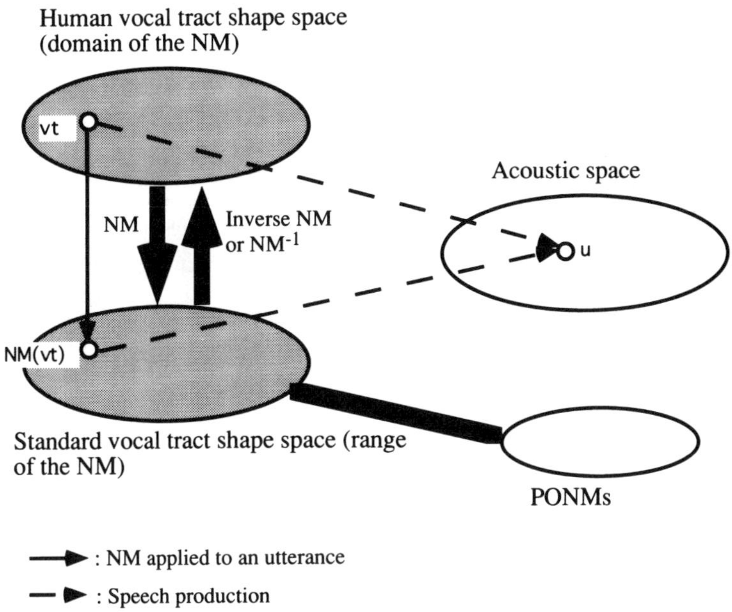

FIGURE 4 The normalizing map (NM) and its inverse, generalized using neural nets. PONS, parameters orthogonal to the NM; vt, vocal tract.

matching. They are both of the form $\alpha^* g^\beta$, where g is the grid segment length between the tongue and either the soft palate or hard palate (Mermelstein, 1973). Both α and β could be varied in both regions so that the acoustic output of the synthesizer matches that of the human over the set of initializing utterances. The radiation impedance model contains one zero and one pole (Rubin et al., 1981), and these parameters can be varied to help the synthesizer match the acoustic output of the subject. Recall that the total vocal tract length and the ratio of mouth-to-pharynx length are also PONMs in the example used here because of the lack of data in the pharyngeal region. The ratio of pharynx length to mouth cavity length would be altered by adding or removing sections to the pharynx tube of the standard vocal tract. To simulate varying vocal tract length, the speed of sound used to calculate the transfer function would be varied to fit the acoustics of the human subject. (This is a convenient means to simulate changes in the total length of the vocal tract. A redefinition of the actual physical speed of sound is not intended.)

11.2.2.4 Step 4: Generalize to the Complete NM and Find the Inverse NM

Once steps 1 through 3 have been completed, a neural net can be used to generalize to complete the NM (Figure 4). The n-tuples in the human domain

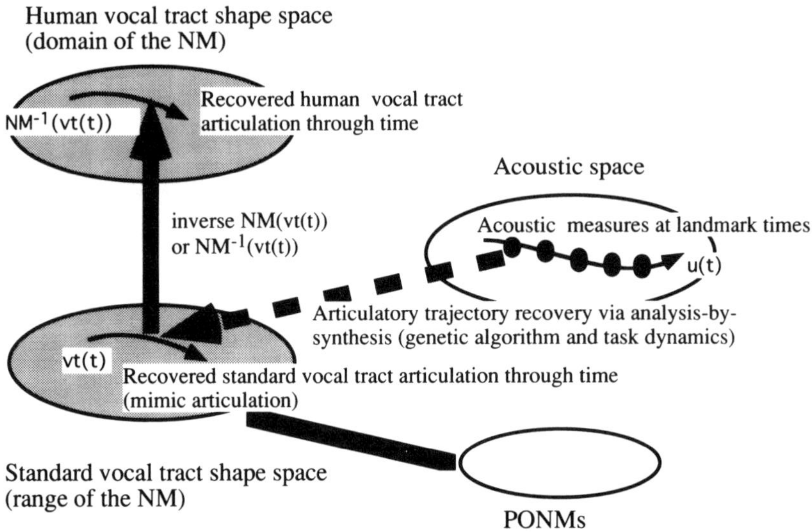

FIGURE 5 Recovery of human articulatory movement using the inverse normalizing maps (NM). PONS, parameters orthogonal to the NM; vt, vocal tract.

space, whether they be tract variables or pellet positions, would be the input to the neural network. The corresponding outputs would be in terms of the standard vocal tract m-tuples. The neural networks would possess an input layer, a hidden layer, and an output layer; and there would be a node for every component of the input n-tuple and a node for every output of the output m-tuple, and the neural network would be trained using back propagation (Rumelhart, Hinton, & Williams, 1986). The training set consists of tokens from the initializing utterances. A neural net for the inverse NM would also be constructed, in a like manner. To check for the homology property of the NM, inputs to the neural nets can be continuously varied while verifying continuous variation in the output.

The procedure for articulatory recovery after the NM for the talker has been constructed is depicted in Figure 5. Given time-varying acoustic data from the talker, the analysis-by-synthesis procedure would find a mimic articulation over time for the standard vocal tract. The inverse NM would then be employed at each frame of the mimic articulation to find the talker's mimic articulation, and this is the recovered articulation.

11.3 ADAPTATION FOR AUTOMATIC SPEECH RECOGNITION

11.3.1 Introduction

The remaining discussion focuses on the how variability caused by individual differences in vocal tract anatomy, and some parts of motor behavior, can be identified to reduce indeterminacy in ASR. The considerations here are very general and without reference to any particular method for ASR. However, some concreteness is attained by relating the discussion back to the steps involved for recovery of articulation in a laboratory setting. There are two points to bear in mind in this discussion: (a) many of the steps could involve machine learning rather than on-line optimization; and (b) articulatory knowledge and constraints can be built into recognition algorithms without explicit recovery of articulation from acoustics, whether on-line or learned.

Basic to all algorithms in ASR seems to be the notion of category neighborhoods of exemplars in a mathematical space parameterized by some physical measures. The phonetic categories of speech are envisioned as regions or neighborhoods of a mathematical space, where acoustic and articulatory parameters provide two possible representations of points in that space. The coordinates of the points are envisioned as real numbers, so that the space of concern can be embedded into a space generated by a multicross-product of the set of real numbers. For phonetic categorization purposes, this space would be endowed with a nonmetric topology that describes relations between the regions or neighborhoods corresponding to different phonetic categories—what neighbors what in this multidimensional space, some sort of nonmetric topology that will be called a *relational topology* here. An example of such a topology is provided by the binary features of distinctive feature theory, where the categories are phonemic, and where there are multiple dimensions that each take two values of off and on, instead of a continuum (Jacobson & Halle, 1971). A continuum of values would be allowed in the space conceived of here. Viewing the same parameter space with a metric topology would relate more to the individual differences between talkers, including aspects of vocal tract anatomy and articulatory behavior, as well as anatomy, and so on. It may be difficult, if not impossible, for a listener to perceive, or an algorithm to recover, one aspect of the space—phonetic categories—without perceiving or recovering the other aspect—individual characteristics—because the categorical properties of speech also depend on anatomy and articulatory behavior (see Remez, Fellowes, & Rubin, in press). In a sense, this is the talker variability problem, where metric, individual-talker properties of the parameter space must be derived in the process of obtaining nonmetric, categorical phonetic properties, and vice versa.

These considerations point to the fact that context is always present in speech and it is never possible to factor out context in the sense of producing a prototypical exemplar of a category. An individual talker provides some of the context for his own speech simply with his own vocal tract and articulatory behavior.[1] *Variability* means that phonetic categories map to neighborhoods in the mathematical space, whether represented acoustically or articulatorily, that is never free of context. The greater the contextual possibilities, the greater the variability and size and potential overlap of these neighborhoods.

[1] Without specifying whether phonemes or /CV/s and /VC/s are used as categories, the term *category exemplar* is used to denote a member of a phonetic category.

The fundamental reason for using articulatory knowledge in ASR is variability due to context of the physical vocal tract and motor behavior. To simplify the pattern recognition problem, it is a good thing to reduce the size or extent and the potential overlap of neighborhoods in the mathematical space corresponding to different phonetic categories. The differences between talkers that create different regions in a metrical topology in the parameter space is an example of context. Reduction of the spread of the neighborhoods used in recognition can be obtained using articulatory knowledge, because the acoustic speech signal is self-consistent. Self-consistency is the result of the speech sound being produced by a single source that is a part of the physical world, and it therefore obeys physical law. This self-consistency may mean that the fastest way to deal with intertalker variability, or to adapt to an individual talker, would be to characterize that individual's vocal tract and aspects of that individual's motor control.[2] Also, other contextual effects can be factored out once the vocal tract is characterized. For example, knowing the mechanism that produces the speech, it is easier to factor out the environmental noise. Environmental noise provides context, and is of great interest in ASR.[3] In summary, variability due to context is inherent in speech production, and some of this variability is the result of context, such as that provided by mechanisms used to produce speech: the human vocal tracts.

The use of contextual knowledge is certainly not new to ASR. It is usually in the form of "higher level" syntactic and semantic knowledge that is used to test possibilities that come from the lower level phoneme recognizer (e.g., Zue et al., 1992). We are proposing the serious use of "lower level" knowledge in the form of articulatory constraint, as have others (Ramsay & Deng, 1994; Randolph, 1994; Rose, Schroeter, & Sondhi, 1994; Shirai & Kobayashi, 1986). Both higher and lower level knowledge are intended to remove apparent variability and ambiguity in the neighborhoods in the mathematical space corresponding to phonetic categories. All these forms of knowledge are knowledge of context—the context provided by words, by parts of speech, by phonemes, and by vocal tract anatomy, physiology, and physics.

Although efforts to incorporate vocal tract constraints into ASR have been mentioned, there is another trend in ASR, which is to use auditory processing to reduce the individual differences due to vocal tract anatomy (Hermansky, 1990). At the same time, dynamic constraints of speech production can be incorporated into these auditory processors (Hermansky & Morgan, 1994). Perhaps a combined approach of using auditory processing to blur some of the individual differences

[2] Some of the anatomical contextual factors include the length of the vocal tract, the wall compliances of the tract, the shape of the hard palate and so forth. Although coarticulation affects the physical realization of category exemplars produced by an individual according to the context of other category exemplars, the anatomical factors depend more on the particular person producing the speech.

[3] In fact, some researchers model effects of environmental noise explicit in a Hidden Markov Model (HMM) (Varga & Moore, 1990), thus attempting to characterize the source of noise itself.

in vocal tracts while adapting to the remaining differences will be the most successful way of dealing with variability.

11.3.2 Implementation for ASR

The notion of recovery for ASR is different from that for the laboratory, because the goals are different. In the laboratory veridical recovery is the goal, insofar as this is possible. For speech recognition, the goal is to efficiently characterize the anatomy and articulatory behavior of any talker whose speech is to be recognized. These characterizations have to be accurate only enough to make the neighborhoods corresponding to different phonetic quantities unambiguous or nonoverlapping. The term *efficient* provides a critical reason for using articulatory characterization instead of a purely acoustic one. To adapt quickly to an individual talker, knowledge of the source, (i.e., the vocal tract) provides a way of inferring aspects of the acoustic signal from other aspects of the signal for a given articulation, as well as ways of inferring the acoustic consequences of an articulatory event based on the acoustic consequences of other articulatory events. Thus, using articulatory characterization, the adaptation process should be speedily performed with a minimum of adaptation parameters.

The "bottom line" is to characterize any talker's vocal tract and to know the acoustic consequences of that characterization. It should be possible to modify the recovery procedure for the laboratory outlined above to meet these objectives. In the remainder of the chapter the steps that were outlined for laboratory recovery will be modified for vocal tract characterization for speech recognition.

1. *Choice of representations.* Choose a system of phonetic categories, such as phonemes or diphones, for the representation in the human and standard vocal tract domains. This means that the NM will no longer be from an n-tuple to an m-tuple, but it is more directly related to the objects of interest: phonetic categories.
2. *Construct samples of the NM.* Take initializing utterances from the human that have been labeled according to the chosen linguistic units and equate them with utterances that have the same label produced by the standard vocal tract. Although there is no visual assurance that like articulations are mapped to one another, the gross relations are likely to be maintained, thus, preserving some semblance of homology between the vocal tracts. For example, /i/ is likely to have a higher tongue position than /ɑ/ in both vocal tracts, and alveolar releases are likely to remain alveolar releases. All that needs to be preserved is the relational topology.
3. *Adjusting PONMs for acoustic match.* The adjustment of PONMs can take place as before.
4. *Generalize to the complete NM and find the inverse NM.* This step is no longer necessary.

The PONMs generated in step (3) contain information about the talker's characteristics. These characteristics are not only anatomical, but also contain aspects of the talker's motor behavior, because the talker's and standard vocal tracts are equated based on categorical equivalence over the set of initializing utterances and the standard vocal tract's articulatory settings would be independent of the talker. Given the PONMs, a choice can be made to perform the recognition in either an acoustic or an articulatory parameter space. For an acoustic parameter space, talker adaptation would be done on the basis of the PONMs. Either it can be assumed that training data for an ASR model has been generated by the standard vocal tract with that particular set of PONMs, or on-line adaptation from a set of training data obtained with a nearby set of PONMs would occur.

A different scenario is to use the articulatory representation, as, for instance, specified in task dynamics. This is the more direct method for using articulatory information. This approach is not necessarily to be preferred compared to working in an acoustic parameter space with articulatory constraints, but it is an alternative that illustrates why this particular normalization procedure could work for ASR. Under this scenario, the representation of the phonetic categories is in terms of the task dynamics with end effectors in the standard vocal tract, which is the range of the NM. The mapping from the task-dynamic parameters to phonetic categories might be accomplished by gestural phonology (Browman & Goldstein, 1990). Perhaps, instead of such expert knowledge, an automatic learning procedure could make the relation between linguistic categories and task dynamics transparent, so that the sequence of linguistic categories could be read right off the standard vocal tract's recovered gestures. (Again, it is not necessarily on-line recovery that is sought here.) Although the inverse NM is never constructed, it would do no good for the inverse NM that could be constructed to be one-to-many because this would imply ambiguity in the linguistic content. Thus, the robustness property for the NM and its inverse is still required. The linguistic content is supposed to be contained in the domain of the NM, that is, the midsagittal section. The assumption that the linguistic content is in the midsagittal aspects of articulation may only be approximately true, but slight modifications to this picture should accommodate any three-dimensional aspects that may become important, such as those for lateral articulations. Again, it is the case that the PONMs characterize the individual talker.

There is research being conducted by others that is related to the above considerations. John Hogden and colleagues (Hogden, Rubin, & Saltzman, in press) have been working with something called a *continuity map*. Essentially, after vector quantizing acoustic speech signals, a random walk through this space is performed to find which regions neighbor one another, thus deriving a relational topology. Perhaps, not surprisingly, there is a close relation between this topology and the physical space the tongue moves through. Jordan and Rumelhart (1992) talk about the use of internal models for their distal supervised learning tasks. They do not require veridical, or even unique, internal models in order to obtain solutions to inverse problems. They do require a certain degree of robustness, and thus take account of nonmetrical aspects of the topology.

11.4 CONCLUSION

The variability caused by the physical context of a talker's vocal tract is a problem to be solved in the process of articulatory recovery via analysis-by-synthesis. A normalization solution has been proposed, based on the construction of an NM between the talker's vocal tract and a standard vocal tract. This solution supposes that a set of simultaneous articulatory-acoustic measures are available, and should thus solve recovery in a laboratory setting. In the case of ASR, a relational topology between the phonetic categories is required. Therefore, a characterization of each talker's vocal tract would help to adapt an ASR procedure by shrinking the extents of the category neighborhood sizes. A veridical recovery of the vocal tract articulations is not required. Therefore, the proposed normalization procedure for the laboratory can be modified for speaker adaptation in ASR.

ACKNOWLEDGMENTS

The work presented here has been supported by the National Institutes of Health through grant DC-01247 to Haskins Laboratories.

REFERENCES

Badin, P., Beautemps, D., Laboissière, R., & Schwartz, J. L. (1995). Recovery of vocal tract geometry from speech signal for vowels and fricative consonants using midsagittal-to-area function conversion model. *Journal of Phonetics, 23,* 221–229.

Beautemps, D., Badin, P., & Laboissière, R. (1995). Deriving vocal-tract area functions from midsagittal profiles and formant frequencies: A new model for vowels and fricative consonants based on experimental data. *Speech Communication, 16,* 27–47.

Browman, C. P., & Goldstein, L. (1990). Articulatory phonology: An overview. *Phonetica, 49,* 155–180.

Hermansky, H. (1990). Perceptual linear predictive (PLP) analysis of speech. *Journal of the Acoustical Society of America, 87,* 1738–1752.

Hermansky, H., & Morgan, N. (1994). RASTA processing of speech. *IEEE Transactions on Speech and Audio Processing, 2,* 578–589.

Hogden, J., Rubin, P., & Saltzman, E. (1996). An unsupervised method for learning to track tongue position from an acoustic signal. *Bulletin de la Communication Parlee, 3,* 101–116.

Jacobson, R., & Halle, M. (1971). *Fundamentals of language.* The Hague: Mouton.

Jordan, M. I., & Rumelhart, D. E. (1992). Forward models: Supervised learning with a distal teacher. *Cognitive Science, 16,* 307–354.

McGowan, R. S. (1994). Recovering articulatory movement from formant frequency trajectories using task dynamics and a genetic algorithm: Preliminary model tests. *Speech Communication, 14,* 19–48.

McGowan, R. S., & Lee, M. (1996). Task-dynamic and articulatory recovery of lip and velar approximations under model mismatch conditions. *Journal of the Acoustical Society of America, 99,* 595–608.

Mermelstein, P. (1973). Articulatory model for the study of speech production. *Journal of the Acoustical Society of America, 53,* 1070–1082.

Ramsay, G., & Deng, L. (1994). A stochastic framework for articulatory speech recognition. *Journal of the Acoustical Society of America, 95,* 2870.

Randolph, M. A. (1994). Speech analysis based on articulatory behavior. *Journal of the Acoustical Society of America, 95,* 2828.

Remez, R. E., Fellowes, J. M., & Rubin, P. E. (in press). Talker identification based on phonetic information. *Journal of Experimental Psychology: Human Perception and Performance.*

Rose, R. C., Schroeter, J., & Sondhi, M. M. (1994). An investigation of the potential role of speech production models in automatic speech recognition. *Proceedings of the International Conference on Spoken Language Processing, Yokohama, Japan.*

Rubin, P., Baer, T., & Mermelstein, P. (1981). An articulatory synthesizer for perceptual research. *Journal of the Acoustical Society of America, 70,* 321–328.

Rumelhart, D. E., Hinton, G. E., & Williams, R. J. (1986). Learning internal representations by error propagation. In D. E. Rumelhart & J. L. McClelland (Eds.), *Parallel distributed processing* (Vol. 1, pp. 318–362). Cambridge, MA: MIT Press.

Saltzman, E. L., & Munhall, K. G. (1989). A dynamic approach to gestural patterning in speech production. *Ecological Psychology, 14,* 333–382.

Shirai, K., & Kobayashi, T. (1986). Estimating articulatory motion from speech wave. *Speech Communication, 5,* 159–170.

Varga, A., & Moore, R. (1990). Hidden Markov model decomposition of speech and noise. *Proceedings on International Conference on Acoustics, Speech, and Signal Processing,* pp. 845–848.

Westbury, J. R. (1994). *X-ray microbeam speech production database user's handbook.* Unpublished.

Zue, V., Glass, J., Goodine, D., Leung, H., Phillips, M., Polifroni, J., & Seneff, S. (1992). The Voyager speech understanding system: A progress report. In P. LaFace & R. DeMori (Eds.), *Speech recognition and understanding* (pp. 413–424). New York: Springer-Verlag.

Index[1]

[1]An "n" following page number indicates footnote.

B

C

Q

R

T

U

V